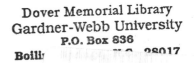
Christian Perspectives on Human Development

Psychology and Christianity

Edited by David G. Benner

Christian
Perspectives
on
Human
Development

Edited by
LEROY ADEN,
DAVID G. BENNER, and
J. HAROLD ELLENS

BAKER BOOK HOUSE
Grand Rapids, Michigan 49516

Copyright 1992 by
Baker Book House Company

Printed in the United States of America

Library of Congress Cataloging-in-Publication Data

Christian perspectives on human development / LeRoy Aden, David G. Benner, J. Harold Ellens, eds.
    p. cm.—(Psychology and Christianity)
    Includes bibliographical references and index.
    ISBN 0-8010-0225-7
    1. Christianity—Psychology.   2. Developmental psychology—Religious aspects
—Christianity. 3. Maturation (Psychology)—Religious aspects—Christianity 4. Belief
and doubt. I. Aden, LeRoy. II. Benner, David G. III. Ellens, J. Harold, 1932-
    IV. Series.
    BR110.C46 1992
    261.5'15—dc20   91-31783
                                                                                          CIP

Scripture versions quoted are the King James Version (KJV); the Jerusalem Bible (JB), copyright © 1966 by Darton, Longman and Todd, Ltd. and Doubleday and Company, Inc.; the Holy Bible, New International Version (NIV), copyright © 1973, 1978, 1984 International Bible Society, and used by permission of Zondervan Bible Publishers; and the Revised Standard Version (RSV), copyright 1946, 1952, 1971, and 1973 by the Division of Christian Education of the National Council of the Churches of Christ in the United States of America.

Contents

Introduction to the Series

This is the sixth volume in the Psychology and Christianity series, a collection of books published cooperatively by Baker Book House and the Christian Association for Psychological Studies (CAPS). Founded in 1952 in Grand Rapids, Michigan, by a group of psychologists, psychiatrists, and pastoral counselors, CAPS is an international society of Christian helping professionals committed to the exploration of the relationship between psychology and Christian faith.

Books in this series draw on the best of previous publications in *The Journal of Psychology and Christianity*, the official publication of CAPS, and supplement these with original articles written for each volume. The purpose of the series is to present psychological and theological reflection on the most important issues encountered in human relationships, particularly relationships of counseling, education, parenting, and ministry.

Further information about the Christian Association for Psychological Studies may be obtained by contacting the head office:

Christian Association for Psychological Studies
Robert R. King, Jr., Ph.D.
CAPS International
P. O. Box 890279
Temecula, CA 92589
(714) 695-2277

David G. Benner
Series Editor

Contributors

LeRoy Aden is Luther D. Reed Professor of Pastoral Care at the Lutheran Theological Seminary, Philadelphia, Pennsylvania.

David G. Benner is professor of psychology at Redeemer College, Ancaster, Ontario, and adjunct professor of psychology at the University of Toronto and McMaster Divinity College.

Donald Capps is William Harte Felmeth Professor of Pastoral Theology at Princeton Theological Seminary, Princeton, New Jersey.

Thomas A. Droege is professor of theology at Valparaiso University, Valparaiso, Indiana.

J. Harold Ellens is Executive Secretary Emeritus of CAPS, Editor in Chief Emeritus of *The Journal of Psychology and Christianity*, a Presbyterian theologian, and a psychotherapist in private practice in Farmington Hills, Michigan.

Gary S. Eller is an ordained Presbyterian minister and pastor in Charlotte, North Carolina.

Mary Gaebler is a graduate student in theology and ethics at Yale Divinity School, New Haven, Connecticut.

Margaret A. Krych is professor of Christian education and theology at the Lutheran Theological Seminary, Philadelphia, Pennsylvania.

Lyman T. Lundeen is professor of religion at Pacific Lutheran University, Tacoma, Washington.

John W. Miller is professor of religious studies at the University of Waterloo, Waterloo, Ontario.

Neil Pembroke is a minister in the United Church Parish of Cairns, Queensland, Australia.

Jared P. Pingleton is a psychologist in private practice in Kansas City, Missouri.

Ronald H. Rottschafer is a psychologist in private practice in Oakbrook, Illinois.

Orlo Strunk, Jr., is professor of psychology at Boston University School of Theology and in the Division of Theological and Religious Studies of the Graduate School.

Harry A. Van Belle is associate professor of psychology at Redeemer College, Ancaster, Ontario.

F. Colleen Zabriskie is a clinical psychologist with the Covina Psychological Services, Covina, California.

The editors wish to express their appreciation to Tracey Hutchison for compiling the initial list of manuscripts and to Sarah Gregory and Beverley Adams for copyediting.

Introduction

In three ways psychology recognizes that we are historical creatures, that our past lives on and influences the present and the future. The first way is found in the psychoanalytic concept of the unconscious. The unconscious means that what we are today has been shaped by, if not determined by, what we were yesterday. The past lives in the present by subtle and hidden means, sometimes giving health but more often yielding neurotic symptoms and pathology.

The second way in which we are seen as historical creatures is through psychology's life cycle theories. Freud proposed stages of human development, but it was theorists like Erik Erikson and Jean Piaget who developed and refined the insight. Erikson, for example, maintained that we develop according to a ground plan and that what we achieve, or fail to achieve, in childhood becomes the foundation on which we build later in life. His theory adds a sequential dimension to our historicity and reminds us that we can get caught in our own history not just by denying it but by failing to achieve appointed tasks at appointed times.

Contextual therapy is the third way in which we are recognized as historical creatures. Ivan Boszormenyi-Nagy, Geraldine M. Spark, Barbara Krasner, and others place us in an intergenerational context and show that we receive from our family of origin a legacy that we pass on to the next generation. Erikson anticipates the interlocking of the generations in his cyclical view of the developmental process, but

11

contextual therapy adds a detailed and intricate knowledge of the way in which we must balance and rebalance giving and receiving in the crucible of the extended family.

The primary concern of this volume is with the second way, with seeing people as historical creatures by recognizing that they go through certain stages of development. The title of the book indicates that it is a compilation of a number of different perspectives on human development. We have included a variety of developmental theories (from Erikson to Piaget) and have opted for a spectrum of Christian viewpoints (from the Reformed perspective of J. Harold Ellens to the Roman Catholic perspective of Karl Rahner). We believe that this diversity throws a great amount of light on the subject. No single perspective is exhaustive of present-day developmental theory or of its implications for our Christian faith and ministry. Each author makes a significant contribution, and together they give a full picture of the terrain.

The diversity leads to some interesting differences. For example, at the end of an extended discussion of faith as a developmental phenomenon in part 1, Mary Gaebler uses Martin Luther's experience of *anfechtung* to propose a paradoxical rather than a developmental view of faith. Or, at the end of part 2, Lyman T. Lundeen criticizes psychological movements that elevate self-development by reminding us that from a Christian perspective the self is basically gift and promise. A third kind of difference is found in the categorizations of Thomas A. Droege and Ellens. Droege makes a distinction between Erikson's life cycle theory and Piaget's structural theory. Ellens contends that Erikson is in the same camp as Piaget and that along with Lawrence Kohlberg and James W. Fowler he represents a structuralist approach to understanding personality development. We make no attempt to resolve these differences. We believe that each viewpoint adds to the dialogue and is an important representation of the diversity that is found in developmental theory.

The book is designed to be of help to those who work in the helping professions, especially if they are interested in exploring the development of faith and the realization of a mature self from a Christian perspective. As one of our authors puts it, "Scholars have shown that there is a definite relationship between faith development and psychological development." If this is true, knowledge of that relationship is vital to counseling, whether it is done in a church or a clinic.

The book is also designed for those who labor on the front line—parish pastors. Whether teaching, preaching, or giving care, pastors deal with people who are at the nexus of life and faith. The book deals with that moment and seeks to illuminate it in ways that are helpful to the practice of ministry. It does not give specific prescriptions for action but critical reflections of faith and development. In this way, it seeks to clarify the milieu in which Christ is engendered in the heart and faith becomes a pearl of great value.

Developmental theory has to do with human fulfillment or, more precisely, with human distortion and repair. Unlike psychoanalysis and contextual therapy, however, it has produced no theory of therapy. It came, not out of any attempt to help people, but out of an attempt to describe human development and to gain a normative view of the healthy personality, of what human life should be. This orientation is still evident in Fowler's attempt to describe stages of faith from the most elementary to the most advanced.

To mention Fowler is to bring up another characteristic of developmental theory, at least in terms of its entrance into the church. It has been used almost exclusively to illuminate the concept of faith, starting with the early work of Droege (1966).[1] Why developmental theory has not been applied to other religious concepts is difficult to assess, but one thing is certain: To focus on faith is to deal with a central and decisive aspect of the Christian faith. Faith is basic to healing and wholeness. By dealing with faith, then, pastoral theologians are addressing the issue of therapy, that is, the issue of how people are helped and healed.

In taking hold of faith, developmental theory has not dealt just with the ideal or normative form of faith. It has seen faith in the context of life or, more specifically, in the context of the developmental stage in which the individual is located. Consequently, it has also seen that faith can be distorted, that it participates in the dynamics of human existence and is shaped by those dynamics even as it may be a profound answer to them. In a word, developmental theory has made faith a very human response. It has added to our knowledge of the human side of faith, sometimes to the neglect or the denial of faith as a gift from God.

Donald Capps is one of the few pastoral theologians who relates developmental theory not just to faith but also to pastoral care. In his *Life Cycle Theory and Pastoral Care*, Capps maintains that there are two ways to relate pastoral care and developmental theory. The first way focuses on particular stages of development and is used to gain a better understanding of people at various ages. The second way focuses on selected developmental theories and is used to understand better "the nature and purpose of pastoral care." While Capps concentrates on the second approach, the present volume by and large focuses on the first one. It describes and critiques major developmental theories, but more important it uses those theories to reflect on, and to increase our

1. See Thomas A. Droege, "A Developmental View of Faith," Ph.D. diss., Divinity School, University of Chicago, 1966, 10.

understanding of, the faith and ministry of the Christian church. Margaret A. Krych and Droege are most explicit in relating developmental theory to ministry, but all the authors are attentive to the need of pastors to gain a better understanding of the people they serve.

This book is divided into three parts. Part 1 deals with faith as a developmental phenomenon. LeRoy Aden uses Erikson's epigenetic theory of human development to describe eight forms that faith takes as an individual progresses through the life cycle. Droege, believing that developmental theory can clarify the dynamics of faith, concentrates on adult faith development and outlines a Christian ministry "that can best nurture faith in periods of transition." In chapter 3, life cycle theory is applied to "lived religion" by Harry A. Van Belle. He finds that religion changes during one's life span if it is responsive to "the stage of development that one has achieved and to the historical-cultural context in which one lives." Krych takes a different developmental approach. She introduces Piaget's stages in cognitive development and applies them to faith by carefully drawing out four implications for ministry. Neil Pembroke follows in chapter 5 with the interesting contention that any person who faces honestly the challenges of each developmental stage eventually comes to faith, at least an implicit and anonymous faith as set forth by Rahner. Gaebler ends part 1 by using Luther to raise a serious question about growth in faith through developmental means. She believes that moments of doubt and growth in faith are inevitable parts of the same dynamic and that therefore a developmental view of faith cannot mean a natural and ascending sequence of growth. Growth in the self does not necessarily yield growth in faith.

Part 2 deals with the mature self as a developmental phenomenon. It is interesting to note that many chapters focus not on the stages of development but on the transition periods between the stages as a time when substantial growth occurs. We start with Jared P. Pingleton's model of relational maturity. He maintains that interdependent relationships more than dependent or independent ones approximate interpersonal maturity. He elaborates the point from both a psychological and a theological vantage point. In chapter 8, Orlo Strunk, Jr., carries the conversation forward by developing the idea that there is no single form of religious maturity and that maybe the idiographic maturity of the Christian transcends the attempt of the behavioral sciences to domesticate it. Ellens, like Droege in an earlier chapter, takes seriously the transition periods between stages of development (Ellens calls them "limit experiences") and maintains that they are opportune times for growth in faith, for the deeper unfolding of the Christian self. Ronald H. Rottschafer helps us to see what that "deeper understanding" may mean. He takes the self from Christian groups who would denigrate and malign it and gives it back to God who in and through grace takes pleasure in "our growth toward fullness." Rottschafer then turns his keen sensor toward the passive Christian (chap. 11). He offers a detailed analysis of passivity and a perceptive application of it to church people. His interpretation of human dynamics and of what he calls "the Christian system" is first-rate.

David G. Benner follows with a penetrating discussion of spirituality and the self. "God meets us within the depths of our selves and it is here that we relate to God and are changed by this relationship." Benner lays bare the intricacies of this encounter and relates it to psychotherapy in ways that revitalize psychotherapy as a genuine care of souls. Lundeen ends the section by seeing the self in the light of God's grace where it becomes both a gift that is received and a promise that is being fulfilled. Lundeen's ability to relate theological affirmations and concrete dynamics is impressive.

Part 3 uses particular situations as a means of discussing developmental theory. F. Colleen Zabriskie brings a feminine perspective to developmental theory and clarifies the various crises that are experienced by mid-life women. From the discussion she draws implications for a therapy that would facilitate positive resolution of the crises. "Religious Ritual and the Excommunication of Ann Hibbens" by Capps is an informative application of Erikson's theory of religious ritual to a famous New England ecclesiastical trial in 1640. In this article Capps makes a good case for seeing the trial as an instance of Erikson's second stage of development when the dynamic of autonomy versus shame and self-doubt is dominant. Gary Eller in chapter 16 follows Capps's lead and considers Jonathan Edwards's dismissal from Northampton church. He too uses the Eriksonian perspective of autonomy versus shame and self-doubt to illuminate the psychosocial dynamics at work in Edwards's staunch stand against Solomon Stoddard, his grandfather and ministerial predecessor. The concluding chapter in part 3 is a developmental study of Jesus at the transitional age of thirty. Recognizing that factual information about Jesus' adulthood is "notoriously scarce," John W. Miller takes a careful and helpful look at the human side of Jesus through the lens of Daniel Levinson's study of adult men. His picture of Jesus adds developmental detail to our understanding of Christ's incarnation into our life and history.

This brief journey through the contents of the book indicates that it is indeed a variety of Christian perspectives on human development. But there is unity within diversity. Each author writes out of a commitment to Jesus Christ who as the giver of all faith and growth is the ultimate perspective on human fulfillment.

Part 1

Developmental Theory and Faith

1

Faith and the Developmental Cycle

LeRoy Aden

Faith as a human response is a dynamic and multidimensional reality rather than a static and monolithic one. This contention can be drawn from the history of the Christian church as much as it can from our own experience. Faith in God has been described variously as trust, as assent, as obedience, and as self-surrender. If there is any validity to these different descriptions, faith appears to be a complex phenomenon consisting of various elements or taking various forms.

Faith is also a developmental phenomenon.[1] It participates in the life cycle of the individual who possesses it. More specifically, the dominant form that faith takes at any one time is determined in part by the particular developmental stage in which the individual is immersed.

It is important to note that both of these contentions focus on faith as a human response and that therefore they neglect, but are not intended to deny, the fact that faith is ultimately a divine gift, a consequence of God's grace.

Both contentions can be explored by using Erik Erikson's epigenetic theory of human development. Viewed epigenetically, faith becomes a dynamic response in which specific elements have a time of special ascendancy, even though in a larger sense all the elements are present in any particular moment of faith. In this approach, faith is taken seriously as a vital part of the life of the individual in whom it appears. It

---

1. The original impetus for this point of view comes in part from Droege (1966).

is not merely a passive response to a particular crisis but is a profound and fitting answer to that crisis.

With this introduction, the eight forms that faith can take may now be elaborated (see table 1.1). In each case, Erikson's psychosocial description will be used to highlight the individual's struggle with an organismic task that, at least in its maximal sense, seems to exert a significant influence on the structure of faith. My discussion is suggestive rather than exhaustive. Furthermore, it emphasizes the healthy outcome of each developmental task, even though in actuality the outcome is at best always ambiguous.

Faith as Trust

In the first year of life, the infant is dominated by the need to receive and incorporate. As Erikson expresses it, "The simplest and the earliest modality is 'to get,' not in the sense of 'go and get' but in that of receiving and accepting what is given" (Erikson 1980, 60). This incorporative orientation is centered anatomically in the mouth, but it is also expressed in the infant's use of eyes, ears, and hands as modalities of "*taking* and *holding on to* things—things which are more or less freely offered and given" (Erikson 1980, 61).[3]

The infant's insatiable need to incorporate is indicative of a radical condition of dependence and helplessness, a condition that immerses the child in, and ties him or her to, an interpersonal atmosphere without which he or she cannot survive physically or psychologically. In other words, the nature of infantile needs binds him or her to significant others as a recipient—initially, a very passive recipient—of their more or less adequate ability and willingness to give. In this transaction, the infant does not need to be conscious of specific impingements, nor does he or she have to go beyond the prototaxic mode of experiencing them, in order to emerge with an organismic feeling about whether or not others are trustworthy, that is, about whether or not they are available and willing to give what is needed. In fact, their trustworthiness, or lack of it, is a crucial and inescapable issue for the infant, for it is the atmosphere in which he or she is rescued from, or is overwhelmed by, powerful needs.

If trustworthiness is a frequent characteristic of the infant's experience of significant others, it tends to create a basic sense of trust toward self and others, for one's needs become acceptable occasions of interpersonal contact and fulfillment rather than undesirable occasions of estrangement and disaster. By the same token, if significant others prove to be frequently untrustworthy, the infant gradually emerges with a deep sense of mistrust toward self and others.

If faith is seen as a differentiated response to God on either a perceptual or a conceptual level, then obviously the infant manifests no

Table 1.1

The Eight Forms of Faith and Their Associated Organismic Tasks

Developmental Stage	Dominant Form of Faith
Infancy	Faith as trust (trust vs. mistrust)
Early Childhood	Faith as courage (courage vs. shame and doubt)
Play Age	Faith as obedience (obedience vs. guilt)
School Age	Faith as assent (assent vs. dissent)
Adolescence	Faith as identity (identity vs. confusion)
Young Adulthood	Faith as self-surrender (self-surrender vs. self-seclusion)
Middle Adulthood	Faith as unconditional caring (caring vs. concupiscence)
Mature Age	Faith as unconditional acceptance (acceptance vs. despair)

faith and what we have said above makes no contribution to its understanding. However, if faith—infantile faith—is seen as a prototaxic state, as an organismic and unreflective response to that which concerns the infant unconditionally, then faith is a vital part of the infant's experience, taking the primal and foundational form of trust.

Faith as infantile trust is a response of openness and receptivity, conceived in a relationship in which the other is trustworthy and manifested in a relationship in which the infant entrusts his or her life to the other. In other words, it is a basic but undifferentiated feeling on the part of the infant that life is basically fulfilling rather than frustrating, that he or she can rest in the structures of life with the confidence that they are finally faithful and dependable. As the child develops, of course, the content of this rudimentary faith should become less amorphous and more centered on God as the Faithful One, but this fact should not cause us to minimize the reality and significance of the infant's organismic response of trust. It is this response, however prototaxic, that may serve as an enduring foundation for the individual's persevering confidence in the ultimate dependability of life or, in less neutral terms, in the benevolent presence and power of God. Thus if this response is not educed in the infant, he or she may later struggle with an enduring sense of doubt and suspicion, making it difficult, if not impossible, for the infant to rely on God's ability and willingness to give what is ultimately needed—grace as pardon where he or she is alienated and guilty, grace as power where he or she is under the mandate of his or her essential being.

Faith as Courage

According to Erikson, maturation of the muscle system moves the two-year-old into a psychosocial stage in which acts of retention and elimination are of central importance. The child becomes the unwieldy possessor of the nascent power to assert himself or herself, and with this power the child interacts with significant others through the social modalities of *holding on* and *letting go*, not only on a physical level but also on an emotional and an interpersonal level. Concretely, every mother knows how lovingly a child at this stage will snuggle and how ruthlessly he will suddenly try to push the adult away. At the same time the child is apt both to hoard things and to discard them, to cling to possessions and to throw them away (Erikson [1959] 1980, 70).

The child's erratic behavior rests on his or her growing ability to choose between alternatives, to assert himself or herself against the will or command of another. This power is exercised in a childhood world that is able to differentiate between self and nonself, and in this world it is appropriate and imperative for the child to begin to manifest a budding sense of autonomy and self-determination. Since the infantile exercise of will, like the earlier struggle with trust, takes place primarily on a prototaxic level, the child does not need to be conscious of particular incidents in order to be influenced and shaped by them. In fact, although specific experiences like toilet training can become pivotal instances of the nuclear conflict, it is the parents' underlying attitude toward autonomy and individuality in both themselves and others that is decisive.

If children are allowed a proper measure of self-determination without the loss of self-esteem, they tend to move toward a sense of responsible self-affirmation in which both self and others can survive and prosper. But if they are invaded by the will of others or made to feel a lack of self-control, they tend to develop a paralyzing sense of shame and doubt. In either case, their ability to affirm themselves in the face of threats, whether internal or external, is the crucial issue at stake.

The child's struggle with autonomy is relevant to his or her response of faith in at least two interrelated ways. On one level, it represents the beginning of a development that reaches its optimal expression only in adolescence—the development of a self that has the proactive ability to respond and initiate rather than the more primitive ability merely to react and receive. It is out of this development that faith as a response begins to take the shape of a truly human and personal response, that it becomes, however prototaxic, the first foundational expression of *my* trust, *my* letting go and holding on. As we will see later, maximal development of this capacity means that the faith of the adult is a centered act, that it is a genuine manifestation of human freedom, even though it is educed by a divine Power that transcends the individual infinitely.

On a deeper level, the child's budding sense of self-determination brings with it the nascent power of self-affirmation: in this stage the child gains, or fails to gain, an organismic and prototaxic power to affirm himself or herself in relation to an impinging world of interpersonal realities. His or her innocent and infantile unity with the world gradually yields to a developing sense of personal power or, in a negative vein, to a developing sense of personal impotence. This development is relevant to the child's response of faith, primarily because it shifts the dominant form of that response from trust to courage.

Faith as childhood courage is a basic but undifferentiated sense of self-affirmation in which the self is grounded in a Reality beyond itself. It is a spontaneous and unpretentious self-confidence, which enables children to be themselves totally, and to give themselves genuinely, rather than to hold onto themselves defensively and to assert themselves defiantly. It is a self-affirmation in which the self derives its power to affirm itself from that which matters infinitely to it. Obviously, as the child develops, the scope of this rudimentary faith must be extended drastically in relation to self and God, but this fact does not negate either the existence or the importance of the primitive roots of faith as a prototaxic and self-transcending self-affirmation.

In adulthood, this primitive faith should become what Paul Tillich calls the courage to be, the courage to affirm oneself "in spite of that which tends to prevent the self from affirming itself." According to Tillich, the self obtains this ultimate power of self-affirmation only as it is grounded in God, a "grounding" that enables it to be itself against all forms of nonbeing that threaten to destroy it. More specifically, "courage participates in the self-affirmation of" God and thereby gives the self a power that transcends "the non-being which is experienced in the anxiety of fate and death, which is present in the anxiety of emptiness and meaninglessness, which is effective in the anxiety of guilt and condemnation" (Tillich [1952] 1977, 155). In addition, courage is an essential form of faith, because it tends to overcome the risk inherent in faith: namely, the shattering risk that the ground upon which one has built one's self-affirmation may prove to be utterly powerless.

Faith as Obedience

Increased skill with language and locomotion expands the imagination and inflames the autonomy of the four- and five-year-old child to a point where he or she possesses an unlimited and undisciplined sense of self-assertion. The child projects himself or herself into the world of parents, desiring to be like them in ways that may even at times frighten him or her. In any case, he or she manifests a dominantly intrusive mode of behavior, invading the interpersonal world around him or her by various means—specifically, through "the intrusion into other bodies by physical attack; the intrusion into other people's ears and minds by aggressive talking; the intrusion into space by vigorous locomotion; the intrusion into the unknown by consuming curiosity" (Erikson [1959] 1980, 90). As Erikson says, there is no simpler or more direct way to describe this undiminished self-assertion than to say that the oedipal child is "on the make," not necessarily in a sexual sense but in the more basic sense of being an active and energetic ingredient in an expanding world of competition and conquest.

The child's manifestation of unlimited self-assertion is countered by an opposite force, initially by the significant others who stand over against him but gradually by the internalization of their standards in the form of a self-governor called conscience. The basic quality of this conscience is decisive in the immediate and influential in the long-term life of the child. On the one hand, an atrophic conscience that is unable to temper unlimited initiative yields an irresponsible and egoistic self-assertion while, on the other hand, a punitive conscience that is moralistic and uncompromising yields a rigid and overly responsible person. Erikson is concerned about the second possibility and its dangers, for he knows that the suspiciousness and evasiveness that is mixed in with an all-or-nothing superego makes moralistic persons a great potential danger to themselves and to others: to others because they are vindictive and unjust; to themselves because they are permeated and often paralyzed by a deep-seated sense of guilt, a basic conviction that they are essentially evil.

Ideally, children should emerge at the end of this stage with what Erikson calls a basic sense of initiative. That is, they should add to autonomy the more active and differentiated ability to project themselves into their interpersonal surroundings in a way that represents a proper balance between possibility and prohibition, between self-assertion and self-discipline.[2]

Although faith is not a creation of will and not at all a mere act of "will power," Erikson's concept of initiative, like his concept of autonomy, implies that faith involves, and is tied up intimately with, our whole conative life, for initiative, like autonomy, deals with the child's will or, more specifically, with his or her self-determination and self-affirmation. Initiative, however, adds to autonomy the oedipal child's tendency toward unlimited and even egoistic self-assertion. Consequently, the development of conscience, that is, the ability to respect and to respond to a demand, is a decisive occasion in the child's life. In a maximal sense it means that the child's intentionality is qualified by, and in part represents a response to, a much larger reality than his or her own inner desires. It is at this point that the present stage becomes especially relevant to the response of faith, for as the child becomes responsive to the claim of a transcending other, the dominant characteristic of his or her ultimate concern becomes obedience rather than courage.

Obedience—genuine obedience—should not be taken in a moralistic sense to mean passive subordination to authoritarian law, whether internal or external, even though many children never get beyond that orientation. Instead it is a holistic response, in which hearing, willing, and doing are all involved. Or as Thomas Oden, following Rudolf Bultmann, says: It is "not a 'work' in the sense of an activity in which the self does not fully participate, but rather must be understood as one's deed, [that is,] an act in which one's whole being participates in one's doing" (Oden 1964, 30).

At its best, then, obedience as a form of childhood faith is a radical

---

2. Stated in the positive terms of Erikson's (1964, 122) scheme of evolving human virtues, initiative is correlative with a sense of purpose, where purpose is defined as "the courage to envisage and pursue valued goals uninhibited by the defeat of infantile fantasies, by guilt and by the foiling fear of punishment. . . . It is the strength of aim-direction fed by fantasy yet not fantastic, limited by guilt yet not inhibited, morally restrained yet ethically active."

change in the child's willing. It is an organismic move from unlimited self-assertion, or even from egoistic desiring, to authentic responsiveness to an ultimate demand without the loss of proper centeredness. For the oedipal child, this move is often not a conscious and really not a very differentiated response. Instead it is a parataxic mode of relating that is probably manifested more directly in the child's spontaneous reaction to the impinging demands and structures of life than it is in his or her verbal and behavioral reaction to a conceptual presentation of God. In other words, faith as childhood obedience is an inward and spontaneous act in which the self submits itself to the concrete claim of an ultimate Other, not as a foreign law that is imposed upon the self but as an inner voice that actualizes authentic self-affirmation. In adulthood, of course, faith as obedience should become more highly differentiated. It should become an explicit and organismic commitment to God as creator and redeemer of life. More specifically, it is life free from any self-assertive attempts to make oneself acceptable, because the self is empowered to give itself to the love of God and to submit itself to his will.

Faith as Assent

Although the child from six through ten is not driven by any great psychosexual upheavals, he or she is still immersed on a psychosocial level in the fundamental and perennial struggle to become an adequate and significant person. During the latency period, this struggle revolves around the child's pervasive need to master important segments of the surrounding world, to master them not by the egoistic assertion of will or imagination but by becoming proficient and knowledgable in the art of doing things. Universal recognition is given to this need in the sense that "in all cultures, at this stage, children receive some systematic instruction" in the technological and cultural aspects of their particular society. Throughout these years, then, the child, whether at school or at play, is caught up in the impelling struggle to gain productive mastery of his or her world. And "this new mastery is not restricted to the technical mastery of toys and *things*; it also includes an infantile way of mastering *experience* by mediating, experimenting, planning and sharing" (Erikson [1959] 1980, 90).

Successful completion of this stage yields a capacitating sense of industry, that is, a basic sense of being not only useful and productive but also insightful and even creative. If the child is made to feel incompetent and unable to produce or to understand, however, he or she arrives at the threshold of adolescence with a paralyzing sense of inadequacy and inferiority.

Obviously, the child's struggle with industry goes beyond mere physical skill and includes the cognitive ability to know and understand, not just on a technological level but on the more basic level of value and meaning. In a maximal sense, it involves the power of the mind to grasp one's technological and cultural heritage and to appropriate and use it in ways that are productive and meaningful. The struggle with industry in this maximal sense is directly relevant to the child's response of faith, for it shifts the focus of that response from obedience to assent.

To clarify this shift it is helpful to recall Martin Buber's contention that "there are two, and in the end only two, types of faith," both of which "can be understood from the simple data of our life: the one from the fact that I trust someone, without being able to offer sufficient reasons for my trust in him; the other from the fact that, likewise without being able to give a sufficient reason, I acknowledge a thing to be true" (Buber 1961, 7). In other words, faith for Buber is two kinds of relationship, each of which in its own way involves "my entire being": the first is a relationship of experiential immediacy in which the individual finds himself or herself in a state of contact with the other; the second is a relationship of organismic acknowledgment in which the individual affirms as true what is said about, or proclaimed by, the other. In a final sense, of course, these two relationships are interrelated dimensions of faith rather than typological entities, for each one tends to involve and move toward the other: a real relationship of trust tends to move toward the acceptance of that which is spoken by or about the other, while a genuine acceptance of that which is proclaimed tends to lead to an organismic trust in the one who stands behind the proclamation.

Granting Buber's distinction, assent is faith in the form of the second relationship. This does not mean that assent is mere intellectual acceptance of certain authoritarian theological propositions. Instead, it is an affirmative response to one's ultimate concern on the representational level of symbolization rather than on the undifferentiated level of immediate experiencing. In less neutral terms, it is a wholehearted acceptance of God as he is disclosed and symbolized in the claim and the confession of the Christian community.

Childhood assent has its technological preoccupations dealing with how God does what he does, but basically it is a desire to know him more fully—a desire that is met more or less adequately by the church's practice of offering the child some systematic instruction in the Christian faith. In other words, it is a serious attempt to move out of the prototaxic experience of religious infancy toward the syntaxic experience of religious maturity. In this struggle, children probe and question not only their own experience but also the verbal and written testimony of others, seeking to gain a mastery of what is proclaimed, not with the sacrilegious purpose of attempting to discredit it but with a sincere desire to try to appropriate and use it. In short, they seek to gain closer union with God—the God of their fathers and mothers —through increased knowledge of him. Thus childhood assent, at least ideally, becomes an organismic acknowledgment of the truth of God as the child moves toward a deeper and more adequate comprehension of that truth. Optimally, of course, this growth should be extended in adulthood so that faith as assent becomes an unqualified yes to God, based on a precise and intimate knowledge of the content and message of God's revelation of himself. Movement in this direction brings assent into dialectical relationship with trust, for, as Buber points out, an organismic acceptance of that which is proclaimed leads to a basic trust in him who is the subject of the proclamation. In this way, trust and assent are interrelated forms of the multidimensional response called faith.

Faith as Identity

As a time of sexual and psychosocial upheaval, adolescence is an age of disruption and consolidation, a developmental season of tearing down and building up. Erikson gathers the numerous skirmishes into a single struggle by saying that adolescents are engaged in a process of developing a basic sense of ego identity, that is, an organismic confidence that they are distinct and centered beings whose self-perceptions and self-evaluations are matched by the way others see and evaluate them. In other words, ego identity is achieved when adolescents possess a realistic knowledge of, and experience a positive correspondence between, their self-meaning and their social meaning. The concept of identity can be clarified more precisely by subdividing it into two interrelated aspects.

First, a mature sense of identity includes a basic sense of inner continuity, not as a mere summation of all childhood identifications but as a selective repudiation and a genuine assimilation of earlier experiences into a new configuration of personhood in which the individual lives out of a basic core. Phenomenologically, it is experienced as a sense of unity and wholeness, as a synthetic, though often a preconscious, feeling of knowing who one is and where one is going. In a word, it is being able to locate oneself and one's direction in an interpersonal world of significant others, because one's multidimensional and often diverse components form a dynamic and identifiable Gestalt called "me."

Second, since personal integration without communal validation is neither complete nor satisfying, a genuine sense of identity includes a basic sense of being confirmed by those who mean most to the adolescent, confirmed not by receiving superficial or spurious encouragement but by receiving authentic recognition for the fact that "his individual way of mastering experience is a successful variant of the way other people around him master experience" (Erikson [1959] 1980, 89). Erikson elaborates: "It is of great relevance to the young individual's identity formation that he be responded to, and be given function and status as a person whose gradual growth and transformation make sense to those who begin to make sense to him." Recognition in this sense is "an entirely indispensable support to the ego in the specific tasks of adolescing" (Erikson [1959] 1980, 95), so much so that an adolescent often fulfills the expectations, negative or positive, that are confirmed, implicitly or explicitly, by a significant adult.

As decisive ingredients in the adolescent's struggle with ego identity, continuity and confirmation indicate that adolescence is a time when the pivotal question becomes, "Who am I in relation to the other?" The other, like the I, has existed and been influential in the child's life for a long time, but it is not until adolescence that the individual becomes intensely conscious and reflective about both of them. This struggle seems decisive enough to influence the adolescent's response of faith, for behind the struggle with ego identity lies the implicit or explicit struggle with one's ultimate identity, that is, with the question, "Who am I in relation to God?"

The meaning and significance of faith as ultimate identity can be elaborated briefly in terms of its two ingredients. In terms of confirmation, a sense of ultimate identity answers the adolescent's need to be recognized and respected as a meaningful and significant person. In a minimal sense, it serves as an antidote to the adolescent's struggle with inadequacy and self-doubt by indicating that he or she is of ultimate importance to God; in a maximal sense, it serves as an antidote to the adolescent's feeling of guilt and failure by showing that he or she is accepted and forgiven by God beyond anything he or she can do or should do. In this sense, confirmation is a central answer to the adolescent's need for authentic recognition, for it identifies him or her as an object of God's unqualified love, as a creature of infinite value.

Unconditional confirmation is essential not only to organismic validation but also to genuine continuity. It resolves the adolescent's nagging feeling of discontinuity by making genuine and complete continuity possible. It undercuts the adolescent's need to deny or distort unacceptable parts of the self and frees him or her to see and acknowledge the multidimensional aspects of his or her existence, no matter how unacceptable they may appear when judged by moralistic standards. Consequently, the adolescent experiences a deeper and more adequate continuity, a continuity that can hold past and present, self and other, possibility and limitation in some kind of vital balance. Phenomenologically, it is experienced as a sense of belonging, as an

oceanic and empowering confidence that one is in tune with the ultimate and underlying structures of life. In less neutral terms, it is a
sense of being whole, because one is participating in the healing and
reuniting power of God as manifested in Jesus the Christ.

Faith as Self-Surrender

With the advent of young adulthood, the adequacy of the individual's sense of identity is put to the decisive test of whether the individual has the self-assurance and the power to go beyond his or her own
boundaries and to give himself or herself fully to other people. At home
and at work he or she is confronted with the challenge and the opportunity to enter into selected relationships of interpersonal intimacy. As
Erikson puts it, the person is faced with the struggle "to commit himself to concrete affiliations and partnerships and to develop the ethical
strength to abide by such commitments, even though they may call
for significant sacrifices and compromises" (Erikson 1963, 263).
Obviously, intimacy in this sense does not refer merely to sexual
encounter, nor does it mean the kind of self-giving that results in the
loss or negation of the self. Instead, it refers to an act of the total personality in which individuals are able to give themselves in love and
devotion to another person, especially to a conjugal other.

Genuine actualization of young adulthood means that the individual
is able to give himself or herself wholeheartedly in a reciprocal relationship, so that there is a genuine "counterpointing as well as a fusing" of two separate identities. Failure to approach this goal means
that the individual tends to move toward isolation and self-absorption,
either by withdrawing from the interpersonal world around him or her
or by establishing impersonal and inadequate relationships.

The organismic struggle with unconditional self-giving is relevant to
the individual's response of faith, for under its influence the dominant
element of faith becomes self-surrender.

Faith as self-surrender actualizes the individual's need to give himself or herself to a Reality that is larger and more basic than his or her
own limited thoughts and desires, a Reality "that transcends him
infinitely at the same time that it fulfills himself completely." In this
sense, faith as self-surrender refers to the proper centering of the self,
and not to its negation or passive submission. The self is turned from a
state of self-seclusion in which the self is centered on itself to a state of
commitment to God in which there is a "whole-souled giving of life
into the keeping of God" as the "absolutely trustworthy source and
redeemer of life" (Williams 1949, 187). In other words, faith as self-
surrender is a direct antidote to estrangement as self-centeredness. It is
an act in which the individual in the totality of his or her being turns
toward and becomes committed to God as the final source of life and

meaning. We can even describe it as the losing of life in order to gain it, and not to negate it.

Faith as Unconditional Caring

If the practice of giving oneself to a conjugal other is really healthy and satisfying, it soon moves the individual beyond mere conjugality and confronts him or her with a new challenge—the challenge of making a significant contribution to humankind by becoming a proactive source of generation and nurture. This challenge may be worked out in nonparental "forms of altruistic concern and creativity," but for most individuals it revolves around the production and care of children. In any case, the basic struggle goes beyond mere productivity to what Erikson calls generativity. It goes beyond the mere desire to bring someone (or something) into existence and includes the individual's organismic desire to guide and nurture one's offspring on the one hand and to perpetuate and enrich one's race on the other hand. Phenomenologically, it is the struggle to become a center for enabling power, to become someone who contributes to the future of one's children and one's community by having something of enduring value to give them.

Optimal realization of this stage means that the individual manifests a basic sense of unselfish caring: the needs of the significant other become a matter of crucial concern to him or her. Failure to develop in this direction means that the individual tends to regress to a state of pseudo-intimacy, "often with a pervading *sense of stagnation*, boredom, and interpersonal impoverishment." In other words, he or she tends to retreat into a world of self-concern and self-indulgence, a condition comparable to the unlimited and self-centered desire that theologians call concupiscence.

In the context of the individual's organismic struggle with unconditional giving, the dominant characteristic of his or her response of faith tends to change from self-surrender to caring. Faith as unconditional caring is an act of the total personality in which one loves God with all one's heart, with all one's soul, and with all one's mind. It is faith in the form of love, an unqualified love in which God and, in a derivative sense, self and neighbor are of infinite concern to the individual.

On a perceptual level, it manifests itself in the fact that the individual sees and responds to God in an extensional rather than an intentional way. That is, one does not perceive God through the distorting lens of one's own self-interests but is able to react to the fullness of God in a concrete and differentiated way, as that fullness is mediated through what one actually experiences and not through what one thinks one ought to experience. On a behavioral level, unconditional caring manifests itself in acts of service in which the will of God and the essential being of self and neighbor are of infinite concern. Thus instead of seeking "to draw the whole of reality" into oneself, the individual sacrifices and serves with a love that in its infinite form is both the ultimate meaning and the ultimate fulfillment of life.

Faith as Unconditional Acceptance

As the individual's potency, performance, and adaptability decline, he or she is confronted with a new and final struggle to become a person of mature integrity. According to Erikson, integrity consists of at least two aspects. On the one hand, it means that one is able to face the ambiguity of life, that one is able to acknowledge and assimilate both the "triumphs and disappointments of being, by necessity, the originator of others and the generator of things and ideas." In short, one can see and experience oneself as a dialectic of success and failure, as an interpersonal nexus of health and disease. On the other hand, integrity means that one possesses a basic sense of organismic satisfaction with one's life, that one is content and able to accept both the determinations that have shaped one and the self-determinations by which one has shaped oneself. Actually, both aspects merge into a single reality, namely, a genuine and deep-seated acceptance of one's life as that life has been lived and experienced.

In a foundational way, then, actualization of old age means that the individual develops a basic sense of unconditional acceptance. An organismic sense of unity and satisfaction pervades him or her, because he or she is able to acknowledge and accept not only what life has given or not given to him or her but also what he or she has made or not made of it. Failure to move in this direction means that the individual tends to develop a basic sense of disgust and despair. The person becomes dominated by a pervasive feeling of bitterness and incompleteness, relatively in terms of fate as a determinative component of his or her life, absolutely in terms of death as its imminent boundary.

The organismic struggle with unqualified acceptance is directly relevant to the individual's response of faith, for under its influence faith shifts from its prior form of unconditional caring and takes the final form of unconditional acceptance. Faith as unconditional acceptance is trust but more than trust, obedience but more than obedience, assent but more than assent, caring but more than caring. It is an ecstatic state in which all of the elements of faith are combined into a deep reliance upon, and a decisive relationship with, the God of life and death. It is a theonomous act of the whole personality in which one is able to affirm both the finite and the eternal value of one's life, not because one's life is meritorious or even especially exemplary but because one is unconditionally accepted by, and is of infinite significance to, the God of love.

Faith as unconditional acceptance is the redemptive experience of being unconditionally accepted, or, more precisely, it is a condition in which the individual is "drawn out of himself and is empowered to trust in and to accept God's love and forgiveness as a pivotal fact in his life." Thus, "the gratuitous and unconditional acceptance of God becomes an organismic truth in the individual's experience, enabling him to affirm himself unqualifiably in spite of the extent to which he is still an estranged and guilty person" (Aden 1969, 271–72).

Conclusion

I have attempted to show that the particular developmental stage in which the individual is immersed influences and in part determines the shape of one's response of faith. If this is valid, faith becomes a dynamic and organized pattern of multidimensional elements, but more important it becomes a healing and fulfilling response that is deeply appropriate to the individual's central organismic struggle. Thus faith is not just a passive reaction to a developmental crisis but is also an active and profound answer to that crisis. It is an answer that heals and transforms, because it is attentive to both God's salutary grace and humanity's deepest need.

2

Adult Faith
Development and Ministry

THOMAS A. DROEGE

The academy, not the parish, is the setting that gave birth to faith development theory, and it is in academic circles that the theory is refined and revised. That is as it should be, since theory construction calls for empirical research and interdisciplinary study. It is the parish setting, however, where faith development theory is applied. When the makers of theory are in the academy and its users in the parish, both theory and practice are in danger of being distorted. The danger for the theorist, of course, is becoming too distant from the setting where faith flourishes. As one who works in the academy, I am very conscious of this danger, but my attention in this chapter will be focused on the problems and possibilities of using adult faith development theory in the parish setting.

The value of faith development theory is that it offers a useful tool for reflecting on the dynamics of faith, both one's own and the faith of others. There are many possible uses of faith development theory for enhancing ministry to adults, but there are dangers as well. One danger is that an inadequate understanding of the theory will lead to distortions and misapplications. Another danger is that the theory will be used for analysis and critique (giving people good and bad grades in faith) rather than for nurture and growth. A third danger is that ministers will use the theory for nurturing the faith of others and ignore the need for nurturing their own faith. We will look at each of these areas in turn.

The Theory of Faith Development

There are two broad traditions of developmental theory that have relevance for understanding faith. Life cycle theory, with Erik Erikson as its leading exponent, provided an impetus to Christians to think about the growth of faith from cradle to grave. Recent studies in adult development have made life cycle theory an even richer resource for reflections on Christian life and faith in adulthood. The other broad stream of developmental theory that has implications for an understanding of faith is a cognitive, structural approach, originating with Immanuel Kant's insight that the human mind acts upon the world to compose it. The mind is not a blank slate which receives and records external stimuli; rather we impose a pattern of meaning on the world as we come to know it. Jean Piaget's structural developmental theory holds that human beings, in interaction with the environment, develop increasingly complex structures to receive, compose, and know their world. Lawrence Kohlberg discerned a similar structural development in the making of moral judgments. James Fowler used a modified form of the same schema in distinguishing developmental stages of faith-knowing.

These two approaches to understanding the developmental dimension of faith are complementary. The life cycle approach of Erikson identifies the issues of faith that are likely to be dominant at a particular stage of life, for example, infancy, adolescence, and mid-life. The structural approach of Fowler shows how faith seeks understanding through the capacities of knowing and valuing which develop in an orderly manner through a sequential progression of stages. The life cycle approach is most helpful for identifying the kinds of faith problems that people are likely to be struggling with in a particular period of life. The structural approach is helpful for discerning how they find and make meaning in these struggles.

Life cycle refers to a way of looking at the course of a human life, taken as a whole, in terms of a succession of phases. Erikson charts what Daniel Levinson has called the seasons of a person's life. Just as there are seasons of the year, each season having its own characteristics, so there are seasons in a person's life, each with its unique life tasks. These seasons, stages, or ages, according to Erikson, are predictable in that they ordinarily come at about the same time in human growth, give or take a few years.

In addition to the idea that every person grows and matures by stages, Erikson emphasizes a proper rate and a proper sequence of growth. Each stage of human development is related to every other stage and depends on the sequential development of each previous stage. I understand this as part of the order of creation, the implanting of a ground plan for the growth of the human personality and the growth of faith.

Furthermore, though all stages exist in some form in the ground plan, a particular stage comes into focus only at its particular time of ascendancy. For example, in the first year of life a child will already have a beginning sense of who he or she is, but it is only in late adolescence that the question of identity becomes the dominant issue.

Usually the idea of growth is that of an unfolding and a smooth transition from one stage to another, as in the growth of flowers. But according to Erikson, human development takes place only in the midst of conflict and its resolution. The conflict normally results in a crisis. Only a successful resolution of the crisis allows the personality to move into the next developmental stage with an increased sense of inner unity and an increased capacity to do well according to personal standards as well as the standards of those whose opinion the person values most.

The structural approach of Fowler helps us to see how the faith unfolding in the life cycle seeks understanding. Faith, which at its deepest level is an experience of trust and loyalty in relation to God, seeks images, stories, and concepts that will express, within the limits of human reason, an understanding of this relationship. Faith-knowing is not a process of indoctrination; the mind is not a blank slate waiting to be filled with all the right knowledge of God. Instead there are patterns of thinking by means of which we construct what we know of God, and these patterns can be charted as predictable, developmental stages.

The way we know God in faith is not different from the way we know other persons and objects in our environment. The object of our faith-knowing is different, but the structures of knowing are not. Knowing is a product of interacting with our environment. God is disclosed to us as loving and merciful through the Bible, through the sacraments, through the liturgy, and through other Christians. Faith-knowing takes place as we respond to the disclosure of God in these means of grace. Our language about the loving presence of God in our lives is a product of our faith-knowing, our making of meaning.

Fowler has discerned six different stages of faith-knowing, each having its place within a sequential order. The sequential order is invariant. No stage can be skipped. Each new stage builds on and incorporates into this more elaborate pattern the operations of the previous stage. This means that development from one stage to the next is always in the direction of greater complexity and flexibility.

Growth from one stage to the next is not automatic and not as directly related to age as the stages in the life cycle theory. Biological maturation, chronological age, psychological development, and mental age are all factors that affect readiness to make a stage transition. The transitions between stages are critical junctures (crises) at which a person's life of faith can be severely threatened. A stage transition means a painful ending as well as a new beginning. It means giving up a total way of making sense of things. It frequently entails confusion, doubt, uncertainty, and what may appear to be a loss of faith.

Thus it is not surprising that we cling to one way of thinking in our faith-life, even when this proves to be constricting and distorted. Fowler's research indicates that many people remain fixed at an early stage of faith development for an entire lifetime, one reason being that churches offer little incentive for progressing to higher stages.

The four stages in Fowler's schema that are most characteristic of adults are

Stage 3: a conformist or conventional stage of faith that is common to adolescence, though it is characteristic of many adults throughout life. Authority resides outside oneself. A person at this stage says: "I believe what the church believes."

Stage 4: the focus of faith shifts from external to internal authority. This can be a period of doubt and soul-searching, but it is an important time for making faith truly one's own.

Stage 5: a stage when faith deepens and becomes more dialogical. Lines of distinction become more fluid, paradox becomes a meaningful expression of faith, and the symbols of faith gain power and resonance.

Stage 6: this is Fowler's highest stage and one that is rarely attained. The longing for moral and spiritual transformation of self and world become actualized in persons like Jesus, Martin Luther King, and Mother Teresa. (see Fowler, 1981, 151–213)

It is important to remember that a particular pattern of meaning making and not the content of the person's faith determines a faith stage. People with widely different theological positions may share a common pattern of meaning making. At the same time two people who make the same biblical or doctrinal affirmation may employ two different ways of thinking about it.

Though the preceding sketch of faith development theory is condensed and abstract, it should suffice as background for a more concrete discussion of adult faith development.

Ministry During Stages of Adult Faith Development

In 1986 the Religious Education Association (REA) completed a five-year research project on "Faith Development in the Adult Life Cycle." The findings of this important research are simply listed here; comment will follow as we reflect on ministry to adults in various stages of adult faith development.

1. Maturity in faith is related to resolving psychosocial tensions in marriage, job, or other circumstances. Psychological and spiritual health are closely related.
2. The period of early middle-age (thirty-five to forty-five) is the time of the greatest struggle with resolutions to life-cycle tensions and is likely to be the most critical time for adult faith development.
3. Men and women experience the faith journey differently. Women reflect on and find fuller dimensions of meaning in experiences they associate with their faith journey, and tend to share faith attitudes with others more than men.
4. Involvement and participation in a religious community is not a determining factor in a person's growth in faith unless the community helps to "sponsor" or encourage that person's spiritual quest.
5. Crisis experiences, both positive and negative, appear to be the major factor in the stimulation of faith development. Most changes in an individual's faith take place at times of life transitions.
6. Two out of three persons believe that faith should change throughout life, although fewer church members than nonmembers hold this view.
7. Higher education leads to more openness to faith change, and also to a weakening of traditional faith orientations. Many regard this as having "less faith" rather than "more faith," a finding that appears to be related to the finding that church members feel that faith should not change.
8. Involvement with social issues and concerns appears to enhance faith development.
9. A balance between the "cognitive" and "affective" dimensions of one's faith development is highly important.
10. Nontraditional forms of education often lead to greater maturity in one's faith development.

This REA research is particularly significant because most of the developmental studies of adulthood completely ignore the religious dimension of experience. A good example is Levinson's research on *The Seasons of a Man's Life*, which is a highly respected in-depth study of forty adult males over an extended time span. None of the stories about these males even mentions faith as a factor in the scheme of life, not because faith was not a factor in their lives but because the research failed to focus on this critical dimension. The REA research is an important corrective to this secular bias.

Adult development is different than child development. You cannot avoid the reality of development in the early years of life, especially when it comes in such dramatic form as in adolescence. In the adult years we are able to ignore the process of development or repress our awareness of it until it hits us with a jolt, most often at the turn of a decade. (Perhaps this is a clue to a point of readiness for reflecting on faith development issues.) The celebrated mid-life crisis is probably the biggest such jolt. At such times all the old questions come back to haunt us. Who am I? Do I still believe in the things I thought worthwhile? How could I spend so much time doing this and have it all seem so fruitless? Is this all there is? Part of the problem is that change catches us unaware, as if changes shouldn't be taking place in our lives, as if we shouldn't be different people with different goals and different meanings at fifty than at twenty-five.

Levinson accounts for three seasons of adulthood: early adulthood (twenty to forty), middle adulthood (forty to sixty), and late adulthood (sixty to eighty). He analyzes the life structure of individuals throughout the seasons of their lives. There are many components to the life structure: occupation, love relationships, marriage and family ties, and the social networks that sustain each of us as individuals. Missing, as I noted before, is any reference to faith as part of that life structure. Just as glaring is the omission of women from this study, which obviously means one must be careful not to assume that the findings apply equally to males and females.

I will use Levinson's (1978, 56–63) three seasons of adulthood as a structure for discussing adult faith development. The REA study shows that faith development occurs at all ages in adulthood and is directly related to the life structure of individuals, even though most people in the study had difficulty seeing their psychosocial development as related to the development of faith. The tradition of faith as "unchanging" makes recognition and acceptance of faith as "developmental" extremely difficult for many people who are aware of the profound social and cultural changes in their lives but relatively unaware that similar changes in faith may be taking place at the same time.

Between each of the seasons exists a transition period in which one life structure begins to deteriorate and a revitalized life structure must be created. These are likely to be periods of upheaval: age seventeen to twenty-two (the early adult transition), forty to forty-five (the mid-life transition), and sixty to sixty-five (the late adult transition). The choices made during the transition periods determine whether the life structure of a particular season will be stable or in turmoil.

To test this, think back to times when you felt you knew least who you were, what you valued, whom you loved, what you wanted to do with your life, what you felt committed to, what or whom you could trust. The probabilities are that these times fell during transition periods, and that the shape your life has taken was largely determined by decisions made at those times. That is why transition periods are periods when faith changes are likely to occur. One of the hypotheses tested in the REA research is that there is a relationship between periods of transition, change, and crisis in one's life and faith development. The evidence supports this hypothesis, and we will explore the forms of ministry that can best nurture faith in periods of transition.

Ministry in the Season of Early Adulthood

The season of early adulthood runs from about twenty to forty. The early adult transition, which overlaps with adolescence, is from seventeen to twenty-two. Gail Sheehy, whose popular book, *Passages,* was based on Levinson's study, calls this transition "Pulling Up Roots." This is the time when most young people leave home, some to enter college, others to get married or to move into their own apartment. It is an exciting time of freedom and independence, but it is also a burdensome time of living with the consequences of the decisions that are likely to be made during the early adult transition: occupation, marriage, where to live.

Faith becomes a matter of personal choice at this time; at least it is an ideal time for the shift of focus in faith from external to internal authority, Fowler's stage 3 to stage 4 transition. If a young person finds a supportive environment when he or she leaves home, there will be less dependence on authorities for right answers to questions of beliefs and values. Healthy development will prompt trust in one's own perceptions, experiences, and understandings. That happens gradually, of course, and needs the support of a caring community of faith.

Not all young people succeed in forming a faith identity that is uniquely their own. They may have been warned against reflecting on their faith in a way that might question any of the time-honored beliefs that they have inherited from the faith community in which they were raised, or it might be that the community of faith which the young adult joins may encourage total dependence on the authorities within the community. Or faith may be regarded with disdain by those with whom the young adult relates most closely and, as a result, faith gets suppressed or at least hidden from public view. Whatever the reason, attacking a new agenda of life tasks with a pattern of meaning making from an earlier era virtually assures that one will settle for a narrower and shallower faith than one needs. It may even mean that faith will never develop beyond the pattern of either passively conforming to or rebelliously rejecting the values and beliefs that were given by external authorities.

The period that Levinson calls "Entering the Adult World" goes from about twenty-two to twenty-eight. The chief task of this period is to fashion a provisional life structure that provides a workable link between the adult society and one of its newest members. It is a time for testing a variety of initial choices regarding occupation, marriage and family, life-style, and faith orientation. There is need for a stable life structure while keeping some options open.

The age thirty transition, which extends from roughly twenty-eight to thirty-three, provides an opportunity to work on the flaws and limitations of the first adult life structure, and to create the basis for a more satisfactory structure with which to complete the era of early adulthood. At about twenty-eight the provisional quality of the twenties is ending and life is becoming more serious, more "for real." This process can be fairly smooth for those who have found a settled place to be, but for most of the men in Levinson's study this was a period of crisis in which they found their present life structure unsatisfactory but seemed unable to form a better one. There was often a sense that "if I'm going to change my life, I'm going to have to do it now before it's too late."

The season of early adulthood is completed at about age forty. The period of time from age thirty transition to forty is a time for settling down or "rooting," as Sheehy puts it. There are two major tasks in this period; one is to establish a niche in society, a place where one belongs, and the second is to make it, to prove oneself, to climb the ladder of success—and to do so without selling one's soul. If all this happens according to schedule, then at the end of the "settling down" period a person has become a senior member in his or her world and can speak more strongly with his or her own voice. It is a fateful time in a person's adult life.

The element that I would like to focus on in Levinson's description of early adulthood is the element of striving. Levinson has a felicitous way of talking about how this striving takes shape in the form of "the Dream":

> In its primordial form the Dream is a vague sense of self-in-adult-world. It has the quality of a vision, an imagined possibility that generates excitement and vitality. At the start it is poorly articulated and only tenuously connected to reality although it may contain concrete images such as winning the Nobel prize or making the all-star team. It may take a dramatic form as in the myth of the hero: the great artist, business tycoon, athletic or intellectual superstar performing magnificent feats and receiving special honors. It may take mundane forms that are yet inspiring and sustaining: the excellent craftsman, the husband-father, in a certain kind of family, the highly respected member of one's community. Whatever the nature of his Dream, a young man has the developmental task of giving it greater definition and finding ways to live it out. (1978, 91)

The Dream is the bearer of striving, and striving is directed toward the achievement of the Dream. There is a danger that the Dream may become one's god, an end in itself. When that is so, the Dream creates the plot of the story that gives meaning to life. In striving for achievement, the Dream can become the substance of faith, the promise which one trusts, and the master to whom one is loyal.

The theology of Luther is especially helpful in exposing the destructiveness of the Dream when it is self-grounded and a slavish master. Luther's life-story during early adulthood is the story of one who lived intensely in the achievement mode of faith. His recognition that the love and mercy of God could not be achieved by anything that he could do triggered the Reformation, the cornerstone of which is Paul's affirmation that we are justified by God's free grace alone (Rom. 3:23). Is it only a coincidence that this shift from a self-grounded to a God-centered faith took place while Luther was a young adult?

Young adults are tyrannized by their Dreams when realization of the dream becomes proof of self-sufficiency, when they look to themselves alone as the source of the dream and the only ones who can make it come true. The REA research suggests that males are more likely to be trapped within the tyranny of their dreams than females. The faith of women is more relational than the faith of men. They are more concerned with meaning than with success. Women are more likely to remain in Fowler's faith stage 3, which is characterized by socialization and dependency.

What is the alternative to the tyranny of dreams? It is a covenant relationship to God in which a purpose and a worth is conferred upon us that we could never generate on our own. Being rooted and grounded in that covenant relationship, we are freed from the tyranny of our dreams and can seek their fulfillment in ways that serve to fulfill the dreams of others as well.

A Dream set within a covenant relationship to God becomes a vocation. Vocation is how you structure your life (work, love, play) in a way that is responsive to the call of God. The call of God can take the form of a dream through which to channel one's energies. Jesus had such a dream; he called it the kingdom of God. And he fulfilled his calling by healing the sick, by feeding the hungry, and above all by dying the death of sinners. Vocation is a way of talking about the difference faith makes in the formation of a life structure in early adulthood. Levinson speaks of one's dream as the key element in the formation of that life structure. When the Dream is given its direction and purpose by the call of God, it continues to provide a powerful motivation toward the achievement of life's goals, but the Dream is grounded in the vision of God rather than in the striving of the self for glory and success.

What kind of ministry is needed for young adults who are attempting to establish a stable life structure? Nurturing by a mentor, one who serves as a role model and guide in the shaping of one's vocation. Jesus was such a mentor for the disciples, even though the deep impact of his mentoring was not obvious until after his death. The lesson in that is about not expecting too much too soon from our nurturing. Throughout his ministry Jesus shares his vision of the kingdom of God and in so doing shapes both the identity of his disciples and their sense of meaning and purpose in life. In spite of the resistance they offer, especially to the idea that suffering is at the very heart of both Jesus' mission and their own, his mentoring had the desired effect, and they prove themselves able leaders in the fledgling church.

Who are the mentors for young adults today? Whoever they are and however they are to be identified, we need to help them reflect on the role of mentoring as a servant ministry. Mentoring as ministry is helping young adults to conceive of their lives as vocation, helping them to find "a purpose for being in the world that is related to the purposes of God," which is the way Walter Brueggemann defines vocation. That is no small task in a world where making it as a young adult often means cutthroat competition in climbing the ladder of success.

How can a life structure be formed so that it conforms to the purposes of God? It is rooted deeply in one's baptism. Here is where we are given our identity as children of God and called to be a people with a purpose. Not just any purpose, of course. Not a self-chosen purpose. In baptism we are called to be conformed to the image of God's Son, Jesus Christ, and to be agents of his loving purpose.

As suggested earlier, Jesus serves as a model for a ministry of mentoring. But we need empowerment as well as example, and baptism is the source of the power to realize the purpose to which we are called. We do not need to prove ourselves as good ministers. In that lies tyranny. Vocation is a gift that brings gladness to the heart, and is at the same time a gift to those who hunger for the care that such ministry provides. As a mentor, you are the apple of God's eye, called to reflect God's love and mercy in service to others. If your faith has been and continues to be nurtured in that love, you will reflect it well. But if you strive to prove to yourself and others that you are the best minister that this world has seen since Jesus Christ, you will reflect only the tyranny of a Dream that enslaves.

The Season of Middle Adulthood

Age forty begins the season of middle adulthood, according to Levinson. The oft-discussed mid-life crisis comes for many between the ages of forty and forty-five, which marks the transition period between early and middle adulthood. One of the ironies of human life is that at the very time when most adults are realizing the full potential of their powers, there comes a corresponding awareness of the limits of those powers. That awareness comes in many ways. The physical evidence is the hardest to deny, especially when you see it in the faces and figures of classmates at a high school or college reunion. But it is not just physical. Reflection on any aspect of one's life structure can trigger awareness of the limits of life. No longer is one up and coming, climbing higher and higher on the ladder of success. Now one is part of the establishment, and a herd of younger people is up and coming from behind. The structure of family life is threatened as children leave home and one's spouse sees an affair as a source of revitalization in life. Suddenly one is aware that there are more yesterdays than tomorrows, that thirty more years of life does not seem all that long.

Levinson uses the term *legacy* to talk about how people cope with the anxieties of the mid-life transition. Children represent that legacy for some people. Parents' concern about "how the children are doing" and the great pride they take in grandchildren makes more sense when one recognizes that their children and grandchildren represent historical continuity, a carrying on of their name. For others work may be the source of their legacy: writing a book, creating a unique product, establishing a company, laying up treasures that will last forever. This is the time of life when a quest for immortality, for some sense of historical continuity beyond one's death, is likely to be at its greatest.

Immortality comes as a gift to the children of faith. Our place in the future is secure, not because of the legacy we leave behind through our children or our accomplishments (all of which could be wiped out with one atomic blast) but because God has promised us and our children a secure future. It is faith that anchors us securely as we weather the storms of mid-life transition, because none of the changes that are taking place can separate us from the love of God in Christ Jesus.

The REA study revealed that there is considerable struggle for meaning clustered around issues in the mid-life crisis period. It appears that mid-life is a critical time during which basic presuppositions are rethought. Some are discarded, and others are restructured in a process of making sense of life's meaning and purpose. This suggests that mid-life is a crucial period of faith development, though not often recognized as such. This may be one of the "teachable moments" which Robert Havighurst speaks of as built-in points of readiness to deal with significant issues.

If our faith keeps us firmly anchored in our baptismal identity in the rough seas of mid-life transition, there is potential for a golden era in middle adulthood. Secure in our personal identity, no longer beset by anxieties about "making it," confident that our life is secure in the hands of God in spite of the losses and limitations that will increasingly be a part of the second half of the life cycle, we can draw on the human strengths and virtues that have accrued over the years and serve the generation to come.

Erikson uses the word *generativity* to account for the mature adult's deepening concern for what a person has produced, be that children or a product of one's labor. In middle adulthood there is a growing capacity to identify with the needs of others and to find personal fulfillment in serving those needs. Productivity comes to full blossom in generativity. The desire to prove oneself matures into a yearning for self-expression and self-fulfillment. The need to be noticed is transformed into a need to be needed. The center of life moves from oneself to the world one cares for and about. Parenthood is the model for such generativity. Any project that is "my baby," however, can be the object cared for and a blessing to others.

The faith term for generativity is care, or what George Forrell has aptly called "faith active in love." Care is an aspect of faith at every stage of life, but it is preeminent in middle adulthood. Children are so needy and egocentric that caring for others is no more than a tiny bud on what will later be the full flower of faith. Thank God for what Erikson calls the interlocking of generations, meaning that the neediness of children is matched by the need of parents to be needed. This kind of caring for the next generation is already coming into bloom in early adulthood, but it does not reach its peak and full flowering until middle adulthood.

Jesus' ministry of healing, his teaching, his style of life, and his dying model is for us what caring is all about. We are the recipients of that care, and our faith fastens onto him as the one who cares for us and models our caring for others. As we feel cared for by Christ, we are freed to care for others. So also those who are cared for by us are made secure enough to care for others. That is the gracious cycle of faith and the reason why it is such an essential ingredient in the unfolding of the life cycle.

It is in this stage of adulthood that Christians can be expected to realize their fullest potential for ministry. The mentors of young adults are most likely to be Christians in middle adulthood. Though there is danger in becoming enslaved to the tyranny of one's Dream, there are also wonderful opportunities for ministry at this stage of life and the fulfillment of a dream that is shaped by the purposes of God. How can adults avoid the danger and make the most of their opportunities? That's the central question for ministry to Christians in middle adulthood.

In some cases that ministry will need to take the form of counseling those who are going through a mid-life crisis and in danger of getting lost, heading down the wrong path, and making self-destructive choices. For the most part, this is growth counseling since mid-life transition is part of normal human development. At the same time it would be a mistake to underestimate the potential for self-destruction in a mid-life crisis, especially for anyone whose life structure has been self-grounded. In such cases the goal may be restoration to wholeness rather than growth in faith.

For those who are not in crisis, ministry that deepens spirituality is likely to be most helpful to people in the stage of middle adulthood. No longer preoccupied with "making it," adults at this stage are often ready for invitations to explore the inner world of their experience. This is Fowler's stage 5 of faith-knowing, where images will be more powerful than concepts, stories more meaningful than doctrine, and liturgy more enriching than preaching. For the most part our imagination gets shut down in childhood, partly because of shifts in mental structures and partly because of a scientific bias in our culture. But the middle years bring the opportunity for the flowering of the imagination once again, and with it a deepening of faith. Among the resources for deepening spirituality and exploring the meaning of life are exercises in guided meditation, journal writing, retreats, and growth groups.

Not all adults at this stage of life will be open to a ministry that is directed toward growth in spirituality. Nor is growth in spirituality limited to adults at this stage of life. Some people are naturally more reflective than others, and women generally are more attracted to a ministry of spirituality. Adults who are inclined toward activism rather than reflection are surely being generative when their activism is an expression of their servanthood.

A ministry of generativity rather than productivity is the appropriate goal for middle adulthood. That calls for a balance between action and reflection. Those who feel primarily called to a life of reflection at this stage may need to be prodded into action, and those who are primarily activists may need to be prodded into periods of reflection. A successful completion of the stage of middle adulthood is most likely when the balance is maintained.

Ministry in the Season of Late Adulthood

The season of late adulthood remains largely uncharted. That should not surprise us since the number of people at this stage of life has only recently begun to match the numbers at earlier stages. Levinson is no help to us since his study stops with middle adulthood. The literature on ministry to older persons has grown significantly in the last ten years, but I am not aware of any longitudinal research like that of Levinson's that can serve as a reliable guide for charting this last stage of the human journey. I am hesitant to say much about late adulthood also, because I am only on the threshold of making the transition into this stage of life.

Retirement is the event that completes the transition into the period of late adulthood and symbolizes the "letting go" that appears to be the dominant image of this season of life. People over sixty-five keep telling me that there is life after retirement, a good life, and that we too often paint pictures of late adulthood that make it seem like a tire that is gradually losing all of its air. As affirmative as I am of the need for a positive view of aging, one must still acknowledge that "letting go" is more characteristic of this stage of life than "taking hold."

Though many people long for the time when they won't have to go to work every day, retirement is often difficult. So much of our identity is locked into what we do, and we work so hard to shape that identity throughout adulthood. When I retire I will no longer be a professor of theology. Who, then, will I be? I don't know, and that's scary.

Only a faith that is rooted in the promise of justification by grace can free older adults and all the rest of us from the threat of worthlessness when we are no longer productive. Worth is based on something other than productivity. It comes as a gift from God. To be a child of God is to be equal to every other child of God, worth no more and no less. We don't have any difficulty saying this about the developmentally disabled. Their worth as children of God is not dependent on what they produce. Why can't we say that about ourselves and others at the point of retirement? Probably because we've lived by another standard, one dictated by society, and it's not easy to lay that aside at an arbitrary point like retirement.

Faith rooted in baptism takes on its deepest meaning in late adulthood. Our baptism is the assurance of our worth in the eyes of God. What God said to Jesus at the time of his baptism is what God said to each of us at the time of our baptism: "You are my Son, whom I love; with you I am well pleased" (Mark 1:11 NIV). And we have the sure promise that the gift of faith which has its beginnings in baptism is a gift for eternity. Jesus says: "He who believes in me, though he die, yet shall he live, and whoever lives and believes in me shall never die" (John 11:25–26 RSV).

A baptismal faith is particularly meaningful at the end of life because the real death of a Christian occurs at the very beginning of life in the rite of initiation into the church. Endings and beginnings are deeply intertwined in the gracious action of a God who puts an end to the power of sin and death at the very beginning and promises resurrection and new beginnings at the very end. This is the deepest meaning of faith—that all of our beginnings and endings, including the beginnings and endings of our faith transitions, are rooted and grounded in the life and love of God.

What are the needs of those in late adulthood that would suggest the shape that ministry should take in this period? If Erikson has correctly identified the developmental task of this stage as integrity versus despair, then one of the needs of the elderly is to have a felt sense of completion and satisfaction about the whole of their lives. They need to have satisfying answers to questions like the following: What will I be remembered for? What does the dream that faith fashioned into a vocation look like as I reflect on it now? Was it a good dream? Did it get fulfilled? What is it about my vocation that I wish I had changed? Was it my dream or someone else's dream for me?

Another need common to the elderly is the grace to receive the care of others gracefully. Most people think that it is much easier and better to receive than to give. As one who has spent a lifetime in ministry, I do not believe that for a minute. It is much harder to receive than to give. I have very little difficulty in reaching out to others in their time of need. I find it exceedingly difficult to ask help for myself. That is why late adulthood can be very trying for those who have devoted their lives to ministry. If we can be more cognizant of our needs and our dependence on others to meet those needs throughout our lives and especially in the period of middle adulthood, we will serve others more effectively and be better prepared for the dependencies we will inevitably face in our later years.

Finally, programs of death education and grief ministry will be particularly meaningful to people in late adulthood. It has been my experience that exercises in guided imagery can be very helpful to Christians as they reflect on the meaning of their dying and the losses in their lives. I have taught a university course, "Understanding Death and Dying," for the past ten years, and guided imagery has been more effective in putting students in touch with their experience than any other kind of experiential exercise. Because it seemed to me that this was such a useful resource for parish ministry, I published a book, *Guided Grief Imagery*, that contains a study of images found in Scripture, liturgy and hymnody, and pastoral care, as well as twenty-six exercises in guided imagery that can be used in adult forums, Bible classes, and homilies.

Nurturing Faith in Periods of Transition

Faith needs nurturing at every stage of the life cycle, but the periods of transition between stages are times when that need is particularly acute. Transitions are periods of high vulnerability, and those who are engaged in ministry need to pay special attention to people in these predictable periods of great stress.

What is involved in transitions? First, they represent an ending. Most of us try to ignore endings by acting as if we can go through a transition without coming to terms with what is left behind. We focus on the challenges of the next stage, the next job, the next marriage. The transition mentioned most frequently in the REA research was the loss of loved ones through death, desertion, or divorce, but we know that loss is a key element in every transition, including the positive transitions like marriage and having a child. In teaching on a college campus, each year I witness the transition that every graduating senior must experience. I have listened to more than twenty commencement addresses at the university where I teach, but I have yet to hear one that mentioned endings, much less one that used it as a theme. Yet nothing is closer to the center of experience for a college graduate than coming to terms with endings: parting with friends with whom one has shared many intimacies, leaving mentors who have modeled a life of faith and hope, and departing from a community in which one's identity was shaped.

The second characteristic of transitions is that they carry people into a wilderness period, a time when nothing is firmly in place, a time when the pervasive feeling is a sense of being on a storm-tossed sea without clear direction. They are no longer who they were. They are not yet who they will be. They are not sure who they are. Though this confusion is a normal and necessary part of a transition, it can be very unsettling, especially when there are no culturally established rituals to facilitate the movement between what was and what will be.

Only after attending to the sense of loss and being lost can a person talk about a transition as a new beginning. Things fall into place, and the way into the future becomes clear. Awareness of the new beginning may come with the realization that there is more order than chaos, more power to act than feelings of helplessness, more acceptance of self and world than self-doubt and self-contempt. As this happens, a surge of energy fortifies the person in transition for the new opportunities that make each new period of life and each new stage of faith exciting and challenging.

The most striking biblical image of transition that I know is Jesus on the cross, a Jesus in need of nurturing rather than being the one who nurtures. Jesus was facing the most difficult developmental transition that any of us will ever face—his own death. We can call it a transition because we affirm that he rose from the dead. But before Easter came Good Friday; the ending was hard and the resurrection not at all obvious. With his mission in shambles and abandoned by the core group that he had so patiently taught and trained, Jesus even felt forsaken by God. Nevertheless he called out, "My God, My God." In this call of faith we can hear the trust that holds on to the promise that there is a power and a love that will carry him safely to the other side.

It is that kind of trust we need to nourish in persons who are going through periods of transition, trust in the promise of a power and a love that will carry them to the other side. At times what is needed may be nothing more than an attentive presence. At other times it might call for an exploration of values and beliefs. At yet other times it might be meeting material needs. Whatever form it takes, a caring ministry needs to make real and concrete the promise of the gospel to which faith clings.

Ministers have always responded in some form to the faith needs of persons in transition, but often it has been an intuitive rather than an informed response. As a result, many faith transitions are understood poorly, and even treated as evidence of a lack of faith by well-meaning ministers. For example, it is a temptation for ministers to reinforce what Fowler calls a conventional faith (stage 3) that conforms to what the church believes. A transition to a more individuative-reflective faith (stage 4) is often accompanied by doubts and feelings of isolation from more conventional believers. It takes an act of courage for a minister to provide a supportive environment to a person engaged in such a transition, partly because the person may become a restless and disruptive influence in the community of faith.

What kind of ministries are needed by people in transition? Consider preaching. I have listened to many sermons in my day, and only rarely do I sense an awareness by the minister of persons in the congregation who are in transition. Some occasions, like a wedding or a funeral, force the minister to address particular people in a specific transition, and those are among the best homilies I have heard. When writing a sermon or a lesson study, simply ask: What might this text or topic mean to someone in transition?

Biographies are a good resource for ministry to people in transition. They can be used in study groups or in a sermon series. They can be biblical accounts or biographies of some of the great heroes of faith in the history of the church. Biographies inevitably lead to a consideration of the role of transition in the lives of the saints. Stories are more helpful to people in transition than doctrines for the simple reason that faith needs a model to nurture its fragile identity in times of crisis.

Programs of ministry in evangelism need to be informed by an understanding of faith development and the needs of people in transition. I am embarrassed to say how insensitive I was as a parish pastor to the needs of people to whom I witnessed. Effective evangelism must always be dialogical. There is no such thing as the gospel in general. The gospel is always good news to a person in need, but the need will vary from person to person, depending both on the stage of life and the particular situation.

Some clues concerning the needs of people in transition come from James Cobble in a timely book on *Faith and Crisis in the Stages of Life*. He reports on a study of the faith responses of 348 adults between age eighteen and eighty-one, 83 of which were in-depth interviews. He notes that seeking direction from God was an important faith need in early adulthood and tended to surface during transition periods.

Discerning the will of God was often related to finding a job, changing careers, or in trying to become reoriented after a divorce or some other personal loss. The age thirty transition and the decade of the forties surfaced as important directional-seeking periods for men. Women, on the other hand, felt that their lives were in the midst of change much more frequently than did men. Thus seeking God's will was a significant response across the life cycle for women. Cobble goes on to note:

> Within any particular period of life, a cluster of responses will emerge in importance. However, this cluster expands and contracts over time as life issues and personal circumstances change. For example, faith seeking direction may emerge as a prominent response during times of transition, but then may rapidly decline in importance once directional issues become clarified. On the other hand, certain faith responses tend to provide stability and are most likely to persist over time. One such response is believing that "God will meet my needs." . . . In a more generalized sense, trust in God also served as a stabilizing expression of faith. . . . More specifically, such trust was related to the Bible. Trust in the Bible was a third stabilizing expression of faith. (1985, 40–44)

Cobble provides many case histories from every stage of adult development to provide illustrations of faith responses of people in transition as well as faith responses of people in periods when their life structures were stable. Not only does he show that periods of transition are times of readiness for the witness of the gospel, but he also indicates that the kind of witness called for is one that will provide a sense of direction in life.

Beyond what I have said about the ministries of preaching and evangelism, an educational ministry can be enhanced by developing programs that meet the particular needs of people in transition. Many congregations sponsor grief groups designed to provide support for people experiencing loss. Usually the goal of such groups is to provide emotional support, but is not this also a wonderful occasion for growth in faith? The same point could be made about programs for young married couples, those facing retirement, and those willing to gather for purposes of reflecting on their life journeys when they cross one of the decade markers. These are periods of high potential for adult faith development, and adult education programs will be more effective if they are tailored to the specific faith needs of people in transition.

3

Adulthood and the Development of Lived Religion

HARRY A. VAN BELLE

Religion is a term that appears to defy definition. It is referred to as one's relation to God, as personal piety, as faith, as worldview, as belief in a set of doctrines, or as those doctrines themselves. Religion has also been identified with a set of social institutions such as churches or religious orders. Finally, it has been described as a subjective "inner" impulse or projection, which comes to expression in a variety of "outer" objective cultic practices or world religions (Smart 1983; Smith 1963).

Perhaps the reason why religion is described in such diverse ways is that it expresses the totality of our lives and therefore resists being boxed in by any one conceptual framework. What we call religion is itself an expression of the religion we live. My understanding of religion is that it concerns both what is basic to, and what is ultimate in, human life. Religion is that which we live out of and that which we live unto. It involves all that we do from the cradle to beyond the grave. Life is religion. Religion that is not lived is no religion at all.

I do not mean to give a definition of religion in general, because I speak as a Christian rooted in the Protestant Reformation. From John Calvin on, a major theme of the Reformation has been that human life is lived *coram deo*, that is, lived immediately before the face of God. Humankind is by nature man of God (Calvin 1960, 1.1.2).

G. C. Berkouwer, a Dutch theologian, echoes this conviction when

53

he says: "The characteristic of the Biblical view lies precisely in this, that man appears as related to God in all his creaturely relationships . . . , the whole Scriptural witness deals with the whole man in the actuality of his existence . . . , its concern is with the whole man, the full man, the actual man as he stands in God's sight in a religious bond between the totality of his being and God" (1962, 32).

My understanding of religion is not an essentialistic view as if religion were an "inner" impulse of the heart which then expresses itself in "outer" behavior or in social structures. I like the formulation of the sociologist Martin Vrieze, who defines lived religion as *"coram deo, cum hominibus, im mundo,* meaning, before the face of God, with others, in the world" (1984, 74). Religion is not an otherworldly, privatistic matter, but a matter of concrete relationships in the everyday world we experience.

To say that the totality of human life is lived before the face of God is to imply that everything we do, think, or say is always and everywhere a response to God. Our capacity to live is a responsibility, that is, an ability to respond to the norms for living revealed by God in his creation, in the Bible, and in his Son Jesus Christ.

As a lived response to God religion is a multidimensional phenomenon, manifesting itself in a variety of ways. It has an integrative, a normative, an individual-communal, and a historical-developmental dimension.

Being the alpha and omega of life, religion is often viewed as the integrator of human existence. A number of personality theorists have recognized this function of religion. Alfred Adler (1927) referred to it as a "guiding fiction." Carl G. Jung (1964) called it the "numinous experience," for Gorden W. Allport (1960) it was a "unifying philosophy of life," and for Abraham Maslow (1968) it was a matter of "peak experiences." Each of these in his own way has understood that religion orders life by offering it a foundation and a direction. Religion provides the conditions that make life possible and it endows life with a unifying goal. Because religion is both basic and ultimate it makes human life whole.

Religion also has a normative dimension. Even the most confirmed relativists have their absolutes whereby they distinguish the good life from the bad life, good persons from bad persons, good behavior from bad behavior. It is generally accepted that religion offers a system of norms or values that allows human beings to make normative decisions. Perhaps the most time-honored function of religion in human life is as the guardian of morality.

We never believe anything by ourselves but always in communion with others. Conversely, no organized religion or ideological camp can maintain itself for long without the heartfelt participation of its members. The way fellow believers live their religion has a profound effect on the way we live our religion. The individual component of lived religion can be distinguished, but never separated from, its communal component. Religion is both private conviction and public display. Together they make up the individual-communal dimension of religion. (First Corinthians 12 describes humankind as a body of which individual persons are members.)

Because of its foundational and directional character religion encompasses human life from the beginning of historical time to the present. It also envelops the life of an individual person from conception to death and even beyond the grave. But the way religion is lived, what is taken to be the basis and goal of life, shifts from one historical period to the next and from one stage of an individual's life to another. The manner in which religion was lived during the Middle Ages differs markedly from the way it is lived in the modern period of history. Similarly, the religion of a child is quite different from the religion of an adult. Religion changes during the course of history and develops over a lifetime.

Contrary to the views of Auguste Comte and of some present-day developmental psychologists, religion is not an archaic phenomenon. Neither is its importance restricted to any one stage of life, such as childhood or old age. Religion is not dependent on historical time or developmental age. These do not determine *whether* a group or an individual is religious but *how* they live their religion. Historical and developmental change are dimensions of religion.

The Development of Lived Religion

The purpose of this chapter is to explore the manner in which religion changes across the life span, and specifically how it is lived during adulthood. What Søren Kierkegaard (1941) held to be true for the life of faith holds true for the life of religion as well: It cannot be passed on full-blown from one person to the next. Each generation must travel the arduous road of appropriating a religion anew, with changes occurring along the way from one generation to the next. Developmentally and historically, religion changes over time. This means that it must be learned, taught, and promoted before it can be passed on to the next generation. This fact has everything to do with the unfolding of religion across the life span.

Some developmental theorists have attempted to investigate the development of those aspects of human existence that traditionally were the intellectual province of philosophers of religion and theologians, that is, ethics and faith. Notable among them are Lawrence Kohlberg (1963), who researched the development of morality, and James W. Fowler (1981), who studied faith development. In their search both these investigators oriented themselves to a cognitive development model, specifically to the theory of Jean Piaget. This approach allowed Kohlberg and Fowler to draw on the wealth of data already collected by Piaget, but it also means that Kohlberg restricted his investigation to the development of moral judgment and Fowler to the development of the cognition of faith. Both theories describe the development of how morality and faith are thought rather than lived.[1]

Kohlberg's and Fowler's approach not only makes how and what we think determinative for the manner in which we behave morally and walk in faith, but also it isolates our thinking from the rest of life. From a cognitive standpoint the dynamics of our thought, developmental or otherwise, including our thinking about morality and faith, are entirely internal to our thinking.

The cognitive model, regardless of whether it is applied to artificial intelligence, computer science, information processing, or cognitive development, can deal only with concepts, constructs, models, schema, and representations, or with models *of* models, representations *of* representations. It does not deny that there is a lived world in which cognition is situated, from which it also derives its representations in the first place, but it cannot explain how the lived world informs the models we make. From the cognitive model's vantage point, cognitions are like the monads of Gottfried Wilhelm von Leibniz (1646–1716)—they have no windows to the outside.[2]

Furthermore, cognitive theory reserves only a marginal place for instruction and nurture in human development. As we will see, I view nurture and instruction as integral components of lived religion during adulthood, so I find the cognitive development model unsuited to my purposes. I find myself much more at home within the psychosocial view of development articulated by Erikson and, as will become evident, his notions of "basic trust" and "generativity" have had considerable influence on my thinking.

Stages of Religious Development

If lived religion encompasses the whole of human life, then it is an abstraction to describe the development of religion as a series of stages through which an individual travels from birth to death. One never lives one's religion by oneself but always in the company of fellow believers. It is the group (the church, the party, or the movement) that believes and confesses as a community of faith.

1. This rationalistic, mentalistic interpretation of religion has a venerable history, dating back to neo-Platonism.
2. Fodor (1980), one of the main proponents of cognitive science, states that the only viable research strategy for cognitive psychology is a form of solipsism that explains human behavior strictly in terms of internal causes.

It is true that the way religion is lived differs from one member of the group to the next, but it is precisely in terms of these differences that members affect one another, and, if things are right, complement (build up, 1 Cor. 12) one another in their faith. This certainly holds true for people at different stages of their religious life. Normally, the unfolding of lived religion in adults complements the development of religion in children and vice versa. Each forms the condition for the other. If we ignore this relational and conditional context of religion by describing its development as a process that occurs internally in individual persons only, then, as we will see, the development of lived religion during adulthood will remain unintelligible.

Trust: The Religion of Childhood

In what follows I will attempt to describe the stages of religious development as I understand them. Customarily religious development is described as the development of faith, where "faith" is a substantive noun denoting one's attitude to life or one's total way of being in the world. I do not use the term in that way. For me, "faith" (or "trust") is a descriptive adjective characterizing the development of religious life during childhood. Childhood existence is trust-full existence. With little to show for itself as yet, childhood religion is an open, receptive, naively accepting, hopeful, anticipatory existence. The end products of its development are confidence, safety, and hope.

Never again can we experience the unconditional trust we feel during childhood. During the first twelve years or so we learn to rely on the constancy and solidity of our physical world; for example, we come to know that the world we cannot see in the dark is the same world we see when the light is on. During this time we also learn to have confidence in our own abilities. We gain the assurance that we are able to do what is expected of us, and we believe that those in whose care we are entrusted are reliable. Finally, if conditions are favorable we develop a basic trust in a providing God who surrounds the whole of our existence.[3]

Both J. Bowlby (1973) and M. D. S. Ainsworth (1970) have demonstrated that the developmental achievement of trust during childhood is important to the rest of our lives. To say that childhood existence is dependent and vulnerable misses the point. Children do not learn to trust because they are vulnerable. Rather, it is because they trust that they can be appropriately dependent on those responsible for their care, even if this also makes them vulnerable to those caregivers who

---

3. "Basic trust" is a term borrowed from Erikson (1963). In connection with religion he states: "Trust born of care is, in fact, the touchstone of the *actuality* of a given religion. All religions have in common the periodic childlike surrender to a Provider or providers who dispense earthly fortune as well as spiritual health."

fail to exercise that responsibility. Pure, childlike faith, unalloyed confidence is a developmental necessity insofar as it provides both the solid foundation for, and the open door to, further stages of growth.

Commitment: The Religion of Adolescence

A childlike faith is an immature faith if it persists unchanged during adolescence. Lived religion demands development as life opens up and unfolds. During adolescence the distinctive character of the development of our religious life is commitment. Adolescence is a time for making choices. Who am I? What is important in my life? What should I do? Whom shall I serve? Where am I going and with whom shall I live? These are the questions of adolescence. Teenagers do not ask these questions merely to satisfy their intellectual curiosity. Rather, these questions betray their heightened awareness that there are difficult decisions to be made up ahead.

The whole of an adolescent's life is focused on the need to make commitments. Every adolescent act is first of all a choice, even the act of whether or not to make a choice. There is a seriousness about adolescent life that is lacking during childhood. Teenagers are busy making the life they live their own, taking responsibility for what they previously took for granted. There is a kind of ethical, moral finality about every choice teenagers make, at least in their own mind. They are involved in a process, the end product of which is a committed life. If we fail to see the centrality of commitment during this stage of development we will never fathom the struggle that being a teenager represents, nor will we understand why some adolescents have to be dragged into adulthood.

Adolescents who have learned to take life on the chin and to revel in the challenges of such a commitment can be said to be adults. They are now able to take care of themselves and are willing to be responsible for their lives. They have come of age and must be respected for it.

There is a world of difference between the trust-full existence of a child and the committed life-style of a young adult. It is, therefore, an obvious pedagogical mistake to treat an adult as a child or to treat a child as an adult. Some denominations fail to recognize the religious importance of this pedagogical fact. It will need little argument that both trust and commitment, faith and obedience, are essential components of, at least, the Christian religion. But not everyone acknowledges that trust must precede commitment in the order of religious development. It may be possible to demand a decision for Christ of a child who has not yet learned to trust. But it is a pedagogical mistake on both developmental and religious grounds because it can only yield an anxious obedience at first, and later, a righteousness based on works. Similarly, to expect no more of an adult than childlike trust is to rob the religious dynamic of its developmental fruitfulness. Trust-full faith comes into its own in committed obedience.

Effective Nurture: The Religion of Adulthood

Childhood religion finds its endpoint in the committed life of young adulthood but this is not the culmination of religious development. If lived religion were a purely intra-individual affair, its development would end with the achievement of adulthood. Lived religion has a communal structure, however, that cannot be accounted for on the basis of individual development alone. If we believed only for and by ourselves, it would be inexplicable why the faith of others, or the lack thereof, would affect us as profoundly as it does. People mutually influence one another for better or worse by the way they live their religion.

During childhood children naively accept the content of their religion from the significant adults in their lives and anticipate the future development of their religion in terms of the patterns of commitments these adults exhibit. Even adolescents do not live out their religion without being influenced by this communal context. Their choices are fashioned from the options available to them in their culture.

Even though children and teenagers never live their religion by themselves, they may be said to live their religion for themselves. They are as a rule preoccupied with themselves. Children may ask, "How can *I* be safe?" but they never question how their sense of trust affects others. Teenagers may ask, "What do *I* believe?" but they do not wonder what impact their commitment has on others. Children and teenagers are concerned about the effect others have on them, but they are not concerned about the effect they have on others. In this sense we can characterize the religion of children and adolescents as a purely intra-individual affair.

The religion of adults, however, is different. To be an adult by definition means that one is able to take care of oneself. This implies that one has developed a religious commitment that one can call one's own. However, for the further development of religion during adulthood it is essential to put this commitment to work for others. Being there for others is inherent to the development of lived religion during adulthood.

There appear to be some developmental factors that distinguish adulthood from both the preceding childhood and adolescent stages and the succeeding stages of life. Researchers of adult development, such as Daniel Levinson (1978), R. L. Gould (1978), and Robert J. Havighurst (1972), all suggest that young adulthood is a period of "making it," a period of realizing a dream. In addition, Erik Erikson (1963) has shown that this process typically culminates in generativity for mature adults. Adulthood seems to be the period par excellence when, to paraphrase Sigmund Freud, we work in order to love.

Faith without commitment is naive, commitment without work is ineffectual, and work without love is meaningless. The dynamic of religion drives committed young adults to develop themselves further. In their marriages, families, careers, and community involvements the push is on to put their newly formulated convictions into practice. Adulthood is the time for demonstrating that the goals one set are achievable, that the choices one made are livable. Making it in all the significant areas of one's life is what adulthood is all about. After a lifetime of learning and preparation the time has come to be productive and successful. Most adults, however, consider themselves successful only when their achievements serve a purpose that extends beyond the goal of personal fulfillment.[4] What one does must not only be done well, it must also be good for others. Adults' work is essentially service.

Children are the special recipients of that service. Much of adulthood is spent having children and raising them. While the primary responsibility for raising children lies with the parents, all the adult members of the community are involved in this task. This fact illustrates a twofold characteristic of development, namely, that at any given stage development always anticipates a later stage and, at the same time, integrates an earlier stage. Anticipation is most evident during childhood, since most children want to be bigger than they are. Integration is most visible during adulthood when it becomes interpersonal and takes on the character of nurturance. To be an adult is essentially to be there for someone who is not yet an adult. To be an adult for someone else is to seek to integrate the next generation into the adult life-style one is in the process of developing.

Religious Nurture

Caring parents want their children to feel secure in the world and to have a goal in life. They want to instill some form of lived religion in their children, usually the form that the parents have made their own. Their sense of success or failure is tied to whether their children are developing the characteristics of trust and commitment. In that respect, children are the report cards of their parents.

Many parents want their children to adopt the religion they themselves have chosen, and these parents feel they have failed if their children choose a different religious path. This desire is understandable since religion deals with what is basic and ultimate in one's life, but such an attitude fails to reckon with the fact that religion differs across historical time periods and from one developmental level to another.

---

4. Robert N. Bellah (1985) has shown that, even though they can only express themselves in the language of individualism, many modern Americans are still guided in their actions by motives derived from a sense of civic duty or the Christian religion.

History does not stand still. Cultures change over time. Different generations have to respond to differing cultural contexts and this change in context induces a change in the form of religious response. So, if religion is to have the centrally important place it deserves in the lives of children, it must be a contemporary religion and not one of times past. One of the most supportive things my father ever said to me was: "Son, you do not live your life the way I do, but I can see in you that the Lord is working out his will in your generation as he did in mine." He understood that there must be continuity and change in matters pertaining to religion.

Parents must also grant that there are genuine developmental differences between them and their children. For adults, religion is a trusted thing and something to which they are committed. It is natural that they want to pass their religion in its adult form on to the next generation. For children, however, religion is something they are in the process of learning to trust and to commit themselves to. It is handed to them from the outside and must be appropriated by them and made their own as they discover its value to their lives. By demanding an adult form of religion from their children, parents fail to encourage them to develop their own sense of trust and commitment to what is basic and ultimate in life.

Parents can live out their urge to make their children conform to their own religion by teaching them its dogma and its rituals. These dogma and rituals are invaluable for children, because they offer them an organized experience of what their parents have come to hold as basic and ultimate in life. Frequently, however, these dogma and rituals are presented to children as intellectualized religious lessons, which, in effect, tell them what to believe and how to behave.

These so-called lessons may have a great deal of meaning for the parents. To them they are living proverbs. However, for their children they are mere statements they will accept and mere behaviors they will perform only out of obedience to their parents. They will not make them their own until they are tested for their trustworthiness in real life. For children the test of the truth of these parental lessons is determined by how they function in the lives of their parents. Even young children have an uncanny, if inarticulate, ability to distinguish what is fake from what is real in their parents' lives. They do not trust statements or customs not evidenced in the lives of their parents. They may go through the motions of praying, of learning Bible lessons, or of attending church services, but they will not stake their lives on these things as long as they remain unconvincing or untested. For adolescents, who are at a stage in life when they must choose a religion of their own, even what is demonstrably true for their parents may not be good enough. They must decide what is basic and ultimate for them in a cultural-historical context that differs significantly from the one their parents grew up in. The erratic behaviors of adolescents often become intelligible when viewed as experimental ways of trying to discover a life-style, a life partner, a career, and a religion that fits in their historical time and place.

Parents provide the right conditions for this developmental process when they take the adolescent's need to choose seriously. Not only should the parents model the behaviors and attitudes their children might choose to emulate, but also they need to provide their children with opportunities to practice the adult behaviors they have tentatively chosen. There seems to be no other way of turning adolescents into adults than by letting them participate in adult society. Finally, parents must be willing to discuss with them the validity of the choices that the adolescents are entertaining. This last step is perhaps the hardest task for parents to learn, especially for parents who insist that their children follow them in the path they have chosen. Discussing with your children the choices they have made is not the same thing as telling them what to believe. It means talking with them person to person rather than as an unquestioned parental authority.

Raising children involves more than the transmission of skills and knowledge. It also involves transferring responsibility from one generation to the next. Giving children the freedom to choose when they reach young adulthood is an indispensable condition for the development of a committed and responsible life-style.

Surrender: The Religion of the Middle Years

The process of religious nurture is such that religion is first passed on, then handed over, and finally surrendered to the next generation. Even during adulthood the nurturing of religion is already a matter of handing religion over to the next generation. One simply cannot successfully dictate the development of religion in one's children. But during the middle years of one's life when one's children have reached young adulthood, the importance of surrendering religion to them becomes all the more pronounced.

If the coming generation is to take up the banner of religion and carry it forward into the future, the preceding generation must surrender its position of religious leadership. Eventually parents must not only give up their attempts to try to change their children but must actively fall in behind them. Parents must let their children lead them into new paths. The act of falling in behind the next generation is an act of courage for people in the middle years because it requires a recognition that what they held to be immutable can be changed, and that what they held to be good can be improved. But such an act of surrender can also be a relaxing gift of grace, if one can discern God working out his will in the coming generation.

Life Review: The Religion of Later Life

As we have seen, developmentally religion goes through various stages: it is first accepted from others, then it is appropriated for oneself, then it is nurtured in others, and finally it is surrendered to others. During the last stage of life religion is simply lived for what it is. Older people live their religion without desiring greatly to change it or to inflict it on others. Their religious thinking is reflective in nature. It dwells on the meaning religion has for their lives, or reminiscently on the meaning it has had in their lives. Most of all, they experience religion as a given, if not always as a gift.

This tendency to review life during the later years is probably due to the realization that the world is changing without one's consent. The realization that one's life is culminating and that what one has come to hold as basic and ultimate is not necessarily so regarded by the younger generations can be a devastating experience. Those who are not desirous of making the world over into their own image may be content to let the world change without being consulted. But the dual awareness that the end of life is immanent and that life goes on in others forces every older person into a life review.

In the course of this review little is changed but much is discarded. Old beliefs that proved to be unreliable and past commitments that failed to bear fruit are discarded as so much excess baggage. Only what has held true through the years is retained. The naive trust of childhood, so full of hope yet so vulnerable to betrayal, is gone. Gone also are the idealistic commitments of adolescence that seemed so rich in promise but proved to have little substance. Even the absolute convictions of adulthood, which worked well enough in one's own life but failed to inspire the next generation, are discarded. What remains is a religion that stood the test of time, seasoned wisdom or, as Solomon called it, "the conclusion of the matter" (Eccles. 12:13 NIV).

Life review cannot be executed on the run. And seasoned wisdom is attained only after days and weeks of reminiscence. In this light the infirmities that afflict us when we are old are not altogether a loss, because they force us to slow down and to reflect on our lives.

Older people have much to teach younger people, but they are less inclined to do so. Though they are always ready to tell stories they are loath to give advice. They will listen patiently to the personal problems of younger people, but they will rarely offer solutions. Instead they are more likely to respond with a story out of their own life. "I used to think that, but then this or that happened, . . . and now I know that. . . ." These stories have the character of testimony. They do not inform people what to do but give them the courage to go on in spite of the problems they face. By placing present problems into a larger time frame they provide certainty for, and openness to, the future.

The changes that take place in a person's life across the life span and across historical time can for the most part be traced back to the changes that occur in that person's religion. Religion is relative to the stage of development one has achieved and to the historical-cultural context in which one lives. It is situated in time and place. Recognition of this fact makes religion more concrete and fosters better intergenerational communication.

If religion is what people count on in life and what they commit themselves to, then we may be asked at any time to give an account of our religion. Is what we count on and commit ourselves to reliable? Does it open a window to the future? These questions become especially pressing as we near the end of our lives because the litmus test of any religion is whether it helps us to come to terms with our own demise. A religion that serves us well enough during our life may not help us to die gracefully or, as the Bible says, "full of days." Ironically, we need an open future at death's door. The Christian religion provides such an open future. It enables Christians at the end of their lives to say, "To be continued" or even to proclaim, "The best is yet to come!"

4

Faith and Cognitive Development

MARGARET A. KRYCH

Faith and cognitive development must never be too closely identified; yet those who deal with faith cannot ignore cognitive development or fail to ask its implications. Unfortunately, some have succumbed to the danger of too closely relating the two or of ignoring their relationship. This chapter studies one influential stage theory of cognitive development, considers how it has been used inappropriately in faith development theory, and makes suggestions for taking account of cognitive development in ministering to those who have faith.

Stages in Cognitive Development

One of the most influential theorists in cognitive development in this century has been Jean Piaget. Piaget's work suggested that children's thinking is qualitatively different from that of adults. He posited stages in cognitive development within childhood. As the brain cells mature, so the quality of thinking changes.

Throughout all stages of maturation there are certain principles of cognitive development. "Cognition always functions within an organization, and it is always an adaptive system, that is, its functioning allows the organism to adapt to its environment" (Lerner 1986, 246). The process of adaptation involves the component processes of assimilation and accommodation.[1] Assimilation is the process by which new items are assimilated into an existing scheme of thinking; accommodation is the process whereby the existing scheme is changed to fit new information. For an organism to be adaptive there must be equilibration or balance between assimilation and accommodation (Lerner 1986, 248).[2] Substitution occurs when a less mature idea is replaced with a more mature idea, the less mature idea still remaining a potential mode of thought. Integration brings together less mature ideas into more complex conceptualities that tend to be stable. Both substitution and integration presuppose readiness to move forward (Elkind 1974, 58–61). Attempting to force development is not helpful. When the child is ready for particular concepts he or she will learn eagerly and quickly with a sense of accomplishment, but when the child is not ready, he or she will be frustrated, and any learning will be temporary.

In his essay, "The Mental Development of the Child," Piaget (1967, part 1) posited six stages of cognitive development that hold true for all children and are invariant and sequential. The ages at which the stages appear depend both on inherited maturational factors and on the environment in which the child is reared.

The first three stages are often treated together as one sensorimotor stage. They last from birth to about two years of age and include the reflex stage, the stage of the organization of precepts and habits, and the stage of sensorimotor or practical intelligence based on the manipulation of objects.

The stage of preoperational thinking lasts from approximately two to seven years of age. It includes the two substages of preconceptual thought and intuitive thought. Preconceptual thought usually lasts from about two to four years of age. It is characterized by developing words as symbols, developing memory of the past, and make believe. The thought is often distorted by a desire to make reality fit the child's desires. It is characterized by egocentricity, the inability to take anyone else's point of view. True concepts (classes) are not formed. Thinking is transductive, reasoning from particular to particular and not from particular to general and vice versa as more mature thinking can do. Intuitive thought differs from preconceptual in that the child can form true classes. However, the child cannot grasp class inclusion. Intuitive thought focuses on part of a problem and ignores other parts or the relation of parts to a whole; this is called centration. In the intuitive

1. Frances Degan Horowitz (1987, 40) explains: "Assimilation and accommodation are represented as follows: The child interprets (assimilates) experience with the environment in terms of his or her existing set of transformation rules; accommodation involves behavior that reflects an alteration of structure (or the transformation rules) to better account for the interaction with the environment."
2. See Piaget (1977).

substage the child focuses on the state of an object rather than on the transformation of the object from one state to another. Intuitive thought lacks logic because it lacks reversibility (the process of reversing an argument to check its accuracy). Thus, young children can hold a number of irreconcilable notions simultaneously.

Preoperational thought does not distinguish between fact and fantasy. Wrong is conceived of in terms of amount of damage done and that for which the child is punished; intentionality is not taken into account.[3] Reasoning from principles to particular instances is beyond the young child.

Somewhere between six and eight years of age most children enter the concrete thinking stage. The child now uses logical operations.[4] His or her thought has decentration. He or she can focus on parts and their relation to the whole. The child's thinking also has reversibility and he or she can check arguments.[5] She can now focus on transformations of objects from one state to another. There is growth in the ability to generalize, and she can see others' points of view. During the concrete stage the child develops concepts of time, space, speed, and causality. The child also begins to take account of intention in judging moral right and wrong. Strong concepts of justice and fairness typify the late concrete stage. Gradually an understanding of death develops: at about six or seven years of age children grasp the universality of death, but it is not until age ten or beyond that the majority begin to understand that death is irrevocable and the cessation of corporeal life.[6]

Despite the leap in thinking ability, the child's concrete thinking is still limited to thinking about what in principle can be perceived through the senses. Children translate statements that have no sensory referent into statements that do. They can grasp simple concrete simile, which does not depend on obvious sensory characteristics, but not metaphor.

Somewhere around eleven or twelve years of age, most children enter the stage of abstract thinking or formal operations. Abstract thinking is able to deal with general ideas and abstract constructions. It uses combinatorial logic and symbols and is able to construct ideals. The abstract thinker thinks about her own thinking, introspects, grasps universal generalizations, reasons about that which is contrary to fact, uses metaphor in sophisticated ways, applies principles in theory, and is no longer limited to reasoning about what in principle is perceivable through the senses. Abstract thinking is typical of teenagers and adults, and clearly is presupposed in formal theological reflection.

3. See Mary Ann Spencer Pulaski (1980, 126–33).
4. On operations see Piaget (1970, 14ff.), and also Charles J. Brainerd (1978, 136–39).
5. See Deanna Kuhn (1984, 143–4).
6. See Edward White, Bill Elsom, and Richard Prawat (1978, 307–10).

Faith

If we are to consider the relation of faith to cognitive development, we need to say something about faith. We shall use Paul Tillich's view of faith as a framework. This will be helpful not only because Tillich has a clearly developed view of faith but also because later we shall discuss James W. Fowler's "faith development" stages and his reference to Tillich's understanding of faith.

Tillich defines faith as ultimate concern,[7] and for Tillich that which is our ultimate concern is that which determines our being or non-being.[8] Such terminal values are gods which may be dehumanizing and idolatrous or which may be directed toward the One who is truly worthy of such centering of one's life. Nothing finite can rightly become a matter of ultimate concern; therefore, to make a finite reality into a god is idolatry (1965, 24). Only ultimate concern with God, who is really God, avoids idolatry (50). And for Tillich true ultimacy, and thus the focus for faith, is to be found in the New Being expressed in Jesus as the Christ. Faith is the certainty that Christ is the center of our history (1964, 2:116). It guarantees the transformation of reality in personal life, which the New Testament expresses in its picture of Jesus as the Christ (123). Faith gives certainty to the victory of Jesus the Christ over the estrangement between ourselves and God, between ourselves and our neighbor, between ourselves and the persons we know we were created to be.[9]

Faith, Tillich asserts, can never be equated solely with cognition. It is a whole-person response, an act of the "total personality, including practical, theoretical, and emotional elements" (54). It occurs when the person in the totality of his or her being turns to God and centers his or her life upon the divine center to which it belongs. It is a total act. "It is not an act of one's volitional, emotive, or cognitive functions alone. Faith is an act wherein all the elements of one's personality are 'synthesized' and 'transcended'. The act of faith embraces such elements (volitional, emotional, cognitive), raising them to a higher unity without being identified with any of them" (Anderson 1972, 4). Faith for Tillich is partly volitional, but never purely so; partly emotive, but not reducible to any sort of feeling; partly cognitive, but never reducible to purely intellectual terms. To reduce faith to any of these functions is to be guilty of distortion, which must be rejected.[10] However, none of these functions can be discarded either since every

7. "If religion is defined as a state of 'being grasped by an ultimate concern'—which is also my definition of faith . . . " (1965, 4).

8. Tillich (1965, 21). See also Tillich (1964, 1:17).

9. See Tillich (1964, 179).

10. See Tillich (1957, 30–40).

function of the human mind participates in the act of faith (Tillich 1957, 30–31). Tillich then preserves a dialectical complexity in the role of cognition, emotion, and will in relation to faith. None of these aspects can be ignored, yet none must be allowed to be separated or to be identified with faith. The gospel must be presented as a message that grasps the person in his or her totality in a response to utter dependence and trust. While retaining a place for cognitive assent to the gospel, Tillich insists that faith is much more than cognitive affirmation. Cognition helps in rationally expressing and communicating the gospel to others, but cognition also participates in the sinfulness of human nature and exhibits the limitations and disruption of the human sinful condition. Reason itself is always in need of the power of the New Being to heal and save.

For Tillich, saving faith does not arise from something in the person but from God. It essentially has a gift quality. Faith is the work of the divine Spirit (Tillich 1957, 2:205). It is the state of being grasped by God and is thus a matter of grace. It is existential, affecting our entire existence, and experiential. The state of spiritual maturity or personal faith can never be fixed with certainty or measured; acts of personal faith are "ever becoming, ever changing, ever disappearing, and ever reappearing."[11] They are preceded by the faith of the spiritual community of believers.

Faith and Cognitive Development

The twin dangers to which Christian thinkers are ever liable is either to identify faith and cognitive development too closely or to ignore any relation between the two. Tillich obviously avoids the latter by asserting that cognition plays an important role in rationally expressing and communicating the gospel to others. However, he also repudiates the suggestion (distortion) of identifying faith and cognition.

Unhappily not all those who quote Tillich are able carefully to preserve this dialectical tension. Fowler, in developing his stages of faith theory, uses a definition of faith as "the dynamic, patterned process by which we find life meaningful."[12] The questions of faith for Fowler

11. Tillich (1964, 3:232) expressly repudiates the idea of quantitative progression in faith. If one is united to God at all in faith, then one "is near to God completely and absolutely" (Tillich, 1968, 229).

12. Fowler (1981, 3) summarizes his definition of faith: "A disposition of the total self toward the ultimate environment, in which trust and loyalty are invested in a center or centers of value and power, which order and give coherence to the force-field of life and which support and sustain (or qualify and relativize) our mundane or everyday commitments and trust, combining to give orientation, courage, meaning and hope to our lives and to unite us into communities of shared interpretation, loyalty and trust" (1980, 137).

"aim to help us reflect on the centers of value and power that sustain
our lives. The persons, causes and institutions we really love and trust,
the images of good and evil, of possibility and probability to which we
are committed, these form the pattern of our faith" (1981, 4). So, for
Fowler, faith is not always religious in content or context; it is simply
"our way of finding coherence in and giving meaning to the multiple
forces and relations that make up our lives."[13] Fowler refers to Tillich's
view of faith as that which has centering power in our lives and
focuses on those things which concern us ultimately (Fowler 1981, 4).
Since all persons are concerned with how to put their lives together
and with what will make life worthwhile, all persons, whether religious
or atheistic, have faith.

Although Fowler refers to Tillich to support his view of faith, he in
fact ignores Tillich's careful and deliberate distinction between those
things which are idols and thus not suitable for ultimate concern and
the One God revealed in Jesus Christ who is suitable. Fowler engages
in a very selective reading of Tillich, adopting those phrases that fit his
own definition of faith and ignoring Tillich's use of the norm of the
New Being to distinguish true faith from those examples of centering
that are in fact idolatry.

Fowler then proceeds to develop his understanding of faith with a
decided cognitive bias. Now Fowler may not have this intention. As a
structuralist he wants to hold that the structures exhibited in faith
organize the person's emotions and social relationships[14] and claims
that his stages cannot be reduced to cognitive or moral stages (1981,
99). In principle, then, he wants to avoid a cognitive bias. In fact, his
stage theory comes across as highly cognitive.

Fowler borrows from Piaget's research in cognitive development and
especially from Lawrence Kohlberg's moral development, which in
turn is highly indebted to Piaget's stage theory. While Fowler's stages 4,
5, and 6 have a social-emotional basis for development, stages 1, 2, and
3 of faith depend on cognitive development. Despite occasional protestations to the contrary, Fowler asserts that there is a qualitative
increase in adequacy in each stage of faith development. He cites with
appreciation the fact that Piaget and Kohlberg "have not shrunk back
from the implication that more developed structural stages of knowing
are, in important ways, more comprehensive and adequate than the
less developed ones; that the more developed stages make possible a
knowing that in some sense is 'more true' than that of less developed
stages." He goes on to say that while in a pluralistic society we may feel
offended by claims such as these, and while in the realm of faith "the

13. Fowler (1981, 4). See also Fowler (1982, 87).
14. See Fowler (1981, 98ff.).

assertion that more developed stages are in significant ways more adequate than less developed ones, has to be made with even greater cautions. . . . Yet we cannot (and will not) avoid making and trying to corroborate that claim" (Fowler 1981, 101). In Fowler's system, the child's stages 1 and 2 are of necessity inferior to the teenage stage 3, and adolescent faith in turn is "less adequate" than the adult stages 4, 5, and 6.[15] Fowler's assumptions about faith in stages 1, 2, and 3 are, then, directly related to and dependent upon his understanding of stages in cognitive development.

James Loder suggests that what Fowler is studying is stages of an aspect of faith, only potentially but not necessarily related to faith in a biblical or a theological sense (Fowler and Loder 1982, 135). Gabriel Moran holds that Fowler is studying those attitudes, expressions, symbols, and such which lead to and from the point of faith (in which faith is a gift and not an object or a human possession), a study of religion and belief (Moran 1983, 122–23) despite Fowler's protest that that is what he is not doing. Whatever Fowler is researching, Robert Wuthnow correctly points to one of the underlying assumptions of faith development theory: "the theory is basically concerned with cognitive processes."[16] While Fowler wishes to avoid the tendency and even criticizes Piaget and Kohlberg for emphasizing cognition at the expense of emotion or affection, nevertheless his faith development scheme clearly follows the pattern of cognitive development and he falls into the same trap.

For Tillich, faith is the work of the Spirit. It is a gift and is inevitably related to salvation. It is the state of being grasped by the New Being in whom the estrangement and conflicts in the human existential situation are overcome. Fowler cannot deal with these aspects of faith without some offensive theological corollaries, presumably that children have less (or less adequate?) salvation than adults, that accepting salvation depends on cognitive development in children and social-emotional experience in adults, and that God apparently gives less adequate faith to the young and more adequate to the older human being.

Fowler is not the first or the last person to relate faith and Piaget's cognitive stages too closely. Some twenty-five years ago, Ronald Goldman led the way in exploring implications of Piagetian theory for teaching religion in England. Using Piaget's stages he found consistent patterns of religious thinking that exemplified the preoperational, con-

15. Craig Dykstra (1982, 58) also notes this characteristic of hierarchy in both Kohlberg's moral stages and Fowler's stages of faith.

16. Wuthnow (1982, 213). The other assumptions that Wuthnow lists (214–18) are the theory's essential humanistic, reductionistic, normative, and individualistic tendencies, and the reification of faith.

crete, and abstract thinking stages (Goldman 1964). Goldman termed the preoperational stage "pre-religious," the concrete "sub-religious," and believed that only the abstract thinker is capable of personal religious thought, the latter becoming well-developed about thirteen to fourteen years of age (1970, 196). Goldman wanted to delay the teaching of theological and biblical content until the child is ready for it. Most content, therefore, would not be taught until the early teenage years and beyond. It is in the adolescent years that Goldman looked for students to exhibit an "act of faith, supported by an intelligent appreciation of why they believe and what it can mean for them," and hoped that they may embrace Christian beliefs either as they leave school at seventeen years or later in adulthood (192). While Goldman is clear that religion cannot be reduced to an intellectual exercise, nevertheless it is also clear that he considers a very large component of faith to be the grasp of intellectually appropriate concepts. Cognition plays too large a role in his understanding of faith.

The current fashion of "measuring mature faith" with lengthy surveys and lists of check-off items, and of producing curricula and programs that are supposed to "mature faith," is probably the latest Protestant attempt to incorporate a heavy cognitive bias into faith. Such approaches are problematic at best and easily open the way to distort faith and turn the gift of God into a human achievement.

Taking Account of Cognition for Ministry

If too close an identification of faith and cognition is dangerous, then the opposite extreme is also destructive. Teaching and counseling that ignore cognitive development fail to show respect for God's creation, human development being part of that creation. Further, to ignore human development is to fail to take seriously opportunities to make the gospel relevant to the hearer, counselee, and learner. If God's Word is to be heard, the development of the hearer is an important factor that must be considered when the Word is to be proclaimed or taught. Since psychological research, such as Piaget's theory, gives no blueprints for Christian teaching or counseling, it is up to the practitioner to ask in what way cognitive development theory may be helpful. A few considerations, chosen rather at random from the myriad that might be given, follow.

First, the Christian practitioner must carefully distinguish between cognitive development and faith as whole-person commitment, trust, and utter dependence as a gift of the Spirit. It will be wise to avoid attempts to measure that gift or rank its adequacy in stages or in any quantifiable way. Especially it will be important to resist the temptation to label a child's faith as less adequate or inferior to that of an adult. By God's grace, a child is as much capable of utter dependence as an adult. The pastor, counselor, or teacher who adopts Tillich's view of faith will take the faith of a child as seriously as that of a teenager or adult. And, by the same token, pastor, counselor, or teacher will take equally seriously the child's rejection of Jesus Christ. We might add that the pastor, teacher, and counselor must likewise take absolutely seriously the faith of the mentally challenged person of whatever age and of whatever cognitive stage and provide for him or her quality pastoral care, time, and opportunities.

A second consideration lies in the area of teaching concepts, a cognitive task and one that is clearly related to cognitive assent to the gospel and to expressing and communicating the gospel to others. This aspect cannot be ignored yet is not to be identified as the sole or dominant component of faith. Teaching concepts appropriately to various age levels requires careful thought since adults tend to treat children and early youth as miniature adults rather than as qualitatively-different thinkers. By and large, we need to teach much less content more thoroughly to little children and then expect to teach much more content to teenagers and adults. In other words, we need to accept children's development and help them deal with concepts when they are ready. The preoperational child, for example, needs only a few concepts clearly presented in straightforward language without metaphors and with frequent repetition. We should not be surprised if children misunderstand, see things only from their own point of view, and pick up parts of an argument but not the whole. These characteristics are typical of the age level. We can help the preschooler build vocabulary; children often use words before they know the correct meaning and at other times have ideas that they cannot express because they do not have the necessary vocabulary. In the case of concrete thinkers we need to accept that concepts of God will be physical or expressed in terms perceivable through the senses. Concrete thinkers will not grasp metaphor, so straightforward language about God will be appropriate rather than parable or analogy. Saying "God loves you" is better than telling a child she is a gem in the Redeemer's crown! We shall expect that concrete thinkers will grasp parts of doctrines, that they will not put the "whole picture" together, that they will have theological questions and sometimes feel uncomfortable because not all their questions can easily be answered in concrete terms. A focus on God's world, the church, stories of Jesus and church heroes, and God's interest and presence in the child's everyday life will be helpful. For the transitional phase between concrete and abstract thinking, the child may feel uncomfortable with previous conceptualities of childhood but find the notion that God may not be physically located "up there" or "out there" strange and foreign. Abstract thinkers will develop mature theological concepts slowly. Abstract thinking enables the adolescent to put together much of the philosophical and theological fragments he or she has heard all his or her life, to follow theoretical arguments, and to have a fuller grasp of traditional religious terminology.

David Elkind reminds us that persons vary in the age that they attain formal operations and that we should not expect that most students will have abstract thinking abilities until about tenth grade or beyond.[17] In addition, teenagers usually need to practice general abstract thinking for a year or two before they can deal easily with complex theological reasoning. All in all, we cannot expect too much too soon of the early adolescent. We need to be prepared to teach and reteach, review often, define terms carefully, explain traditional terminology, and teach from the more concrete concepts to the more universal and abstract ones.

A third consideration has to do with counseling. Cognitive development has emotional and social repercussions. For example, a child's understanding of death has consequences for the way in which he experiences bereavement. Without the ability either to grasp the irrevocability of death or the cessation of corporeal life, the child under ten years of age may well assume that the dead loved one is able to come back to life. Bereavement for the child is more akin to a loved one leaving the country either deliberately—"she has gone away"—or against her will—"God took her." In either case, the child is often angry at the dead person for such abandonment or angry at whoever is preventing the person from returning. The counselor may gently insist that the loved one is not going to return. It need not be a surprise if the child wants to keep the person's room ready and persists in asking how long it will be before the loved one comes back. Watching earth being put into a grave can be a frightening experience for a child: How is Mommy going to dig herself out from under all that earth? When the child reaches adolescence, the parent and pastor need to be ready for a second grief experience. Abstract thinking brings with it the ability to grasp the future and realize a life ahead without the loved one, and, if not before, along with that understanding comes the realization that death in fact is irrevocable. The adolescent now experiences the finality of the bereavement. He ceases to hope that Mom will come back. If the death of the loved one occurred several years before, the young teenager's second grief reaction can be puzzling and distressing to the family and to the teenager himself. A parent may have worked through the grief process a long time ago and now moved on in life. It can be embarrassing and upsetting when the adolescent suddenly begins to relive the grief experience. The parent may wonder if there is some-

17. See Elkind (1984, 152).

thing wrong with the child. A stepparent may resent the sudden focus on the dead person. Well-meaning adults may try to gloss over the grief: "Why bring it all up again now? You should be over that long ago." It is helpful if pastors expect this second grief and are ready to deal with it and treat it as seriously as it deserves; for the individual, the pain of the finality of bereavement is new and vivid. Pastors can warn parents to expect this second grief experience. And young adolescents are often relieved to discover that such an experience is normal and that they are not "crazy" to be mourning someone who died years before.

A fourth consideration has to do with ministry with adults. Cognitive development theory emphasizes the abstract thinking ability of all adults with normal development. This means that all adults need to be challenged to learn about and wrestle with the Scriptures and the depths of the Christian faith. Of course, persons have varying intellectual ability, but all can be challenged to careful thought and learning, in keeping with their talents. Most are far more able than either the church or they themselves believe! A person who left school after ninth grade may have had less practice in reading books but may be just as capable of formal operational reasoning and theological reflection as the college graduate. Many adults who left Sunday school at age ten or eleven have had little opportunity since to reflect seriously on the Christian faith; they often still operate in concrete thinking mode in church. They need helpful teachers and pastors who will challenge them to use their abstract thinking skills to reflect on the Scriptures and to relate theology to their daily experience. On the other hand, pastors also need to be able to communicate with concrete adult thinkers; not only with those who are impaired but with the average adult who, in times of emotional distress, may revert to concrete thinking. It is the caring and astute pastor who knows when to work with the adult in concrete terms and when to challenge the adult to use formal operations and examine facets of the faith which he or she has not yet explored.

Many more considerations can be drawn from cognitive development theory than have been given. And that is the task of the Christian practitioner: to draw implications while preserving carefully the important distinction between faith and cognition. The whole-person commitment of faith includes the cognitive dimension but is not defined by it; volitional and emotional dimensions are equally important. The practitioner must, therefore, take all of these aspects into account and preserve a healthy skepticism of faith stage theory and other approaches that give too much weight to the cognitive dimension or which attempt to measure or quantify faith. While recognizing the limitations of cognition and its participation in the disruption of the human condition, the practitioner also recognizes the role of cognition in clearly expressing and communicating the gospel. To take the communication of the gospel seriously means to explore ways in which the good news may most effectively be communicated and received. In this task cognitive development research can be immensely helpful. If human beings think and develop in particular ways, then it is appropriate for us to examine those ways and ask what they might mean for communicating the gospel through teaching and counseling and preaching.

5

Anonymous Faith and the Psychology of Identity

NEIL PEMBROKE

The Jesuit theologian Karl Rahner has issued a challenge to traditional Christian thinking on salvation through his concept of anonymous faith (Rahner 1974, 1979). His theory is that adherents of non-Christian religions, and even atheists, respond implicitly to saving grace. The aim of this essay is to show that Erik Erikson's (1977a, 1968) description of the identity crisis fits with Rahner's understanding of anonymous Christianity. The thesis argued is that in honestly struggling with the identity crisis, one experiences God's grace. If this is in fact the case, new light is shed on the nature of the development of the personality: God is the stage on which the developmental drama is acted out.

The major problem associated with any attempt to integrate a theological and a psychological concept is that one is confronted with the gap between the transcendent and the immanent. Put differently, theologians are concerned with discourse on God; the focus of psychologists is discourse on the human mind. Where, then, is the meeting point? The reality, of course, is that we can never completely close the gap. Rahner's theology, however, presents itself as particularly amenable to integration with psychology since it has an anthropological starting point. In his theological reflection, Rahner is concerned with "faith as experience of myself and with reference to my own life" (Weger 1980, 9). The struggle for a sense of personal identity is clearly

an important dimension of human experience; consequently, we would
expect Rahner's approach to have some application here. We will not
be able to overcome the difficult problem of psycho-theological integration. Rather, we will be content simply to use Rahner's theology to
deepen our understanding of the identity crisis.

Anonymous Faith

Rahner (1979) defined anonymous faith as a faith that is necessary
and effective for salvation, but which occurs without an explicit and
conscious relationship to the revelation of Jesus Christ. By adopting
the position that anonymous faith is indeed legitimate, Rahner is in
accord with the teaching of the Second Vatican Council. According to
the traditional neo-scholastic theology, an atheist must, in the long run,
incur guilt. The fathers of the council opposed this view by stating that
even the long-term atheist is capable of living in faith, hope, and love.
Rahner's perspective is that Christians can never deny others the possibility of salvation. To do so would be to violate the biblical principle
that we should not judge others.

The idea of an anonymous faith is an extension of Rahner's concept
of the "supernatural existential" factor. Because there is this factor in
human existence, there is no dualism between nature and grace.
Humans do not operate according to two distinct drives—one toward
purely natural fulfillment and the other toward the vision of God.
Rather, human existence is graced existence. We have a capacity to
receive God's loving gift of himself. "This 'existential' is a permanent
modification of the human spirit which transforms its natural
dynamism into an ontological drive to the God of grace and glory"
(McCool 1975, 185). The fact of the supernatural existential means that
there is no aspect of human action in which God's grace is not communicated to us. Thus, whenever we act in good conscience we are experiencing—albeit implicitly—God's grace.

The anonymous Christianity thesis is based on three pieces of theological data: the unlimited, transcendent nature of the human spirit;
the fact that God wills the salvation of all humans; and the fact that
grace is always mediated through Jesus Christ (Rahner 1979). The
human, first, is the being who has the capacity for unlimited transcendence of knowledge and freedom. In our human existence we are oriented to God. This transcendent reference of the human to God is
mediated through what Rahner calls "categorical" reality—through the
concrete, everyday stuff of life. The aspects of this categorical reality do
not have to be religious. Thus, whenever we face up to moral decisions
honestly, we accept ourselves in our self-transcending subjectivity, and
so we accept God. For example, Rahner refers to the fact that when we
act responsibly in relation to technology we are accepting God through

accepting ourselves completely. He also speaks of the implicit acceptance of God when persons go about their daily lives patiently, lovingly, devotedly, and caringly. The mother who gives herself fully in love and patience to the little ones in her care; the student who is guided in his or her pursuit of knowledge by the principles of truth, honesty, and integrity; the worker who carries out allotted tasks in a spirit of responsibility and cooperation; the captain of industry who responds to the call to care for people and the environment; the Hindu who is absolutely true to his or her faith—these are the anonymous Christians.

The second piece of theological data that is relevant to the thesis is the universal salvific will of God. This is expressed concretely in God's free gift of grace—the gift of God's self-communication. This is not a gift that is given periodically; rather, as we have seen, God's grace is involved in every human act of knowledge and freedom. This offer of grace—this supernatural existential—can be accepted, in which case there is justification, or it can be deliberately and directly rejected. Where there is deliberate rejection it is not possible to speak about implicit faith. Thus Rahner does not say that every person is an anonymous Christian.

Further, this grace transforms human consciousness. When God gives God's self to a person he or she comes to a conscious, though nonthematic, knowledge of his or her unlimited transcendence. That is, there is an awareness of the radical nature of the transcendence of humanity, but this fact is not necessarily thought through. In consciously grasping one's nature, one grasps God's gift of God's self. Rahner (1979, 57) writes:

> The process by which human transcendence is given new depth and purpose and is ordered to the direct presence of God is universal in time and place, because God's saving will is universally operative, even if it cannot be distinguished or given conceptual shape by individual reflection. If God's self-communication is free and if it is consciously grasped by a person, even if this occurs without thematic reflection, then the two conditions for supernatural revelation are realized in the strict sense of the term.

The final factor in the anonymous faith equation is the fact that grace is always mediated through Jesus Christ. Thus, the implicit acceptance of grace leads not just to anonymous theism, but to anonymous Christianity.

In attempting to draw this theological reflection together, it can be said that the kernel of the teaching on anonymous Christianity is the idea that in completely accepting oneself and in becoming conscious of one's unlimited transcendence—even though this consciousness is nonthematic—one is accepting God.

A number of objections have been raised to Rahner's thesis. The following relies on Weger's (1980) excellent treatment of the debate. One criticism is that the idea of anonymity is quite foreign to Christianity. The Christian faith, it is argued, is about an explicit association with the person of Jesus Christ. Weger (1980, 116) points out that though there may be a better term than "anonymous Christianity" to describe what Rahner is referring to, one has yet to be developed. One wonders whether this response really answers the objection. Perhaps the real point of this criticism is that the New Testament knows nothing of an implicit faith. Thus, while Rahner can point to 1 Timothy 2:4 in support of this thesis, it is not possible to establish a direct link with the Scriptures. Rahner is a philosophical theologian. From the point of view of those who see the Bible as the primary datum for theological reflection, his work necessarily involves an element of speculation.

Another objection is that the concept represents an offensive taking over of non-Christians. For instance, would a Christian like to be called an anonymous Buddhist? It must be remembered, though, that Rahner is writing for Christians. It is our question, not that of the non-Christians (Weger 1980, 117).

Some object, finally, that the thesis relativizes the value of the Christian faith to the extent that there appears to be no reason to preach and to evangelize. That is, if non-Christians are already experiencing God's grace, if salvation is already open to them, why try to lead them to Christ? Rahner responds by pointing out that explicit knowledge of God's revelation in Christ is not "academic" knowledge, but rather knowledge that leads to personal transformation and growth (Weger 1980, 121). There is real value in knowing God explicitly. One experiences a depth of relationship with God that is simply not a possibility for the anonymous Christian.

Faith as Courage

Rahner's (1977) teaching on "faith as courage" represents an explicit working out of the general principle behind the anonymous faith thesis. He begins his discussion on faith and courage by observing that courage is really the same thing as hope. And he sees hope as ultimately hope for God.

Courage, says Rahner, is necessary when there is a risk involved in a certain action or process. There is risk involved when there is no guarantee of success. This occurs when there is a gap between what, on the one hand, one plans for and hopes will happen, and what, on the other, might in fact happen. Rahner (1977, 15) states that "courage certainly can, even should, coexist with planning, with working out the chances of success. But where courage is really required is when there is a gap for rational consideration between the calculation of the possibilities of success and the actual performance of the task, where success is not known for certain before it is actually achieved."

Of course there are activities and processes involving different degrees of courage. For example, there is certainly a gap between what can be reasonably planned for and controlled and what might actually happen in the experience of the (not so proficient) home handyperson who embarks on the task of tiling the bathroom! However, Rahner is speaking about "radical total" courage. This is courage that involves the whole person. It is the kind of courage Tillich ([1952] 1977) refers to in *The Courage to Be*. Tillich speaks of the courage required to affirm one's existence in the face of the threat of nonbeing. The whole person, the person in the totality of his or her existence, is involved in the courage to be. Rahner (1977) makes reference to the way in which the whole person is involved in the courageous act of facing up to the challenge of self-realization: "He [the human] has to realize himself as a whole person in and through all these individual episodes of his life, whether he knows it consciously or not. Because of his freedom man is himself, by definition, both subject and object. He has not only a great number and variety of things to do in his life, but he has to be concerned about himself as an individual, a task which in theological language we call salvation."

Rahner calls this concern for oneself as an individual "one's first and last task." In this task one is wholly and completely oneself in freedom. However, the fulfillment of this ultimate task depends on a whole host of conditions and causes that cannot be controlled. There is an experience of one's freedom as "limited and threatened." Here, then, is the gulf, or gap, that we have been referring to. The only way that the gulf can be bridged is by absolute hope.

Rahner acknowledges that most theologians would not want to call such hope a revealed faith. Rahner *is* prepared to step out on a limb and make this claim. His rationale is as follows: Freedom always involves the taking of a risk. In the experience of risk one comes "face to face with the incomprehensibility and freedom of God" (Rahner 1977, 22). The hope that bridges the gulf is ultimately hope for God.

Grace, says Rahner, makes it possible for the human to reach out for the goal of hope, God himself. Here is true revelation, though it need not be consciously understood as such. This is not a revelation involving the communication of particular dogmas; rather, it "springs from the heart and soul of the free person" (Rahner 1977, 22). Thus, grace drives this inner dynamism of hope, making the courage to hope for everything—for God—possible. "This inner spiritual dynamism of man should be accepted and not retarded and reduced by any false modesty . . . so that no other good is sought as the final goal of life. If it is accepted, then what we call faith, in theological terms, is already present" (Rahner 1977, 22–23).

Identity and the Life Cycle

Since it is likely that the reader is more familiar with Erikson's life cycle theory than with Rahner's theology of anonymous faith, a detailed discussion of Erikson's theory is not necessary. In analyzing the various stages in the development of the personality, Erikson seeks to identify the characteristics of a healthy personality. He adopts M. Jahoda's definition of healthy functioning: "a healthy personality *actively masters* his environment, shows a certain *unity of personality*, and is able to *perceive* the world and himself correctly" (Jahoda 1950, as quoted by Erikson 1968, 92).

Erikson's understanding of the growth of personality is based on the epigenetic principle. According to this general principle, everything that grows does so according to a ground plan. Each part grows according to this inbuilt schedule and has its own particular time of ascendancy. Once each part has been through its key time, the parts are brought together to form a functional whole. At a given stage of development a particular crisis (in the sense of a turning point) has its time of ascendance and is resolved toward the end of the stage.

Of the eight stages identified by Erikson, the first four are infancy and childhood stages, the fifth is the adolescent stage, and the last three cover the period from young adulthood through to old age. The crises associated with the various stages of development are described in terms of the following polarities: basic trust versus basic mistrust, autonomy versus shame and doubt, initiative versus guilt, industry versus inferiority, identity versus identity confusion, intimacy versus isolation, generativity versus stagnation, and integrity versus despair. In the early sixties Erikson added a schedule of virtues or strengths to his theory of ego development. The eight virtues correlate with the eight stages and are as follows: hope, will, purpose, competence, fidelity, love, care, and wisdom.

It is important to note that the decisive element in the development of a healthy personality is the ratio of the positive and negative poles. That is, the ratio needs to be in favor of trust over mistrust, autonomy over shame and doubt, and so on. Erikson stresses that he has not endeavored to develop an "achievement scale," according to which a person "achieves," for example, initiative (Evans 1969, 15). The negative components are also important in one's social attitude. The experience of a degree of mistrust, shame, or guilt are part and parcel of normal human functioning.

The identity phase is actually the bridge in the life cycle. It involves both a reaching back into the past of childhood experiences and a reaching out toward an adult future. Erikson (1968, 87) points to the bridging function of identity when he writes: "The wholeness to be achieved at this stage I have called a *sense of inner identity*. The young person, in order to experience wholeness, must feel a progressive continuity between that which he has come to be during the long years of childhood and that which he promises to become in the anticipated future. . . ." The sense of identity, then, is the bridge across the chasm between childhood experience and an adult future. The adolescent must let go of his or her childhood and reach out toward adulthood. The image used by Erikson is that of a trapeze artist letting go of one bar and reaching out for another (Erikson 1964, 90). Thus, the identity crisis is a time of transition; and as such it is the most critical time in the whole of the life cycle.

At this stage there is a heavy preoccupation with how one appears to others. More specifically, there is a deep concern with how the perceptions of others fit with one's perception of oneself. The adolescent is searching for a new sense of sameness and continuity, including also the new sexual dimension. "The sense of ego identity, then, is the accrued confidence that one's ability to maintain inner sameness and continuity . . . is matched by the sameness and continuity of one's meaning for others. Thus, self-esteem, confirmed at the end of each major crisis, grows to be a conviction that one is learning effective steps toward a tangible future, that one is developing a defined personality within a social reality which one understands" (Erikson 1959, 89). It is vitally important for adolescents to come to a sense that their way of mastering experience is a "successful variant" of the way significant people around them master experience.

It is important to note the relationship between identification and identity formation. While the final identity as fixed at the end of adolescence includes all significant childhood identifications, it is not simply the sum total of those identifications—a new and unique configuration emerges. "Identity formation . . . begins where the usefulness of identification ends. It arises from the selective repudiation and mutual assimilation of childhood identifications, and their absorption in a new configuration . . . " (Erikson 1959, 113).

The estrangement of this stage is identity confusion. Youths experience an inability to come to any clear definition of who they are and of where they are going. That is, they have no coherent sense of "I," and they just cannot settle on a vocational direction.

Adolescents, on the other hand, who successfully resolve their identity crisis emerge with the virtue of fidelity. Despite the fact that they are faced with a whole host of competing value systems and ideological perspectives,they find that they are able to maintain the loyalties they have pledged; they are able to resist the temptation to jump from one to another.

Integration of Faith and Identity

The concepts of conscience and courage will be used to facilitate a linking together of anonymous faith and personal identity. These two concepts will act as "third terms" in the equation. The argument is that they are central aspects of both faith and identity.

Identity, Conscience, and Anonymous Faith

The suggestion here is that the life cycle theory, with the identity crisis as its focal point, is the image of the life of anonymous faith. In other words, Erikson's life cycle theory is a psychological description of the way of living Rahner has in mind when he makes the theological statement that in accepting ourselves completely we implicitly accept God.

When Rahner refers to the notion of accepting self completely, the key terms are "conscience" and "moral decision." Of course these terms are intimately related to each other. When we follow our conscience "with free consent" we accept ourselves in our unlimited transcendence. "To this extent the acceptance of human transcendence in faith . . . can be found in an atheist . . . given that he is absolutely obedient to the dictates of his conscience and so accepts himself and God, at least unreflectively, insofar as he actually realizes his own transcendence" (Rahner 1979, 58). Following one's conscience when faced with the decisions of everyday life is, then, the essence of what it means to accept oneself completely. One must accept duty responsibly: " . . . this acceptance can be present in an implicit form whereby a person undertakes and lives the duty of each day in the quiet sincerity of patience, in devotion to his material duties and the demands made upon him by the persons under his care" (Rahner 1974, 394).

Now, Peter Homans (1976) points to the fact that identity is Erikson's term for conscience. Actually he suggests that identity lies midway between the two Tillichian concepts: the bad, moral conscience and the good, transmoral conscience. If we can accept Homans's suggestion, and I think that we can, then it is possible to see the identity crisis, to the extent that it is faced honestly, as an image of what it means to accept oneself, to come to faith anonymously.

Further, it is important to recall that Erikson has a "schedule of virtues" to go with his eight stages in the life cycle. This addendum was added to his basic theory in 1963. In 1966 he added a sequence of "ritual elements" (something that we did not consider). The fact that he included these theoretical addenda to his life cycle theory prompts

Capps (1984) to make this comment: "While it [the life cycle] technically remained a theory of 'ego development,' these two conceptual additions transformed it into an image of the religious and moral life" (121). We can take Capps's observation one step further and suggest that Erikson's life cycle theory, with the identity crisis as its focal point, is an image of the life of anonymous faith. If Rahner were to reflect on Erikson's life cycle theory, one could imagine that he would say something like this: When we honestly face the task of coming to a sense of "I" (identity and fidelity); when we lovingly commit ourselves to others (intimacy and love); when we truly care for what has been generated (generativity and care); and when we courageously look at "life itself in the face of death itself" (integrity and wisdom) . . . then we accept ourselves completely and we come to faith.

Identity, Courage, and Anonymous Faith

Our approach here will be to inquire as to the extent to which Erikson's description of the identity crisis matches with Rahner's conception of courage. A close match between the two would indicate that one may properly speak of the identity crisis as an experience of faith. Attention will be given to the two key elements in Rahner's analysis of courage: the fact that the whole person is involved in radical total courage; and the notion of the gap between what might actually happen and what one plans to happen.

Recall, first, that when Rahner refers to radical total courage he is referring to an act of courage that involves the whole person. The identity crisis is an existential crisis; it involves a person in the totality of his or her being.

Indeed, Rahner's comment that the human "has to realize himself as a whole person . . . , whether he knows it consciously or not" (1977, 17) is descriptive of the identity crisis. Whether or not we are consciously aware of it we must come to a sense of sameness and continuity in our experience of the world; we must establish our wholeness as a person. Erikson (1968) defines wholeness in contrast to totalism. Totalism involves a very definite, though quite arbitrary, delineation of boundaries. That which is seen to be outside is repudiated with a vengeance, while that which is seen to be inside is obsessively appropriated. Wholeness, on the other hand, "seems to connote an assembly of parts, even quite diversified parts, that enter into fruitful association and organization. This concept is most strikingly expressed in such terms as wholeheartedness, whole mindedness, wholesomeness, and the like. As a Gestalt, then, wholeness emphasizes a sound, organic, progressive mutuality between diversified functions and parts within an entirety, the boundaries of which are open and fluid" (80–81).

Identity formation, then, is a process in which the whole person is engaged in the quest for wholeness, for "wholeheartedness, whole mindedness, wholesomeness." When we take up the challenge posed by the identity crisis with the totality of our being the first of the conditions for a radical total courage is fulfilled.

We focus, second, on the fact that adolescents, in moving through the identity crisis, are confronted with a gap between their "now" and their adult future. There is no guarantee of success for them as they work toward their future. This means that in facing up to the adolescent crisis courage is required.

It is important to note, however, that though the identity gap has the basic characteristics of the Rahnerian gap, it is also somewhat different. As we have seen, Rahner defines the gap as "a gap for rational consideration between the calculation of the possibilities of success and the actual performance of the task, where success is not known for certain before it is actually achieved" (1977, 15). Obviously he has in mind a concrete task or action: undertaking a course of study, a Gandhian act of civil disobedience, the decision of a couple to have a baby, etc. One decides to take on this task, to engage in this action, and one plans for it as best one can; without, however, having any real guarantee of success. Now one does not decide to have an identity crisis! The identity crisis does not involve rational consideration of a gap between what is planned and what might actually happen. It is not a concrete task, but rather an existential task. Hence, the nature of the identity gap is somewhat different from that of the Rahnerian gap.

The fact is that whether or not there is a specific awareness of the nature of the existential task to be completed, the adolescent is aware that he is confused and anxious, that he is going through a difficult stage. He is aware of his existential questions: "Who am I really?" "Where am I going?" "What do others think about me?" "What will my future be?" "Will I have a future?" The youth thinks: "I am certain that one day I will be an adult, but I am not at all sure about what kind of adult I will be." The adolescent is engaged in building a bridge over the yawning gulf separating a childhood past and an adult future. It is a scary experience. The challenge is to let go of childhood and to reach out for adulthood. As noted earlier, Erikson (1964) has compared this experience of transition to that heart-stopping moment when a trapeze artist lets go of one bar and reaches out for another. This letting go and reaching across the gulf requires courage; radical, total courage. It requires courage because of the great risk involved.

For some, the risk that is associated with the identity crisis is the ultimate risk. We have referred often to the bridging function of identity. During adolescence the ego works to synthesize and resynthesize the capacities, roles, sublimations, identifications, and defenses of childhood. This synthesis and resynthesis results in an "evolving configuration"; and it is this evolving configuration that is the basis for a sense of sameness and continuity in the way one experiences the world. This sense of sameness and continuity is, in turn, the basis for a confident anticipation of the future. If the attempt to build a bridge between childhood and adulthood fails, there is acute identity confusion.

Identity confusion involves the loss of one's past (one senses discontinuity between who one is now and who one was as a child). It also means that one has no future (the confusion of identity prevents any positive steps in the direction of one's future). The stakes are indeed high. Consider Erikson's (1968) description of youth suffering from identity confusion: "Such complaints as 'I don't know,' 'I give up,' and 'I quit' are by no means mere habitual statements reflecting a mild depression; they are often expressions of the kind of despair discussed by Edward Bibring as a wish on the part of the ego 'to let itself die'" (169).

Of course, for most adolescents there is very little chance that the bridge-building exercise will fail altogether. There is a very real chance, though, that the bridge that is finally built will not be as solid as would have been hoped. In this case, though there is still a way forward into an adult future, that future looks somewhat shaky. When the bridge is weak the adolescent feels confused and anxious; he or she experiences a high degree of emotional pain. Identity and risk are cognate terms.

Our analysis in relation to these two aspects of the identity crisis—the involvement of the whole person, and the importance of the gap—indicates the extent to which it calls for radical total courage. Consequently, it is quite proper to think of identity as faith.

Conclusion

One concludes that anonymous faith and personal identity can be linked together via the "third terms" conscience and courage. It is appropriate to view an honest struggle to come to a sense of identity as an experience of anonymous faith. New light is shed on the nature of the developmental process: it is a process in which God offers his saving grace.

6

Moments of Doubt
and Growth in Faith

MARY GAEBLER

Traditionally, religion has maintained that a person who is gifted by grace tends to move from hating a God who limits us to accepting and loving a God who preserves and supports us. It is also maintained that at any given time we can locate ourselves somewhere along the continuum, for we are moving either toward faith in a God who loves us or toward doubt in a God who does not. In this scheme, we can never move far enough to the left or the right to negate the other stance. If, for example, we are filled with doubt, even to the point of thinking that God has abandoned us, we still manifest faith, not in a good and loving God but in a God who has turned away. In other words, we cannot live without having faith. And traditionally religion says that during the course of a lifetime we tend to move progressively, even if erratically, from doubt to faith.

This view of our growth in faith is primarily developmental. Experiences are arranged along a continuum of chronological stages, and according to the ground plan we become increasingly more mature in our faith.

There is another way to understand our moments of doubt and our growth in faith. Martin Luther exhibited this alternative model in his life and proposed it explicitly in his work. He struggled with what he called *anfechtung*, meaning bouts of despair when he feared that God hated rather than loved him. In this struggle, he never experienced a steady progression toward emotional peace and confidence in God's love. Instead faith was characterized by a paradoxical situation in which Luther knew simultaneously both doubt-filled despair and ecstatic certainty. Growth in faith became not a progressive horizontal movement but a deepening paradox in which the goodness and efficacy of God's gift in Christ was grasped ever more profoundly as the only response to an otherwise overwhelming and ever-present doubt.

In this chapter I want to consider Luther's paradoxical understanding, primarily because I think it is a profound and adequate way to conceptualize growth in faith. Using his thought, I will pursue the idea that moments of doubt lead to growth in faith or, even more paradoxically, that moments of doubt and growth in faith are inevitable parts of the same dynamic.

In some sense, Luther's struggle with anxiety and depression was unique to his time and circumstance, but in a larger sense I think it has something to say to us today as we, too, struggle with existential or even cosmic anxieties. His theological response to the problem may be helpful in our age as we try to identify the source of sustenance and meaning in a world that sometimes seems to have been abandoned by an apparently indifferent God. In any case, the discussion will show us a different model of our growth in faith than may be available in a developmental approach to the problem.

We can begin the discussion by focusing on Luther's *anfechtung*.

Luther's Moments of Doubt

Luther used the word *anfechtung* to describe both his experience of God's apparent abandonment and the external cosmic forces that he believed lay behind that experience. He traced the source of *anfechtung* to God and Satan, to two different powers that generate a single emotional event. These two powers are locked in combat to gain possession of the individual. Roland H. Bainton says of Luther's experience: "It may be a trial sent by God to test man, or an assault by the devil to destroy man. It is all the doubt, turmoil, pang, tremor, panic, despair, desolation, and desperation which invade the spirit of man" (Bainton 1950, 31).

Some Luther scholars theorize that his *anfechtungen* were caused, at least in part, by the terrible physical health that he endured throughout his life. Bainton is critical of this explanation. "The attempt to discover a correlation between [Luther's] many diseases and the despondencies has proved unsuccessful. . . . One must not forget in this connection that his spiritual ailments were acute in the monastery before the physical had begun." Bainton suggests that we should look to the external events of Luther's life for the source of his despair, events like the trauma of the thunderstorm, the saying of his first mass, and later the fact that he "was still sleeping in his own bed while his followers were dying for the faith" (Bainton 1950, 281–82).

Neither the physical nor the historical explanations take seriously the source behind these experiences that Luther himself pointed to, namely, the theological. In the words of Bernhard Lohse, Luther saw his bouts of despair as "spiritual temptations." He refers to them in his *Explanation of the Ninety-Five Theses:*

> I knew a man who claimed that he had often suffered these punishments, in fact over a very brief period of time. Yet they were so great and so much like hell that no tongue could adequately express them, no pen could describe them, and one who had not himself experienced them could believe them. And so great were they that, if they had been sustained or had lasted for half an hour, even for one tenth of an hour, he would have perished completely and all of his bones would have been reduced to ashes.

Immediately, Luther reflects theologically on the experience:

> At such a time God seems terribly angry, and with him the whole creation. At such a time there is no flight, no comfort, within or without, but all things accuse. At such a time as that the Psalmist mourns, "I am cut off from thy sight" (Ps. 31:22). . . . In this moment the soul cannot believe that it can ever be redeemed other than that the punishment is not yet completely felt. (Luther 1957, 129)

Luther was aware of the fact that not everyone experienced such despair. Nevertheless, he maintained that everyone is acquainted with the underlying struggle, the struggle with law and death, if not during the course of life then certainly at the end of it. The church of Luther's day, with its theological emphasis on the necessity of human participation in the work of salvation, encouraged this feeling of eternal uncertainty. Consequently, many people in that age dealt with bouts of anxiety, which were manifested in such things as the flourishing purchase of indulgences.

Luther tried to help other people as well as himself face this awful hour. His intense reaction to death is seen in the way in which his wife and students chose to hide the sudden death of his friend Nicholas Hausmann. They initially kept the news from him, and then "took turns—his wife, Phillip, Jonas, and I—in telling him, first, that his friend was not well; second, that he was gravely ill; and finally that he died quietly" (Luther 1967, 319). Luther's radical experience of terror before the yawning jaws of eternity may have led to his equally radical solution—sheer trust in God's promise of eternal reconciliation in Christ.

Luther found that any reliance on his own resources did not help but in fact often aggravated the despair. In his *Table Talks*, he indicated that he often questioned whether God was gracious to him. If he tried to reassure himself by recalling that "he who loves God will inherit the kingdom of God," Satan would return to raise a question about his love of God. Or if Luther found himself doubting his worthiness as a recipient of God's forgiveness, he was not consoled by the thought that he was a diligent reader and preacher of Scripture. The only thing that sustained Luther in these moments of despair was to rely totally on the external promise of forgiveness that God had given in Christ. He would remind himself as he struggled to fend off the voice that accused him, "Christ died for me" (51) or again "I have been baptized and by the sacrament I have been incorporated [into Christ]" (86).

Luther was convinced that one thing was especially unhelpful in dealing with doubt. He described it as arguing with the devil—an experience we might put in psychological language today, suggesting that Luther was simply castigating himself for not meeting the demands of the law, not measuring up to God's standards that had been written on his heart. But it was precisely Luther's understanding of the devil as an objective reality who spoke to him from beyond himself that provided the free ground from which he might withstand the devil's disputation. This struggle, Luther realized, was the critical moment when faith stood fast in the promises of Christ or fell before the devil's persuasion.

If, for a moment, an individual succumbs to the disputation of the devil who argues that Christ's promises are not personally applicable, then all is lost. Hope and confidence in God's promise become despair if one grants authority to the demonic voice that says one is ultimately the recipient of cosmic wrath rather than love. The biblical story of the Canaanite woman who trusted in God so she could eventually hear God's yes behind what sounded like his no was a source of great comfort to Luther. He maintains that the answers we hear in the world, even those that come through our own reason, often sound like no but that we must turn "to a deep hidden 'yes' under the 'no' and hold with a firm faith to God's Word" (85). Only trust in God's promise of absolute reconciliation in Christ will rescue the individual from *anfechtung*.

Contemporary Moments of *Anfechtung*

In the twentieth century, can we still speak of *anfechtung*, of spiritual temptations? I think we can, especially if we recall that the demonic intention behind Luther's *anfechtung* was to drive Luther away from God, to alienate him from the reassuring Word, and to move him toward death rather than life. We may not ascribe the evil forces to Satan as readily as Luther did, but the forces are there and the anxiety is real. Luther would say that the anxiety and the alienation come ultimately from our failure to keep the law of God and from our inability or unwillingness to hear the external Word of grace that comes to us as a lifeline. Because we are created beings in God's world, we alienate ourselves from God and create a gulf when we do not conform to God's law. We experience that alienation as anxiety and fail to see that God's reconciling love is seeking to draw us back to himself in trust, contrary to the apparent no that appears to us as God's judgment.

God's law is more inclusive than our usual understanding of moral injunction. We experience it in several forms. The first, and most basic, form is our mortality. We are born into a world and come to consciousness only to discover that we are already staring into the face of a death that will consume us. In our age, we live with the muted horror of atomic war which lurks in the background as an awesome and unpredictable possibility. Like Luther himself, we experience "the heart-ache and the thousand natural shocks that flesh is heir to" (Shakespeare 1917, 1145). In many different forms, then, we are reminded of our mortality, even if it is in the relative sense of being confined by our limitations, by boundaries we cannot get beyond.

Second, our sense of guilt, often masked behind a generalized anxiety, may be a witness to God's law. Many people today are not impressed by the moral injunctions that we have learned to identify as God's rules. They are neither sure that God is really out there nor are they convinced that the rules have any merit in our day. There seems to be no reason to feel guilty, especially since we bear little personal responsibility for who we are. After all we have little, or no, control over our genetic structure and our psychological conditioning.

The problem is that we do feel the results of choices that conflict with God's expectations for humankind. Inevitably, we bump up against the structures of creation and find ourselves wanting. We look in a mirror and find unlived, or even disowned, dimensions of our God-given potential. More concretely, for example, we may assert that human sexuality provides an opportunity for pleasure that can be enjoyed apart from any integral association with our whole person. But what of the lingering anxiety, the residual alienation as we retreat further and further in an attempt to protect ourselves against the pain of being objectified by another human being? The law of creation demands that we be in relation to other human beings, and it tells us that human sexuality is the vehicle provided for our most intimate relationships. We feel its quiet fury when we attempt to set it aside.

Finally, we know the anxiety of failure and rejection when we do not or cannot participate in the normal structures of society—in work, in family, in community. We feel thrust out, broken against the laws that govern human interaction. We stand on the outside looking in, wanting to belong not just to our immediate surroundings but also to the very source of life and fellowship.

In all of these instances we feel the brunt of life, the anxiety of alien-ation and despair. For some of us these instances easily turn into moments of *anfechtung* when we doubt the goodness of God and even feel the heat of his retributive wrath. We rebel against a God who seals our death on the very day that we are brought into life. We stand before the infinite possibilities of our being and find it difficult to accept the divinely ordained limits of our creatureliness. We think it is a cruel joke to be called beloved children of God when we are despised and forsaken by those around us. Sometimes the moment of *anfech-tung* feels like the absence of God, but often it is God's presence, the countenance of his punitive displeasure, that torments our tranquility.

In any age, the human situation can be found where Luther found himself—at the point of doubt and despair. The sensitive person is aware of the ever-present reality of God but is uncertain of just where he or she stands in this relationship. On the one hand life has been given; on the other hand tribulation and death are inevitably included with the gift, seeming to negate that very life. It is this terrible chasm of despair—a despair that leads ultimately to death—that can become the occasion for growth in faith. Despair and hope, doubt and faith linger in a single moment. We need to return to Luther to see how that is possible, at least as far as he is concerned.

Anfechtung and Faith

In the midst of despair and confusion, Luther clung to God's promise of reconciliation in Christ as a point above the storm. This gave him a stance beyond his own inner confusion and doubt to see that God had not abandoned him but had supported him all along in the struggle against doubt. He had the assurance in his baptism that Christ's promise was his and that he was an object of God's particular concern. He could look back and cling to Christ's promise, acknowl-edging both the promise and his faith in it as a gracious act of God on his behalf.

How Luther could find God's loving concern beneath the pain and doubt is of particular interest to us, because it is an ultimate affirma-tion of trust to say that God lies not only behind the solution but also behind the pain. To find an answer we turn to the cosmic dimension of the problem where Luther locates the principalities and powers that operate behind the pain. Luther believes that "God tempts no one to sin" (1959, 347), but he also believes that God does not hinder or stop the devil from putting temptation in our path (1967, 128). In a sense, God looks the other way and allows the devil to do his work. Luther ends up with the idea that the pain we experience and attribute to Satan is actually perpetuated under the all-powerful hand of God. His answer to the problem of theodicy preserves an all-powerful and good

God but at the same time comprehends the reality of evil without giving the demonic dualistic power equal to God.

Apart from this theological achievement, Luther affirms the living and active presence of God in our pain and maintains that that presence has a salutary intent. God's intent is to direct us in our despair back to himself through Christ's promise. In other words, God is a loving and healing presence in the midst of judgment and evil or, as Luther says, "God uses all evil for good" (1967, 99). Luther presses the point. He maintains that it is the "saints," the baptized believers, who are especially tempted by the devil even as they are especially loved and supported by God. Satan tries to lure them away from God by increasing their despair; God protects and sustains them or, if their faith is weak, tries to increase and strengthen their trust in him. Moments of *anfechtung*, then, become decisive turning points. They represent an opportunity for a renewed faith in God's forgiving love in the midst of great pain and doubt.

Luther did not think that growth in faith comes easily or that it is automatic. By understanding the struggle in cosmic terms where the devil seeks to alienate and divide the creature from the Creator through despair and death while God simultaneously draws the individual toward himself in faith, Luther posits an intense and profound cosmic conflict that is ultimately reflected within each individual. "The darts of the devil cannot be removed pleasantly and without effort when they are so deeply embedded in your flesh. They must be torn out by force" (1945, 89). Luther counsels courage and perseverance. He pleads for faith in the promise of God. He finds comfort and empowerment by resting on the assurance that God does not desire one's death but one's salvation.

Practical Solutions to *Anfechtung*

As we have seen, Luther's first line of defense against *anfechtung* is to receive and to grasp onto the external promise of God revealed in Christ. That promise can be delivered to us in different ways, from the preached Word to "the mutual conversation and consolation" of fellow believers. Luther himself was comforted by the living, spoken Word that came through a friend: "I have often been refreshed by the words which Bugenhagen once spoke to me: 'You ought not despise my consolation because I am convinced that I speak words of God from heaven'" (1945, 118). Luther, in turn, sought to be that "living voice" to other people on many occasions. To a friend who was suffering from *anfechtung*, he said, "Listen then to what we are saying to you in God's name: Rejoice in Christ, who is your gracious Lord and Redeemer. . . . Let him bear your burdens for he assuredly cares for you" (1945, 96).

Luther recommended other means. Referring to the devil, he said to a friend, "Laugh your adversary to scorn," mock and despise him instead of trying to argue with him. He also suggested that people flee solitude and enjoy the company of others, for he thought that the devil increased melancholy dramatically when people were alone (1945, 85–86). Finally, he called music a "divine and most precious gift" (Buzin 1958, 4). He thought it was especially repugnant to the devil and particularly effective in lifting us out of *anfechtung*, especially if it served as a vehicle for communicating the empowering Word of God (11).

While Luther applied these practical measures to *anfechtung*, he was convinced that their efficacy resided in the Word of God. The content of that Word, and the faith with which he grasped onto it, gave him power not only to survive his own moments of *anfechtung* but also to be an effective carer of souls.

Conclusion

Luther's belief that faith emerges and deepens only in the context of paradoxical tension stands in contrast to a developmental approach to faith. While both perspectives emphasize moments of crisis as the context of growth, the locus of that crisis differs in each. Developmental theory locates the source of conflict and the occasion for progressive growth in faith in the internal autonomous disjuncture between a new developing self and the self that has been outgrown. Luther's paradoxical view proposes two different but intrinsically related contexts of conflict. The first is between the self and the world. As the self bumps up against the limits imposed upon it from without, either in the form of God's law in creation or in the form of evil in the world, conflict is induced. The second locus of crisis occurs in the process of interpreting this first one. Luther calls this crisis *anfechtung* or temptation and indicates that it is a crisis within faith itself. It is an internal struggle between doubt in a God who seems to have abandoned us and faith in a loving God who overcomes pain and death in Christ's promise. This second crisis is not only the context for faith but is a decisive event in faith itself.

The contrast between Luther and a developmental approach comes to an apex in the issue of autonomy. Developmental theory maintains that growth in faith is occasioned by biological and psychological factors. If it grants that these factors are divinely bestowed in our origins, it implies that they function autonomously thereafter. Growth in this autonomous self leads to growth in faith.

Luther reverses the formula. He maintains that growth in faith yields growth in the self. This growth may not take any outwardly identifiable forms, for principally it is a widening and deepening of the self's ability to see Christ's promise in the midst of pain and confusion. Each time we see and claim the promise of Christ in moments of doubt, we experience the final triumphant resolution of Christ's promise over evil. God's love and abiding presence breaks into our lives anew, both as consolation now and as hope for the future. The pain of apparent divine abandonment is overcome, and we live in the hope of the eventual defeat of death and despair.

Part 2

Developmental Theory and the Mature Self

7

A Model
of Relational Maturity

JARED P. PINGLETON

Relationships are central to human existence. Not only are our lives composed of them, it is only through the functional meaningfulness of interpersonal relationships that life itself is derived and perpetuated. The significance of human relationships is vividly exemplified in the fact that they were originally designed to counteract the only aspect of creation which God declared to be "not good"—namely, the condition of loneliness (Gen. 2:18). The intent of this chapter is to analyze human affiliations from a maturational perspective in order to determine optimum potentials for fully integrated interpersonal growth.

The elusive and subjective properties of maturity are by nature culturally bound and determined (Kao 1981). Therefore it is ironic that while in an increasingly technologically complex and productive age of scientific inquiry and specialization, little emphasis has been placed upon the acquisition and cultivation of the inner strengths and maturation of character necessary to live effectively in it! Though difficult to conceptualize and systematize in this stressful, mechanized, fractured society, the bulk of the research and writing on maturity tends to ascribe greater importance to individualistic interiority or autonomy than to one's relational context or style. Erik Erickson, Harry Stack Sullivan, Alfred Adler, and Karen Horney all discuss growth from a psychosocial perspective and Gordon W. Allport, Abraham Maslow, and Carl Rogers explicate healthy personality and maturity from a humanistic-existential orientation, but they all more heavily emphasize the intrapsychic and and intrapersonal qualities in proportion to the interpersonal dimensions of maturity (Hall and Lindzey 1970). In essence, most personality theorists that postulate models of maturity tend to characterize growth as consisting of the individual in autonomous isolation, whereas the biblical focus depicts maturation in terms of relationship and community (Kao 1981).

The theoretical schema proposed here for the conceptualization of relational maturity was stimulated by J. D. Carter's (1980) model for biblical counseling. Systematically analogous to that model, interpersonal relationships will be considered along a tripartite continuum for the purpose of delineating qualities of maturity from those of immaturity. The following dimensions of maturational dynamics are assumed to be operant in some form within typical interpersonal relationships: dependence, independence, and interdependence.

From a psychological perspective dependence and independence are merely counter-manifestations of immaturity, in that they operationally deny one's true need for others, whereas interdependence connotes relational maturity. The process also will be explored theologically, involving an evaluation of the model's implications and potential for explicit integration and interpersonal application.

A Psychological Perspective

Dependence

Biologically, socially, and emotionally the necessity of one's utter reliance upon others to initially fulfill one's needs is apparent. Developmentally, this helplessness is present at birth and the formation of a trusting relationship in which an individual can experience satisfactory need resolution is crucial to his or her very subsistence, growth, and well-being. These dependency needs which are so obvious during infancy are a naturally vital and indispensable component of growing up, and are normatively present in humans throughout life (Parens and Saul 1971). Therefore, it can be seen that "because the human condition requires an infant to be dependent upon parents for survival, dependency becomes a fundamental denominator in life" (Leader 1976, 639).

According to psychodynamically-oriented object relations theorists (Bowlby, Mahler, Spitz, Jacobsen, Winnicott, and Fairbairn) the infant's dependence upon the caretaker is characterized by a desperate, anaclitic fusion (Guntrip 1971; Rosen 1973; Shackleford 1978). This symbiotic attachment is a primitive life force from which a sense of self-identification and basic trust through perception of the love, constancy, and superiority of the parental figure is progressively elicited. Ironically, however, the very strength and intensity of this nurturant attachment later serves to undermine its genetic advantages and complicates further optimum psychosocial development. According to psychoanalytic theory a dual affective crisis ensues in the dependent, from the fear of the loss of the object and the equally devastating feared loss of the object's love (Parens and Saul 1971).

Consequently, a powerful sense of ambivalence is created within the infant and is always indicative of one's enmeshment in an overly dependent interpersonal relationship (Leader 1976). No matter how necessary or mutually satisfying the relationship may be, the fear of separation at some level generates anxiety concomitant with feelings of rage that one might lose the other, and thereby, oneself. As deprivation and dissatisfaction inevitably occur in the maturation process, the infant's ambivalence escalates dramatically and he or she may experience intense affects pertaining to basic questions of identity, self-worth, anxiety of nonbeing, fears of rejection and engulfment, chronic alienation and emptiness, frustration, resentment, and guilt. It is precisely at this momentous juncture that the most serious pathological fixations or adjustments can occur. Henri Parens and Leon Saul clinically diagnose that "some of our most serious disorders, schizoids, borderlines, and 'oral dependent' character types, stem, to an important degree, from defects in normal dependence upon the object" (1971, 6).

Clinically and theoretically, the tremendous ramifications of one's early interpersonal relationships possess extensive psychotherapeutic import. The vicissitudes and frustrations of attempting to work with these difficult clients and their frequently schizophrenogenic and boundarily diffused families are widely documented and several conflicting inherent processes and interactional patterns can function to mitigate against successful therapeutic interventions.

For example, the overly dependent position offers certain advantages or secondary gains for the compliant individual. He or she is awarded the gratification of infantalized nurturance; freedom from adult decision making, pressures, and outcomes; and little personal responsibility for thinking, feeling, acting, and therefore, few of the relational risks of being self-directed. Additionally, by attempting to unilaterally please the caretaker, who in an opposite manner correspondingly senses the need to be depended upon and may therefore implicitly foster an incipient dependency, he or she offers them the gratifications of a sense of power, control, and pseudo-omnipotent vitality.

Unfortunately, however, this position distorts true relationship and neediness in that the dependent person, while on the one hand enjoying the benefits of his or her egocentrism, is simultaneously forced to deny the very limitations in himself or herself which contribute to his or her fused position. The caretaker also utilizes denial by avoiding coming to grips with his or her respective limited power and superiority and need of the dependent to perpetuate it. A reticence is produced by the dual fear of exposing one's own disappointment in not having one's needs met and of the awareness of the limited nurturance capacity in the provider which caused it. Then the hostility awakened by the insufficient gratification must be contended with along with the double-binding subsequent fear of potential rejection by the parent figure if the hostility felt toward him or her is displayed. This process is unconsciously formulated by reasoning: better to stay with what one has, bad as it is, than to risk utter abandonment and annihilation. Since one's formative, rudimentary identity and very sustenance is contingent upon the other, one is forced to cling desperately in some extreme instances to a pathological, abusive, neglectful, or scapegoating relationship rather than to acknowledge one's internal basic neediness that would be consciously intolerable due to its abject emptiness.

The end result of this dynamic, according to A. L. Leader, is that "people with excessive dependency needs tend to either become locked into complementary dependent-independent [symbiotic] relationships, or more often, rejecting relationships" (1976, 638). In either case, a dire price is paid: Individual growth in the first instance is sacrificed for periods of comfort, even though they are inconsistently maintained; and in the second case, growth is thwarted because of the natural preoccupation with excessive frustration and hostility. Typically then, a destructive reciprocal cycle operates in which the demands of the extremely dependent person are possibly perceived by the caretaker as encroachment, excessive expectancy, and an overwhelming threat to one's own existence. This feeling tends to generate a withdrawal or rejecting counterattack by the parental figure, ironically leaving the dependent even more lonely, afraid, and angry than before—thereby intensifying the demands of a mutually and viciously destructive cycle.

Although some people unfortunately become enmeshed in this dysfunctional pattern, at this stage, or before, one hopes that the dependent denial involves a reaction formation. The dependency strivings are reactively glossed over by their opposite action: exaggerated claims, pursuits, and feats of unusual autonomy which serve to conceal the underlying needs and fears of the more primitive relational closeness in addition to the residual hostility for its failure. Normally this process occurs in the child's development at approximately two to three years of age but it is more fully exhibited in adolescence. Again it should be emphasized that relational dependency needs are normal and present throughout life. Even though dependency is viewed rather negatively in our culture, because of the association with the vulnerability and helplessness characteristic of childhood, those needs naturally resurface throughout all interpersonal developmental stages, particularly acutely in late adulthood (Parens and Saul 1971).

Independence

While it is understood that excessive dependency needs are often associated with volatile interpersonal and familial conflict, it is evident that their attempted denial or avoidance breeds even greater internal and interactional disharmony (Rosen 1973). As the child begins to separate from the caretaker and progressively individuate, there is typically a diametrically opposed reaction in the child's behavior *vis-á-vis* his or her felt need to relate to others. In the ensuing struggle to emancipate oneself from a fused identity an extremistic movement toward isolation is not uncommon for the child, which can likewise result in pathological relational adjustment (Guntrip 1973). To complicate matters, as parents experience their child's relational ambivalence "children are often pushed prematurely toward independence and conflicts arising from excessive frustration of dependency needs may be disregarded" (Parens and Saul 1971, 6).

Developmentally, this relational conflict the child experiences in the separation-individuation process is recapitulated in adolescence. Viewed from a psychodynamic orientation, Parens and Saul (1971, 194) submit that "the inevitable dependence-independence conflict of adolescence results as the efforts to individuate come up against the resistance and regressive pull of former cathexes." So an internal and external struggle results during an attempt to emancipate oneself and mature. At this time the adolescent may exhibit tendencies toward overreactionary independence.

Rather than maturely recognizing, accepting, and integrating their dependency needs, adolescents may try to eliminate them as though the two cannot coexist. This is because in separating "one has to deny and cut off dependent feelings and attachment to the world you leave behind or you could not leave" (Leader 1976, 638). The forces of the intensity of their neediness, their ambivalence toward parents, and fear of separating from their original sources of gratification may aggregately create a tough, hard, rebellious facade—both protecting and hiding a soft, vulnerable, frightened interior in children, adolescents, and young adults.

It should be emphasized, however, that this frequently defiant revolt can serve a healthy purpose in one's maturation process. C. C. L. Kao (1981) recognizes this principle in observing that the major developmental task of adolescence is to complete the unfinished tasks of childhood and therein to formulate one's own identity as personally distinct from one's parental figures. He states "although adolescent independence is not as mature as adulthood interdependence [because while rebellious behavior is reactive and over-directed, truly autonomous behavior is inner-directed], it has a considerable degree of maturity in itself" (173). Though often turbulent, this dynamism can help facilitate the separation process and lead to healthy individuation.

Several other realities may help perpetuate this extreme striving for independence. Persons may experience conflicts about dependency needs not only because some can continue unresolved from childhood, but secondly, a combination of severe environmental crises and/or losses may in actuality leave one alone and helpless, contributing to the reaction of denying one's need to be cared for to avoid feeling any further hurt. Since it may be too painful to realize that gratification may not be forthcoming or is out of reach, in order to survive all defensive energies within the self are summoned in a desperate attempt to attain self-sufficiency.

A poignant illustration of this isolated relational type was captured by Charles Dickens's classic depiction of Ebeneezer Scrooge. His embittered schizoid-like detachedness was derived from a denial of the pain of an early broken love relationship and his need of it or of a similar one. The reaction-formation was diametric—then he depended exclusively upon money, not people, for his self-sufficient security.

Cultural pressures also strongly impinge upon the reaction-formation of independence. Assigned social roles of parent, older sibling, employer, or leader all assume inherent expectations of certain caretaking and autonomous functions and capacities. In the fulfilling of these roles, caring for others' needs may seem appropriate but in contrast the existence or expression of one's own needs and weaknesses can become too threatening and appear to be incongruent with all the power and autonomy attributed to the individual.

Finally, present society, in stressing aggression and comparative competition and performance, especially in men, and in placing a highly desirable premium on independent qualities, tends to ascribe fairly negative values to dependency. This makes it quite difficult for many adults to admit its existence and validity in themselves and in their relationships. It is taken as a threatening verification of the childishness and weakness already feared to reside within them, honest acceptance of which would be viewed as humiliating or potentially disastrous.

However, both extreme states of dependent and counterdependent behavior are relationally immature in that they each functionally attempt to deny one's true need for relationship. In actuality "both types lead to maladaptive character formations and represent some of our most difficult psychiatric problems, such as alcoholism, drug addiction, various forms of other pathologic dependent characters, as well as some antisocial character formations and the dramatic childhood psychoses, autistic and symbiotic" (Parens and Saul 1971, 243).

The same authors finally conclude "problems of insufficient dependency . . . are as difficult as those arising from excessive dependency" (221). Therefore, neither symbiosis nor isolation offers the potential of rewarding, balanced, mutually fulfilling interpersonal relationship.

Interdependence

The quality or state of interdependence has been described as preferring to be together, but being able to stand alone (Carter 1980). Relationally this principle becomes actualized as one progressively becomes aware that "others are as dependent upon us as we are upon them. The lives of other individuals in various aspects are dependent upon our being and doing . . . they trust us to sustain their being and doing" (Gustafson 1977, 160).

This reciprocity of dependence-needs being expressed and met in a mutual relationship is the ideal of the notion of interdependence. This process is open-ended in terms of growth potential and, as such, encapsulates the essence of interpersonal maturity. Basically "the individual capable of accepting his needs for objects can be called mature" (Parens and Saul 1971, 231). In terms of relationships "maturity brings an awareness of one's needs for others and an acknowledgement of mutuality, give and take, communion, and dialogue in interpersonal relationships" (Kao 1981, 173).

The very simplicity of the concept in theory belies its difficulty in practical application. It is precisely the simplicity of this reality-based orientation that for many precludes its actualization in relationship. Before one can become interdependent one must have successfully differentiated oneself from the other, yet simultaneously be cognizant of one's needs in addition to one's assets. This requires an objective awareness of one's own identity, which in turn can be realized only through relationship. Thomas Merton (1955, xvii) has a fine and simple aphorism for this : "we cannot find ourselves within ourselves, but only in others, yet at the same time before we can go out to others, we must first find ourselves. . . . The best way to love ourselves is to love others, yet we cannot love others unless we love ourselves." He goes on to say "this is not merely a helpful suggestion, it is the fundamental law of human existence" (19).

It is within the marital relationship that the elements of and necessity for interdependence are perhaps most acutely manifest. In order to engage in and maintain meaningful relations with the opposite sex one must be willing and able to risk personal vulnerability in order to experience closeness and intimacy. Unfortunately, many persons are unable and/or unwilling to express their love to the other and receive it in return. In fact, many marital relationships are characterized by unbalanced dependent-independent interactional patterns in which both persons fear the openness indicative of true, mature love (Hodge 1967).

Gradually, one must learn to accept his or her authenic need for others, to receive affection and care, balanced by an increasing demonstration of giving to the other. Optimally this process develops into "being able to stand alone, but preferring to be together." The separateness involved in this form of relational maturity is perhaps best crystallized by M. B. Hodge's citing of Gibran's *The Prophet*: "Let there be space in your togetherness . . . for the oak and the cypress grow not in each others' shadow" (1967, 178). Families would do well to cultivate a sense of identification from which members can eventually individuate and establish a feeling of separateness within the secure context of lovingly belonging.

When relationship and maturity are considered in this light, human existence begins to assume a new and greater meaning. We truly need others, and they truly need us. This kind of conceptual model is very systematic in that mature relationships will reinforce progressively even more mature ones. An increasing awareness of one's own needs and of those in others can lead not only to need-satisfaction but reciprocity. J. M. Gustafson applies this principle broadly to all human life.

> Probably the experiences of dependence and interdependence led to the ancient observation that man is a social or political being and to the use of the body metaphor to gain insight into human societies. These experiences of dependence and interdependence are surely premises of an observation that has been basic to social morality, namely, that the common good and the welfare and duties of individuals must somehow be kept in mutually contributing relationships. (1977, 160)

The ramifications of this relational schema will now be explored from a theologically oriented point of view.

A Theological Perspective

Dependence

Jesus made it clear that in order properly to respond to him and ultimately enter the kingdom of heaven a person must become as a little child (Matt. 18:3). Spiritually, development is initiated with a process analogous to birth (John 3) such that one's infantile dependence upon God and his body, the church, for one's theological livelihood is not only understandable but essential. Unfortunately, however, as is frequently the case, the theory or principle can become distorted or neglected in actual practice. A. W. Tozer notes that so often in contemporary evangelical Christianity "everything is made to center upon the initial act of 'accepting' Christ (a term incidentally not found in the Bible) and we are not expected thereafter to crave any further revelation of God to our souls" (1948, 16). Scripture does not indicate the necessity of one's initial spiritual dependence as a natural element in the process of Christian development, but its broad scope is on continuously evolving growth and maturity, not on a fixated, clingy symbiosis (1 Cor. 3:1–2; 14:20; Heb. 5:11–6:1). When this occurs there can be no true spiritual relationship sustained on a healthy level, with God, or among his body.

The Bible authoritatively declares that God is a completely good and stable object (Mal. 3:6; Heb. 13:8; Matt. 28:20) upon whom one can depend, whom one can love, and trust. Unconditional love and discipline for God's children is assured and evidenced by a parental relationship to them (Heb. 12:5–11; 1 John 3:1–2; Rev. 3:19). Furthermore, God is characterized by the maturity of his personality with which his children are encouraged to identify and which they are called to imitate (Matt. 5:48; Eph. 4:13–15). While these distinctives of the heavenly parent are crucial when compared to one's earthly parents, as fallen creatures it is inevitable and unfortunate that one's residual pathological distortions of human relationship will be projected upon God.

It is here that the problems associated with blind, symbiotic dependency upon God can ensue. By introjecting and fusing with parental or societal religious values and moral standards, God is omnipotently converted into one's own image and the true need of relationship with him is thereby perverted (Kao 1981). It is in this way that strict allegiance to authoritarian, extrabiblical codes of conduct or morality, all of which are humanly and self-righteously controlled, can be rigidly imposed and confused with God's person or identity. By so doing, the distortions of human fallenness, for example, the sophisticated idolatry of legalism, can impede or even preclude mature relationship with God. Ideally these spiritual and emotional dependency needs can be met through a personal relationship with God, since he is not a symbiotic or schizophrenogenic parent who will perpetuate pathology but rather permits his children to differentiate from him.

In the church, though, there certainly exist potentially the same distortions as the familial development, with it becoming enmeshed into a dependent-independent cycle. C. S. Lewis (1960) identified this selfishly directed power tendency of the independent person, which seldom respects the rights of others to be fully functioning autonomous persons but instead subjugates dependence inappropriately upon oneself as a "need-love," which vividly evidences the unhealthy element within the relationship. This same vicious reciprocal cycle delineated in human relational development is ripe for spiritual repetition along with all its concomitant denied feelings and fantasies, exemplified possibly in the systematic "pedestalizing" of certain leaders in many churches.

It seems reasonable to assume that persons with excessive and/or unresolved dependency needs would carry this psychological relational pattern into their theologically oriented ones, even more firmly entrenching them. The allure of having a truly perfect, omnipotent Caretaker, or his designated servants, sublimely fulfill one's every ego-centric whim and to provide idyllic bliss, is indeed acknowledged. But it is precisely in this way "our relationships with others easily become needy and greedy, sticky and clingy, dependent and sentimental, exploitative and parasitic" (Nouwen 1975, 30), destructively reinforcing and thereby perpetuating immaturity. Even though all the accompanying fears and hostilities may well be duplicated in religious relationships, they can likewise be readily rationalized, if not completely denied, in a manner parallel to those familial psychological relationships. After all, what well-intentioned Christian wants to consciously form a restrictive stance against God and his body to the extreme of becoming unhealthily independent from them?

Independence

Whereas dependence is a distortion of community, independence is a perversion of individuality. A most conspicuous illustration of this phenomenon for the Christian has been pinpointed by Tozer (1948, 104). He declared "the sinner prides himself on his independence, completely overlooking the fact that he is the weak slave of the sins that rule his members." This arrogant denial of one's dependency needs can be easily and rapidly, if not hostilely, projected outward and identified with another person as a "sinner." How quickly many Christians forget that if it were not for the mercy of God's grace, they too would be in the same category!

The Christian's hang-up here is instead much more stable, and therefore of greater potential destructiveness, than that of the simple unrepentant sinner. Salvation will cure the latter's malady whereas a pharisaical nonacceptance of the Christian's limited humanness lies hidden beneath a cloak of insidious self-sufficiency and pseudosanctification, alienating the self-righteous who may really be just "Christian Scrooges." In this manner one can become prone to project one's fears and hostilities upon others, under the thinly veiled guise of "spiritual" correction, criticism, and fault-finding, all of which, if done in an arrogant fashion, will create and maintain relational distance and alienation due to its judgmental attitude of superiority.

This independence can actually be a prideful overt denial of humankind's need to be dependent in a healthy way upon anyone, including God, and therefore in a reaction-formation one may attempt to meet all their own needs narcissistically. This immature omnipotent effort to be "as God" ironically aberrates the Christian's dependence needs to a level approximating that of "the sinner's," if not worse. Tozer wisely advised "the whole course of life is upset by the failure to put God where He belongs. We exalt ourselves instead of God and the curse follows" (1948, 107). The ramifications of that curse—omnipotent, self-perpetuating sin—lay bare the pitfalls of alienated pseudomaturity in which healthy interpersonal relating is obstructed (Heb. 10:21–25).

It should be cautiously stated here, however, that a degree of risky independence from God and his church can ultimately function to be the pathway toward the promotion of greater relational maturity (Clines 1977). While rebellion and acting out are sinful, perhaps a disenchantment with the hypocrisy and duplicity of rigid, legalistic morality can fuel the push away from a foreclosed anaclitic attachment to it, leading to the eventual formation of a healthy identity-achieved status with God, by divesting him of our distorted projections. By gaining some distance, the individual can then be freed to see the loving truth about God, oneself, and others. This rebellion or moratorium can be a sufficient, if not necessary, factor in helping one to realize one's true sinfulness and be a reminder that one only becomes saved by admitting that one is not saved (Rom. 10:9–10). Likewise, perhaps one becomes mature only by paradoxically admitting that one is not mature and needs relationship to God and others.

In any event, the lack of genuine *koinonia* and relational *teleios* in the church has emerged from what R. Welch has labeled "an overemphasis on individualism in evangelical Christianity" (1973, 27). The point is "since we do in reality need one another ('it is not good for man to live alone'), then the failure of this need . . . is a bad spiritual symptom" (Lewis 1960, 13). Maturely accepting oneself and the other by choosing to be together in essence reflects the willful healing ability which God created in man. In recognition of this fact, Hodge asserts that "God risked creating persons so independent they could love him or thumb their noses at him" (1967, 270).

Interdependence

As people become increasingly aware of the reciprocal vertical relationship with God as it is inseparably linked with their horizonal relationships with his other children inside whom he also dwells, they can be free to meet their needs through his body, which is to be by nature functionally interdependent (1 Cor. 12; Rom. 12; Eph. 4). If we as Christians actually are synergetic then we can humbly accept and internalize that "in Christ we belong together and we really do need each other" (Welch 1973, 11). In so doing, we are enabled to confront ourselves as we are, eliminating the temptation to isolate ourselves by denying, defending, rejecting, and otherwise trying to ignore our humanness with its needs, faults, guilt, weaknesses, failures, inconsistencies, limitations, and fallenness. In fact, without this freedom which the truth brings (John 8:32; Ps. 51:6) "I cannot discover God in myself and myself in Him unless I have the courage to face myself exactly as I am, with all my limitations, and to accept others as they are, with all their limitations" (Merton 1955, xvi).

This attitude toward God, oneself, and others is positively infectious. In fact a plethora of scriptural teaching emphasizes this relational interdependence. R. J. Salinger (1979) establishes that repeatedly scriptural directives demonstrate "clear emphasis on mutuality and interdependence" (244) and notes how "Paul challenged the believers at Corinth to fully accept their interdependence" (248). G. A. Getz (1973, 58) expounds the meaning of twelve "one another" New Testament principles within the metaphor of the body and concludes "we are responsible before God to become mature in Christ so we in turn can help others become mature in Christ." J. R. Beck likewise observes "this emphasis on mutuality permeates all the gospels and epistles. It extends into all relationships in which Christians participate" (1978, 173).

It is logical that this process should hold true for the psychotherapeutic relationship as well. J. F. Shackleford (1978) pointed out the lack of substantive integrative theoretical work in the areas of how dependency needs are met developmentally as well as how maturity can be facilitated in therapy. In this respect C. Barshinger (1977) argued that intimacy is a prerequisite for personal and spiritual growth and is promoted only within the security of a loving relationship. This seems to be consistent with Christ's command in John 15:9, where the context is the interdependent vine-branch analogy: "As the Father has loved me, so have I loved you. Now remain in my love" (NIV). It is suggested here that perhaps this epigenetic principle of *agape* encapsulates both how interdependence is perpetuated and how maturity can be fostered in therapy.

Therefore because humans are not exclusively dependent or independent and "since no man is an island . . . we all depend upon one another" (Merton 1955, 64), mature interpersonal relations become possible. Instead of the egocentric constraints that the states of immaturity promulgate, the intimacy of loving and being loved enables one to reach out in *agape* to others. However, lest we naively assume maximal relationships will be simplistic, Dietrich Bonhoeffer reminds us of the nature of interdependency, that is, preferring to be together but able to stand alone. His caution sounds paradoxical: "Let him who cannot be alone beware of community . . . likewise let him who is not in community beware of being alone" (1954, 77). Interdependence is not a fixed entity; rather, it is an ongoing process of "lived integration" that progressively recognizes, accepts, appreciates, and synthesizes the elements of one's relational differences and immaturities throughout human existence and development.

Both extremes of dependence and independence are inherently precariously imbalanced and consequently preclude the healthiness and rewards of loving relations in practical application. Ideally "one grows from childish dependence and heteronomy to adolescent independence and autonomy, and then to adult interdependence and mutuality" (Kao 1975, 147). Possibly the clearest example of this progression is seen in the account of the prodigal son and his father (Luke 15:11–32). The story traces the son's development from his dependent narcissism to his rebellious counterdependent separation, and finally to his individuated loving reunion. Henri Nouwen (1975, 77) grasps the essence of this notion of relational maturity, which he concludes actually "creates community since it is not in self-sufficiency but in a creative interdependency that the mystery of life unfolds to us."

8

Religious Maturities
of the Adult

ORLO STRUNK, JR.

Contemporary behavioral sciences are not content to be exclusively descriptive endeavors. Nor is it realistic anymore to insist that psychological science ought only to be preoccupied with understanding, prediction, and control, the traditional canons of science. Though these intentions may be noble and valid, they are not exhaustive. The sciences of human behavior have become normative in design, if not overtly and conspicuously then insidiously and mildly. The fact is that in the case of psychology and psychiatry, especially as they are practiced in the clinic and in the marketplace, normative propensities were there from the very beginning, although practitioners have frequently refused to acknowledge them.

Even today it is possible to find psychotherapists who argue that their personal values play no part in the therapeutic relationship. Or they contend that the wholeness they wish for their clients is strictly a self-determined objective, devoid of their own normative criteria. Though we have no great pyramid of empirical research to refute these claims, the research we have appears to indicate that the patients who are rated "most improved" by their therapists tend to hold the same values as their therapists (Welkowitz, Cohen, and Ortmeyer 1967, 48–55). There are many possible interpretations that can be applied to such findings, but one of them, that psychologists provide a normative model for their clients, cannot be dismissed as an unlikely possibility.

115

In my own special branch of psychology, religious psychology, the point is perhaps even more debatable and touchy. Traditionally, workers in the psychology of religion have insisted that the psychologist as psychologist is not able to draw conclusions about the truth or falsity of religious factors. A typical passage, one I require my students in the psychology of religion to read at the beginning of the course, is from the classical period of religious psychology. It argues:

> The psychology of religion, by its very nature as a science, is bound to restrict itself to a limited area of fact in order to explain it. In the total fact represented by the religious experience of prayer and conversion, psychology can take note only of the human, psychical side. The activity of God as such cannot become an object of scientific inquiry. Hence, the conclusions of psychology, as applied to religious experience, will be like all other scientific conclusions—true so far as they go, and within the limited area of the interest involved; but they are relative and not absolute. They need to be supplemented by and coordinated with other conclusions reached along philosophical and theological lines. The psychology of religion can never take the place of the philosophy of religion, nor can it render theology otiose. It can show us that religious experience is normal, and, by tracing the human mechanism of such experience, it may even encourage us to believe that the working of the normal mind, in this sphere as in others, may be trusted. It will still leave to the philosophy of religion the task of considering the final implications of such experience. Hence, while the mechanism of the psychology of religion may be granted for its own particular purposes, theology may still claim the right to consider the same facts under their divine aspect, so far as this lies open to us. (Price 1959, 273)

This is an appealing explanation of the peculiar place the psychology of religion can play in the structure of the human sciences. It is essentially an acceptable and trouble-free point of view, but in actuality things do not, strictly speaking, work out this way. For example, when Sigmund Freud in *The Future of an Illusion* went to great pains to define illusion as a belief having its roots in a wish, he did acknowledge that an illusion might indeed correspond to reality (Freud 1964). He was also making some rather clear and firm statements of a normative character, albeit through the use of inferences and inuendoes. The point is that the normative tends to find its way into our sciences, no matter how strongly we may insist on our innocence in such matters.

I conclude this opening augury with a personal witness: Several years ago I undertook the audacious task of defining religious maturity within a psychological framework (Strunk 1965). In the writings of Freud, Carl G. Jung, Erich Fromm, William James, Gordon W. Allport, and Viktor E. Frankl, I found numerous normative leanings, either directly stated or strongly implied. I then made the enigmatic leap: I tried to synthesize these insights into a meaningful definition of religious maturity.

If I learned one thing from that exercise, it was that religious maturity as a category is in essence quite mysterious—something perhaps I should have learned from Rudolf Otto or Jung a long time ago. I also learned that religious maturity itself lies beyond the ordinary theories of psychology and psychiatry. Since then I think I have discovered something else too: Religious maturity, as a dynamic of existential states and processes, lies beyond the reach of any discipline, including theology as the "queen of sciences." While these conclusions need not deter the attempt to understand the characteristics and dynamics of religious maturity, psychologists, psychiatrists, and theologians involved in such a quest ought to know that religious maturity, even on a level considerably below the ultimate, is not only an incomprehensible abstraction but also a nonexistent category. There are religious maturities, as there are religious individuals, and these are open for us to discover, handle, analyze, even perhaps befriend, but we must guard against taking any one of them and assigning it any kind of singular, normative position.

Let me elaborate on these theses and convictions at the same time relating them to our contemporary situation as behavioral scientists and applied theologians.

Psychological Maturity and Religious Maturity

In the development of the psychological sciences, especially as related to the psychology of personality and to counseling and psychotherapy, the idea of maturity has taken strange turns. The term *maturity* itself has come to mean "the state or condition of complete or adult form, structure, and function of an organism, whether in respect to a single trait or, more often, all traits" (English and English 1958, 308). Though such a connotation is not desperately controversial, the real rub comes when we wish to add content to the general concept. What are the characteristics or traits of this state or condition? How do we recognize the distinctive attributes that separate maturity from immaturity?

When he was asked by a Harvard sophomore to explain the difference between a normal and an abnormal person, Allport paused to struggle with the complexities of the question. Then he said, "This is an institution, and all of you are members of this institution. Not far from here is the Boston Psychopathic Hospital. It too is an institution, and it has its members. You are different from them. They are different from you." Allport then returned to his lecture notes. He knew that his answer was unsatisfactory. Later in his lecture he reminded the class of the tremendous complexities involved in making meaningful differentiations in the areas of "normal" and "abnormal" and "mature" and "immature."

Allport was one of the most adventuresome behavioral scientists in facing the issue of normative definitions. In his Personality: A Psychological Interpretation (1937), he maintains that the developed person is one who has a variety of autonomous interests and can lose himself or herself in such things as work, contemplation, recreation, and loyalty to others. He gave his definition specific content by describing the characteristics of self-extension, self-objectification, including insight and a sense of humor, and, finally, a unifying philosophy of life. In his 1961 revision of the book, he gave even more space to a discussion of the mature personality, listing as criteria extension of the sense of self; warm relating of self to others; emotional security; realistic perception, skills, and assignments; self-objectification; and a unifying philosophy of life (1961, chap. 12).

Allport's contribution to the literature on religious maturity is valuable, because he was willing to go beyond a description of the mature personality and propose a list of characteristics that are essential for the mature religious sentiment. For him, the mature religious sentiment is well differentiated, dynamic in character in spite of its derivative nature, productive of a consistent morality, comprehensive, integral, and fundamentally heuristic (1950).

Abraham Maslow offers another understanding of religious maturity in his concept of self-actualization (1954, 1968). I should like to illustrate his theory by referring to an inventory that purportedly measures self-actualization. This will add practical dimension to our concern, since this inventory has been used in counseling, in industrial situations, and in educational settings. The instrument, called the Personal Orientation Inventory, was developed by Everett L. Shostrom, director of the Institute of Therapeutic Psychology at Santa Ana, California (1966). Though relatively new, its uses in showing relationships between self-actualizing persons and pathological subjects has been impressive (Shostrom and Knapp 1966). It measures in terms of ratio scores time competency, inner directedness, self-actualizing value, existentiality, feeling reactivity, spontaneity, self-regard, self-acceptance, nature of man, synergy, acceptance of aggression, and capacity for intimate contact. An analysis of a profile of these various ratio scores gives an index of the degree of self-actualization that has been achieved by the subject.

What is the relationship of Allport's and Maslow's notions of maturity to religious maturity? In the case of the Allportian criteria, we find an interesting state of affairs. A caustic critic has observed that what we have is not a concept of religious maturity but instead a picture of a liberal Episcopalian. There is truth in this charge. If we apply Allport's characteristics to an evangelical Disciple of Christ member, for example, we might have some severe difficulties. Or trying to fit a practicing Hindu into the model becomes an impossible exercise.

There is one consistency, though, that shows itself when we take Allport's mature religious sentiment and relate it to his concept of mature personality. In this psychological conceptualization, we find a place for religious maturity, but we must note that the religious factor finds its niche within the broader notion of mature personality. Specifically, we note that a unifying philosophy of life may contain the religious factor. In fact, Allport, though admitting of many possible cognitive orientations, gives special weight to Eduard Spranger's belief that the religious orientation is the most comprehensive and integrative of all value orientations. Nevertheless, we must be cognizant of the fact that religious maturity is viewed within the larger concept of mature personality.

When we turn to Maslow's model of self-actualization, we discover a similar assumption. Although the Personal Orientation Inventory does not treat religion as conspicuously as Allport's approach, it includes several traits or factors that carry a religious overtone. For example, the nature of man scale deals with what we might call proceptive directions or proceptive sets. Frequently these are religious in tone and content. In fact, a clear normative and evaluative factor is present in this scale, for those subjects who see humankind as essentially evil or bad hurt their chances of being defined as self-actualizers. Though this point is worth discussion and offers problematics of no little consequences for the religious practioner, it is noted here only to point up the tendency to include the religious dimensions within the concept of psychological maturity—in this instance, self-actualization.

I do not present these illustrations primarily as criticisms of the propensity to place religious maturity under the psychological categories, though I am certain that such a tendency lends itself to attack from theologicans and philosophers and others who perceive their disciplines as having a wider and larger purview. My point is that when this is done—and, frankly, I see no way of avoiding the practice—we should be aware of what is being done and should appreciate the limitations in such tendencies. An even more severe warning seems legitimate in view of what we often find in the literature: We ought to state as clearly as we can the context in which we speak of religious maturity. If this is done with insight and openness, we will reserve the term *religious maturity* for very special usage. We might even bring forth a wise sort of humility capable of handling the facts with sympathy and care, and those of us who are behavioral scientists might be willing to embrace a more humanistic aura in which to make our studies. Indeed, there are some current signs that humanistic psychology already recognizes the complexity and multidimensionality of the religious problem (Bugental 1967). Perhaps its extension will help to deter the chances of premature closure that seems to be characteristic of the psychology of religion and the other sciences of religion.

Nature of Religious Maturity

I need to clarify my understanding of the concept of religious maturity. In another place I have offered a definition of mature religion based on the opinions and inferences of psychologists and psychiatrists:

> Mature religion is a dynamic organization of cognitive-affective-conative factors possessing certain characteristics of depth and height—including a highly conscious and articulate belief system, purged, by critical processes, of childish wishes and intensely suited and comprehensive enough to find positive meaning in all of life's vicissitudes. Such a belief system, though tentative in spirit, will include a conviction of the existence of an Ideal Power to which the person can sense a friendly continuity—a conviction grounded in authoritative and ineffable experiences. The dynamic relationship between this belief system and these experiential events will generate feelings of wonder and awe, a sense of oneness with the All, humility, elation, and freedom; and with great consistency will determine the individual's responsible behavior in all areas of personal and interpersonal relationships, including such spheres as morality, love, work, and so forth. (Strunk 1965, 144–45)

The definition may be helpful for those who are content, or tolerant enough, to accept religious maturity as a circle within the much larger circle of mature personality. Despite this positive possibility, I should like to suggest a slightly different approach to viewing religious maturity, one that has not been taken seriously by those who are willing to speak of religious maturity or comparable notions.

We can consider religious maturity in terms of a comprehensive stratification scheme (Gilbert 1967, 3–19). Ordinarily, when we Americans import stratification concepts from Germany, we fragment the theories or, perhaps more kindly, we select what we want in such theories and conveniently overlook or forget what we do not want. It is not difficult, for example, for those of us outside the behavioristic stream to accept the ideas of the unconscious, the preconscious, and the conscious. But most of us find it uncomfortable to assimilate the notion of a collective unconscious and even more distasteful to speak openly about such notions as cosmic consciousness or universal consciousness.

Ironically, in our depth explorations we contribute toward accomplishments of height. That is, if we take seriously the individuation process as described by Jung, we arrive at wider consciousness (Jung 1940, [1938] 1958; Goldbrunner 1964). Thus, religious maturity may be seen as having its basis in how well the individual has been able to become aware of the religious archetypes of the collective unconscious. This, it seems to me, is still a fruitful way to approach an understanding of religious maturity, especially if we take seriously James Hillman's recent suggestion that we learn to "befriend" the inner workings of our unconscious, to become, in a sense, our "own mythologist" (Hillman 1967). But I am convinced that a comprehensive stratification approach must also take into account many "not-self" categories—areas of potential acquisition that rest outside and beyond the unconscious, personal or collective, but that through a befriending process add to our range of awareness.

One attempt to articulate a level of awareness conceptualization comes from a Canadian psychologist, Joseph R. Royce (1964). A fellow countryman, Richard M. Bucke (1901), had introduced the concept of cosmic consciousness more than sixty years before, but he is not mentioned by Royce. In fact Bucke's work is amazingly absent from the literature of religious psychology generally, although William James in his *Varieties of Religious Experience* (1961) refers to Bucke's *Cosmic Consciousness* with serious intent. Bucke wrote, "Cosmic consciousness in its more striking instances is not simply an expansion or extension of the self-conscious mind with which we are all familiar, but the superaddition of a function as distinct from any possessed by the average man as self-consciousness is distinct from any function possessed by one of the higher animals" (Bucke 1901, 2).

Cosmic consciousness, then, cannot be contained within the ordinary meaning of the individuation process, because this stratum of awareness has to do with the life and order of the universe. It is associated with a kind of knowledge that transcends the self and in this sense it belongs to another stratum and represents another dimension of being. In Royce's approach this stratum is called ultimate consciousness and is characterized as a psychic state that places persons beyond their encapsulated condition. Royce's guarded comment on the mysterious nature of this ultimate consciousness is especially relevant for the entire question of religious maturity: "Presumably, ultimate consciousness is synonymous with God or ultimate reality, implying omniscience or complete awareness. If there are states of awareness which come closer to ultimate reality than what we have described as individuated consciousness, we in the West are not sufficiently cognizant of such states" (1964, 172–82).

Royce is driven to the East and to the Eastern religions for some assistance and hope, a move that Jung was also forced to make early in his research. The move demonstrates just how complex the question of religious maturity becomes when it is faced in an open and realistic fashion. Complexity and idiomorphic forms become integral with the subject of religious maturity. There is no escaping these characteristics, no matter how much we as psychologists, psychiatrists, theologians, and behavioral practitioners may wish to do so. Those who choose to escape these factors deliberately encapsulate themselves. They may do so for good and respectable scientific reasons, but they have a responsibility to be aware of what they are doing.

Religious Maturity and Christian Maturity

What we have said about religious maturity is a necessary prerequisite for our consideration of Christian maturity and of the Christian's quest for maturity. Sooner or later we need to confront the issue of the relationship between a developed notion of Christian maturity and of religious maturity itself and of psychological maturity in general. "Is the mature Christian ipso facto religiously mature?" is an important question. Even more stimulating and controversial is the question, "Is the religiously mature individual necessarily psychologically mature?"

We ought to begin the discussion by recognizing that there are Christian maturities rather than a Christian maturity. No matter how irritating this pluralistic thesis is, I see no way of ignoring it without oversimplifying the issue or deliberately overlooking what we already know of the religious sentiment and of the history of religion. The point was brought home to me in a dramatic and concrete fashion. My denomination invited me to write a curriculum consisting of twelve brief biographies of twentieth-century Christians (Strunk 1969). In preparing to write the volume, I read scores of biographies, autobiographies, and letters of different people. What struck me most decisively was the complete absence of any kind of uniform or common core of characteristics of these people. The mere mention of their names tends to make the point: Rufus Jones, Simone Weil, Mary Bethune, Toyohiko Kagawa, Angelo Roncalli, Thomas A. Dooley, Dietrich Bonhoeffer, Francis J. McConnell, Joseph Gomer, Evelyn Underhill, Frank Mason North, and Helen Keller. We could argue about the degree of Christian maturity of these persons, but we might agree that each one of them is in some sense worthy of emulation. In any case, my point is that it appears hopeless to find a set of neat and common characteristics that can be found in all of them. The idiographic factor dominates the problem.

In *The Choice Called Atheism* (1968), I said, "When the gospel is translated into personal acts, it loses something in the translation. . . . At the same time, it is enriched and made unique by the personality of the Christian. He communicates his translation in a way peculiar to him, and since no two people are alike, the characteristics of the witnessing Christian must be seen as variable and flexible." As behavioral scientists we are uncomfortable with this kind of statement, and yet the complex-idiographic propensities of our problem cannot be dimmed or we risk losing the heart of the matter. As Rollo May says:

> One can gather empirical data, let us say on religion and art, from now till doomsday, and one will never get any closer to understanding these activities if, to start with, his presuppositions shut out what the religious person is dedicated to and what the artist is trying to do. Deterministic presuppositions make it possible to understand everything about art except the creative act and the art itself; mechanistic naturalistic presuppositions may uncover many facts about religion, but, as in Freud's terms, religion will always turn out to be more or less a neurosis, and what the genuinely religious person is concerned with will never get into the picture at all. (1966)

May is pleading for a more existential stance on the part of behavioral scientists, but I think the principle is true for all who seek to identify the marks of Christian maturity, whether they are behavioral scientists or theologians. I do not want to degrade or discourage the many attempts to come to some agreement on a style of life for the Christian. These exercises can be both productive and creative but I think we need to know the peculiar nature of these findings and to use them with extreme care and insightful timidity. For example, it is possible for a group of knowledgeable members of a Southern Baptist congregation to sit down and work through a list of traits characteristic of Christian maturity. They might even find empirical ways of translating these traits to IBM cards and with enough ingenuity to define individuals on a continuum ranging from immature to mature. There is one sense in which this practice is legitimate. We do it in other areas of behavioral science, and talk of our operational definitions and findings. But, as we have seen, the mature religious sentiment is far too complex for such gymnastics. The same thing can be said of any attempt to designate traits of Christian maturity.

This "agnostic" stance may be bothersome and irritating, but I believe that it is the only realistic position we can take in view of the reality that we are just beginning to discover about religion and the human personality.

The Christian's Quest for Maturity

We have discussed the topics of religious maturity and of Christian maturity but have not really dealt with the issue of the Christian's quest for maturity. To speak of the latter issue is to raise the question, What kind or kinds of maturities? Are we saying that the Christian's quest ought to be for a general psychological maturity? Are we saying that the Christian's main quest ought to be directed toward the notion of Christian maturity? Or is a mature Christian already both religiously and psychologically mature?

Frankl insisted that self-actualization, pleasure, or power cannot be sought directly but are by-products of the search for meaning (1962, 1967). I believe this same principle might apply to the spiritual quest for maturity. Religious maturity and Christian maturity, and maybe psychological maturity, are not goals resting at the end of an uphill climb. Instead they are a part of life—givens, if you will, that are there in their magnificence and diversity and that are available to us if we can find ways of befriending them. Whatever the meaning of Christian maturity, religious maturity, or mental health may be, we can befriend these meanings if we are open to life and to reading it with insight, patience, and vigor.

To return to my original assertion in regard to religious maturity, the process of awareness in which we participate gives us also our maturity. The process itself helps to condition the content, and this content is, as I have said, unique for each one of us. That such processes transcend the tools of the behavioral sciences or of science in general ought not to surprise us. As human beings, however, we have a responsibility to see that we and others do not reduce these processes to fit a reductionistic method or some pathetic assortment of psychiatric or metapsychological assumptions.

Orville S. Walters made this point in his review of the tendency of theology, or certain contemporary theologians, to accept and make full use of the Freudian notion of the unconscious. He observes, "The generous use of psychoanalytic terms by [theologians] bespeaks premature and overenthusiastic commitment to a sectarian psychology that has not been able to win itself a comparable acceptance within science" (1968, 125). I suggest that the same tendency may be at work when we consider the relevance of such processes as self-actualization, peak experiences, and individuation as appropriate processes in understanding religious and Christian maturities.

David Bakan has called such a tactic a form of idolatry:

> If it were possible to root out idolatrous tendencies in both science and religion, then the singularity of the impulse expressed in both would emerge clearly. It is not that religion, as some have maintained, supplies mythical answers until science can provide more valid ones. Rather, it is that both religion and science are attempts on the part of mankind to search out the nature of himself and the world in which he lives. But it is *search* rather than answer which is significant. Indeed, as soon as either the scientist or the theologian allows himself to fix upon an answer as if it were the ultimate fulfillment of his impulse, he stops being either scientist or theologian and becomes an idolater. (1966, 9)

Bakan's comment reminds us that it is the quest itself that may be of primary value.

Maturity and the Church

I will not offer extended commentary on the role of the church in the Christian's quest for maturity, but I want to introduce a personal conviction on the subject. Bishop Robinson may be right when he observes that in the years ahead more and more people will need to work out their spiritual survival and development outside the organized church (1963, 1965). Nevertheless, the fact remains that it is in the church, especially in the local church, where many individuals first experience the nature and mystery of the religious question. It is in the church, too, where they may be conditioned to the notion of a mature religious sentiment or to a model of Christian maturity. There may be many places where spiritual development begins, but the church remains one primary locus.

I believe an authoritarian-moralistic orientation in the church is less likely to provide the individual with the atmosphere most capable of exposing the fullness of God's world and that therefore this kind of structure is an inadequate resource in the search for maturity of any kind. In *The Choice Called Atheism,* I use J. H. Oldham's (1959) words to describe the church at its best: "The church is most true to its own nature when it seeks nothing for itself, renounces power, humbly bears witness to the truth but makes no claim to be the possessor of truth, and is continually dying in order that it may live." This kind of church can play a significant role in providing the sort of atmosphere that is especially suited for the discovery of all maturities and in assisting individuals to find their unique style of participating in such maturities.

I think the clergy play an important part in assisting individuals to open themselves to the fullness of faith and the world. It seems to me that there has never been a time in the history of the church when the pastor and priest have been called upon to represent so much and to do so much, especially in that area which we once called spiritual direction. My point can be made by quoting again the Jungian analyst Hillman:

> Where the analyst only exceptionally meets with his analysand outside of his consulting room, and the physician makes house calls ever more rarely, the minister has the unique opportunity of entering the home and performing his pastoral function within the natural habitat of his charge. The discussions which take place about "visits" of the minister, whether he may telephone a member of the congregation if he is worried about him, whether he ought to call on a woman when her husband is at work and she is alone, whether the children should be allowed in or not—in

short, the entire question of managing the spatial problem of the human connection—may better be seen as one of attitude rather than as one of technique. Under the influence of psychotherapy and the medical model of the analyst, ministers tend more to see their troubled parishioners in their studies. This only cuts the ministers off further from their charges, turning parishioners indeed into patients, owing to the anxiety of the minister about handling the human connection on the spot, where the action is. The minister has a unique opportunity of entering the home, the family itself, where the soul goes through its torments. The tradition of pastoral care shows that the minister not only may make visits, he must make them. . . . The task of the [pastoral] counselor is essentially different from that of the analyst, the clinical psychologist, and the academic psychologist. And his tradition goes back to Jesus, who cared for and cured souls in many ways: preaching, wandering, visiting, telling tales, conversing, arguing, touching, praying, sharing, weeping, suffering, dying—in short, by living to the full his own destiny, true to his life. (1967, 31–32, 46)

This is not an argument against psychological or psychiatric sophistication on the part of clergymen. Ministers need all the knowledge of psychological dynamics they can get, but they need much more. They need to be experts, for example, in "God's forgotten language." The church needs what I like to call a shamanistic ministry, a ministry of people who by training, experience, and temperament are more than psychologists in clerical garb. Through complex and variable psychic integrations they are, like the shaman in primitive societies (Eliade 1960), peculiarily sensitized to the human condition and are devoted existentially to the befriending of all those forces that determine an individual's destiny. This kind of ministry, if an integral part of the church, would serve as an invaluable resource in the individual's entrance into the complex and idiographic processes that we try to glaciate in the concepts of psychological, Christian, and religious maturity.

9

The Unfolding Christian Self

J. Harold Ellens

The unfolding of the Christian self is a precarious and enchanting thing to see in others and to experience in ourselves. It is a mystifying, though not particularly mysterious, process of human growth and development. It includes the entire person—body, mind, and spirit—and drives always toward perfection in the sense of wholeness or completeness of personhood. It has mainly to do, however, with the spirit, that is, with those aspects of our persons to which we usually refer with such terms as spirituality and psychology.

Undoubtedly, we should learn more and more to see the psychology and spirituality of human persons as involving the same domain or operation of the human spirit. The two terms should likely be interchangeable, each encompassing all of what we have historically meant by both. Surely this is the biblical way of referring to and dealing with the functions of the psyche.

The unfolding development of the psyche, in all of its aspects, is mystifying in the sense that it is so wonderfully distinctive in each individual human that it is never possible to predict just how the world of the inner person will take its shape for each of us. On the other hand, the process is hardly mysterious. We know a very great deal about it, particularly in terms of the history of psychological research. We can, in fact, predict a great deal about the patterns the development will take and the behavior individual persons will manifest at various ages and stages of the unfolding. These predictable patterns are present in the growth that we customarily call spiritual as well as that which is referred to generally as psychological.

In chapter 4, Margaret Krych has pointed out in some detail the very helpful research of Jean Piaget regarding the stages of cognitive development in the unfolding human person. She presents a critique of the applicability of the work of Piaget and the assumptions upon which that work was built. Such challenges are, perhaps, a useful chastening of the excessive psychologizing of human personality that is sometimes the result of failing to appreciate adequately the degree to which spirituality and emotionality are essential aspects of the function of the human psyche and, therefore, of a comprehensive psychology.

However, the real value of Krych's contribution is to point out the structural framework of human growth in which the various attitudes and functions typical of specific ages and stages of human development can be understood. Piaget (1969) is the father of the contemporary structuralist approach to understanding personality development. He is joined in that perspective, notably, by Erik Erikson (1964), Lawrence Kohlberg (1974, 1976), and James W. Fowler (1981). Daniel Levinson (1978) has done significant research in this area as well and has published it in his worthy volume, *The Seasons of a Man's Life*, popularized in Gail Sheehy's *Passages* (1974).

Piaget demonstrated empirically the predictable structural stages through which human cognitive development moves as the self unfolds year by year, from birth to death. Kohlberg's contribution was to describe the comparable developmental stages that could be predicted for human moral development. Erikson has taught us that the stages of psychosocial growth are predictable corollaries of the cognitive and moral development patterns unveiled by Piaget and Kohlberg. Fowler has done us the incomparable favor of successfully applying structuralist theory to the patterns of religious or faith development. He has demonstrated that these structural patterns are as predictable in spiritual formation as in cognitive, moral, and psychosocial growth.

More recently, Robert C. Fuller, in *Religion and the Life Cycle* (1988), has published a unique and crucial contribution to our understanding of the unfolding Christian self. It is the burden of this chapter to present a studied appreciation of that work of Fuller and point out its relationship to his antecedents, particularly Fowler and Erikson.

Structuralism

The valuable work of Piaget, Kohlberg, Erikson, and Fowler was studied in some detail in a previous volume in this series (Ellens 1988). A cryptic summary of the structuralist framework may best be provided here, therefore, in the form of five tables (9.1–9.5), drawn from that study.

Table 9.1

Piaget's Cognitive
Development Stages

Years	Stage
0–2	Primarily sensorimotor
2–7	Preoperational and intuitive
7–13	Concrete operational
13–21	Formal operational: dichotomizing
21–35	Formal operational: dialectical
35–	Formal operational: synthetic

Fuller provides a well written and persuasive heuristic argument, backed by a wealth of convincing empirical evidence and rational analysis, that religious insights and ideas function crucially to mediate the healthy movement of human personalities through the transitions we make from one developmental phase to another and through the life-shaping trauma that often confronts us. Indeed, Fuller contends that religious ideas and experiences facilitate these growth transitions better than any other factors shaping our sense of meaning and our worldviews.

Fuller makes it plain that human maturation, fulfillment, and self-actualization depend upon values and experiences that are religious in

Table 9.2

Kohlberg's Moral Development Stages

Years	Stage
0–2	Response to positive and negative reward
2–7	Preconventional: heteronomous morality
7–13	Preconventional: instrumental hedonism
13–21	Conventional: mutual interpersonal concord, law and order morality
21–35	Conventional: social system priority, conscience dominant, class-biased universalism
35–	Postconventional: social contract, individual rights, principled higher law
60–	Postconventional: universal ethical principles, loyalty to being

Table 9.3

Erikson's Psychosocial Development Stages

Years	Stage
0–2	Basic trust vs. mistrust: hope
2–7	Autonomy vs. shame and doubt: will initiative vs. guilt: purpose
7–13	Industry vs. inferiority: competence
13–21	Identity vs. role confusion: fidelity
21–35	Intimacy vs. isolation: love
35–	Generativity vs. stagnation: care
60–	Integrity vs. despair: wisdom

character. Employing modern psychological theory and clinical research he establishes a model of the structure of human life cycle development, giving particular attention to Erikson's eight stages of psychosocial process. Fuller places great emphasis upon the way religion emerges in the lives of individuals and the role it plays in our development. He evidences a rich appreciation of the religious dynamics that are necessary for human growth to achieve the objective of wholeness and completeness in human personhood.

Table 9.4

Fowler's Development
Stages

Years	Stage
0–2	Infancy
2–7	Early childhood
7–13	Childhood
13–21	Adolescence
21–35	Young adulthood
35–	Adulthood/maturity

Translated into biblical language, Fuller's thesis is that faith in God and the providence and grace to which the Bible directs us is the key concept that incites our healing and growth in the adaptive process of achieving a mature and creatively fulfilling life. Fuller addresses religion and childhood development, belief and identity formation, values and mid-life transitions, aging, dying, and integrity, and religion and

Table 9.5
Fowler's Taxonomy of Faith Development by Ages, Stages, and Aspects: A Comprehensive Structuralist Model

Years/Stages	A (Piaget) Form of Logic	B (Kohlberg) Form of Moral Judgment	C (Erikson) Form of Psychosocial Function	D Bounds of Social Awareness	E Locus of Authority	F Forms of World Coherence	G Symbolic Function
0–2 Infancy	Primarily sensorimotor	Response to positive and negative reward	Basic trust vs. mistrust: hope	Family, primal others. Significant object relationship	Attachment/dependence relationships. Size, power, visible symbols of authority	Fragile, episodic, vacillating	Magical numinous
2–7 Early childhood Intuitive and projective	Preoperational and intuitive	Preconventional: heteronomous morality	Autonomy vs. shame and doubt: will initiative vs. guilt: purpose				
7–13 Childhood Mythic-literal	Concrete operational	Preconventional: instrumental hedonism	Industry vs. inferiority: competence	Like self in family social and religious terms	Authority figures based upon personal relatedness	Narrative dramatic (histrionic)	Literal one-dimensional
13–21 Adolescence Synthetic-conventional	Formal operational: dichotomizing	Conventional: mutual interpersonal concord, law and order morality	Identity vs. role confusion: fidelity	Composite of group in which one has interpersonal relationships	Consensus of valued groups of worthy representatives of value and belief system	Tacit system, felt meanings, symbolic, global import but clear boundaries	Symbolic, multidimensional
21–35 Young adulthood Individuative-reflexive	Formal operational: dialectical	Conventional: social system, reflective relativism, conscience, class-biased universalism	Intimacy vs. isolation: love	Ideologically congruent communities and self-chosen norms	Own convictions with self-ratified ideology. Authority and norms judged on congruency	Multisystem symbolism and concepts	progress from symbol adherence to meaning commitment
35– Adulthood Paradoxical-consolidative	Formal operational: synthetic	Postconventional: social contract, individual rights, principled higher law	Generativity vs. stagnation: care	Disciplined, ideological. Vulnerability to other's "truths" or "claims"	Open to dialectical interaction with other perspectives on human wisdom and worldviews	Unity in experience and concept	Postcritical reunion of symbol and meaning. Reality perceived beyond both
60– Maturity Universalizing	Formal operational: synthetic	Postconventional: universal ethical principles, loyalty to being	Integrity vs. despair: wisdom	Identification with species. Trans-narcissistic love of being	Commitment to intuition, principle of being, and personal judgment		Evocative power of truth and reality experienced in unification of symbol, symbolized and self

self-transcendence. His concern is to locate the place of religion within the overall structure of mature personality and to reexamine modern attitudes toward human nature by investigating the religious aspects of personal development. So we are here concerned with the way psychological understandings of human fulfillment enable us to understand the role faith and spirituality play in our lives.

Fuller's Thesis

Science and technology have devalued the role given to religious considerations in Western thought in the last two centuries, largely because spiritual function is less easily quantified in cause-effect equations than are the more tangible things we study or experience. In the effort to use the empirical model of physics the social sciences have sometimes overlooked their significant linkage with theology or philosophy. The structuralists have given us a great advantage in providing a framework within which psychology and the other social sciences can study the issues of cause and effect in human development while at the same time affording substantive address to matters of meaning and purpose. In the end, it is the resolution of meaning and purpose issues that people seek and hunger for, in terms of which we fashion life's satisfying psychological solutions, and which provides the force that moves us from one structural stage to the next in our growth process.

The original aims of the empirical method that natural and social sciences employ are "shaped by the desire to derive public and definitive information" by selecting out those data from life's total range of experience which can be objectively discerned (Fuller 1988, 5). Structuralism, particularly as articulated by Fowler and Fuller, provides a mechanism for reenlisting these sciences in the task of giving us a well-rounded vision of human nature and its complex functions, including those of faith and religious desire.

Fuller notes that four kinds of causality need to be addressed in order to understand honestly and comprehensively humanity's interaction with the universe: material (physiology, instincts, and genetics), environmental, mental/attitudinal, and spiritual or ultimate. General psychology addresses the first two. Speculative philosophy and religious research address all four and make a special contribution regarding the last two. Clinical and other research evidence indicates that a comprehensive appreciation of how humans function and how religious factors influence the course of human development requires us to focus upon the "extent to which humanity's pursuit of happiness and fulfillment is contingent upon 'adapting' to a spiritual environment beyond the limits of our physical and social worlds" (7). The evidence currently available demonstrates an inherently and inescapably religious dimension of human experience that is accessible to and consistent with the methods and spirit of comprehensive scientific inquiry.

David Tracy, in *Blessed Rage for Order* (1975), makes a point of special usefulness at this juncture in our discussion. He raises the notion that in our process of growth and development we frequently arrive at locations in the unfolding of our selves at which we confront what he engagingly calls "limit experiences." Such experiences arise in us when we reach the point in any stage of our growth at which our rational or doctrinal framework, our worldview, will no longer adequately accommodate or account for the actual data of our experience or learning.

> The limit dimension of human experience refers to those situations in which persons find themselves confronted with an ultimate limit or horizon to their experience. A "limit experience" is any moment of life that forces us to acknowledge the limits or limitations of a strictly rational or empirical approach to life. They impart an awareness that many of life's most profound challenges prompt us to look beyond the resources and perspectives of the finite personality . . . some limit experiences arise during periods of intellectual reflection and are thus of a more or less calm, even sedate character. Others occur amidst highly emotional moments and thus partake of the dramatic quality of either ecstasy or despair. Whichever the case, what distinguishes a limit experience from other types of experience is that it forces the individual to the recognition that reason, logic, and worldly resources are alone incapable of adjusting us to some of the most recurring themes in human experience. (Fuller 1988, 10)

Positive limit experiences, as in rewarding worship, conversion, or significant bursts of illumination, have a revelatory character insofar as they afford persons "a direct experience of a More or Beyond." "Negative limit experiences emerge amidst feelings of grief, confusion, or meaninglessness." Positive "limit experiences impart sensations of bliss, ecstasy, euphoria, and contentment. They impart to the conscious personality a firm conviction in the existence and even availability of a supersensible reality," such as God and the divine providence and grace insinuated into our lives and experience. In this regard, William James declared that the "heart of religion . . . is the conviction that (1) the visible world is part of an unseen spiritual universe from which it draws its ultimate meaning or purpose, and (2) that union or harmonious relation with that higher universe is our true end as well as the key to achieving personal wholeness and well-being."[1]

---

1. Fuller (1988, 11). See also James (1961, 377).

Limit experiences confront us with the awareness that there is some power and dimension of reality and potential experience, or some higher level of consciousness, namely, our hunger for and perception of God's grace and providence. This and this alone can resolve those disharmonies and feelings of incompleteness which occur in us when we are at the "limits" of our human comprehension and condition.

> They bring us to the conviction that *if* our lives can continue to be meaningful, *if* we can successfully handle the full gamut of mental, emotional, and moral challenges that typically confront humans over the course of their lives, and *if* we wish to interpret the relevance of a religious or mystical experience for our everyday life, *then* we must recognize that the "secret" to a life of maximum richness and fulfillment lies beyond the limits of the world known by (natural and social) science and beyond the limits of the self known by academic psychology. (Fuller 1988, 11)

Fuller's conceptualization of religion, as he acknowledges, will not satisfy those who think of it as a formal process of ritual behavior or as a functional process of dogma with its role in instruction and illumination. Fuller's perspective, as that of James, anchors religion "not in God but rather in a certain dimension of experiences common to individuals as they pursue their various courses of life" (12). Fuller is quite correct in this approach since notions about God are second-level content in our religious experience, derivative from that experience, whether it is learning in Sunday school, reading theology, or personal conversations. That is, concepts of God are the human experiences by which we name and structure our deeper, primary-level spiritual hunger and revelatory perceptions. The primary-level structure and content of religious perception is that afforded by our direct experiences of faith, trust, assurance of the "More or Beyond," and projections of God concepts upon our limit events. These primary religious experiences develop their structure in infancy and childhood out of ingrained hunger for God, for ultimacy, and for meaning. This hunger is invested in all of us by our creation in the image of God. We develop the content out of experiences of faith, trust, and assurance in relationship with such significant others as parents, teachers, and friends. Saint Augustine was psychologically as well as spiritually correct in his doxological confession, "You have made us for yourself, and our souls are restless until they rest, O God, in you!"

The Thesis Applied

True faith always exists only in the context of honest doubt, and Fuller helps us focus the fact that the personal empirical approach to religious conceptualization "permits us to view religious faith not as a set of unproven beliefs that we either do or do not hold but rather as a style of living influenced by the kinds of insights that occur just beyond the limits of either reason or sensory experience" (12).

The pragmatic application of Fuller's thesis is persuasive.

> At crucial stages in our course through life our happiness and fulfillment are dependent upon our ability to "adapt" not to the sensible world, but to the supersensible world; not to structures of physical and social reality but rather to that which lies just beyond the limits of the physical, (i.e., the metaphysical) . . . such experiences as midlife identity crises, moral struggles, and the need to embrace the aging process as a path toward continued personal development all lead individuals to the limit dimension of human experience. And for that reason they lay the foundation for a modern, co-scientific view of the nature and relevance of religiousness in human experience. (1988, 12–13)

Fuller recognizes Erikson's structuralist framework as a model of the way humans gain skills to cope with the expanding experience, opportunity, and responsibility that life affords. Erikson rejects Freud's pathology-oriented view of human personality, placing the primary emphasis not on the role of instinctual drives but upon conscious ego formation. He credits the ego with the capacity to regulate a person's relationship with the environment in ways that "not only achieve personal wholeness but make positive contributions to the fulfillment of others as well" (Fuller 1988, 17). This gives attitudinal causes a greater role in shaping our well-being, adaptation, growth, and faith.

Each of Erikson's eight stages describes how a person is presented with a "new developmental challenge," requiring a new developmental method for relating with the internal and external environment, for the purpose of successfully resolving and integrating the perplexities and growth possibilities of new experiences. In our progress from one stage to the next we discover dimensions of reality which do not integrate well in terms of our previous framework of understanding. We arrive at the horizon of our understanding and perception—a limit experience. This crisis requires a rethinking and "refeeling" of our framework of understanding and meaning—our *Weltanschauung* or worldview.

At Erikson's first level the human infant must resolve the crisis of trust versus mistrust, and so acquire hope: "the belief that our wishes can be obtained in spite of difficulties. Hope is the virtue that makes faith possible, and adult faith in turn nourishes hope and inspires us to care for others." At the second stage we must process a crisis of will: "the unbroken determination to exercise free choice as well as self-restraint, in spite of unavoidable moments of shame and doubt." The third stage deals with personal initiative and with rising above a sense of guilt. It resolves the crisis of purpose: "the courage to envisage and pursue valued goals without being inhibited by fear of punishment or guilt." These three initial stages are the crises of infancy and early childhood which we negotiate during the ages of birth to two years, two to four years, and four to five years, respectively (Fuller 1988, 19–23).

Erikson's fourth stage confronts us at six to eleven years with the crisis of inferiority versus industry, and challenges us to acquire the virtue of competence: "the free exercise of intelligence and physical skills to complete tasks unimpaired by feelings of inferiority" (Fuller 1988, 23–24). This completes what Erikson sees as the childhood process. The progress from stage 1 to 4 is a progress from coping with primal physiological maturation to coping with psychological and spiritual maturation. "And, importantly, as the life cycle progresses the triggering experience of human development and transformation is increasingly likely to come in the form of a limit experience" (Fuller 1988, 25). Early human development is shaped largely by imitation and identification. Other significant personalities impact us. The notion of God is a cultural-symbol concept mediated to us by that imitation and identification process; however, we acquire such symbol concepts because of an inherent appetite for the meaning that the symbols afford us. "As childhood gives way to adolescence and young adulthood, pressures come to bear upon a religious faith acquired from without on the basis of parental authority. The late teens and twenties afford individuals their first opportunities to make the somewhat turbulent transition from a secondhand to a firsthand religious faith" (33).

Thus Erikson's stage 5, age twelve to twenty-two, leads humans to deal with the crisis of identity and the acquisition of the virtue of fidelity: the ability to sustain loyalty to an important commitment.

> Fidelity is the cornerstone or foundation of identity and the mark of maturity. It is also the precondition of true love. . . . Much as the infant confronts the disruption of continuous attachment to the nurturing parent by creating a safe "transitional space" into which she or he might trustingly engage life, so must the adolescent utilize nonrational mental processes to create an ideological matrix that can make life appear trustworthy and true. Religious faith of course is a primary source from which (or possibly in contrast to which) individuals turn their world into a living whole which they might meet in a mutually enhancing manner. This is especially true for those to whom the need for cognitive certainty carries with it an ultimacy that drives them to the "limiting" questions concerning the origin and meaning of human existence. Religion draws upon the deepest yearnings humans have for aligning their lives with that which is central to existence and symbolizes what feels profoundly true even though it is not demonstrable. From a psychological perspective, religious faith can thus be viewed as an ongoing expression of those psychological processes that make it possible for humans to venture forth into life on the basis of trust. As Erikson remarks, "It translates into

significant words, images, and codes the exceeding darkness which surrounds man's existence, and the light which pervades it beyond all desert or comprehension." Religious faith operates within the emerging identity as an adaptive and integrating force. Because religion roots the meaning and purpose of life in the transcendental reality of God, it makes it possible for individuals to locate themselves and their actions within a larger frame of reference. Religious doctrines enable individuals to make confident choices about who they are, what they stand for, and what they stand against. Religious faith also frees individuals from being at the total mercy of events in the outer world . . . to bring their own set of values and goals to bear upon the interpretation of everyday life . . . the kind of mature and self-controlled behavior that the psychologist Gordon Allport calls "propriate striving"—conduct motivated by self-chosen values rather than by environmental or instinctual forces . . . religious faith reinforces a positive sense of self-worth by aligning our personal identity and moral outlook with an understanding of God's creative activity in the world. (Fuller 1988, 38–39)

Serious doubt is the essential matrix of great faith. The human personality that is encouraged and stimulated to full maturation ultimately experiences faith resurging and reasserting itself over doubt under the suasion of pragmatic, mystical, or intellectual/contemplative/reflective experience. Personalities that do not come to this fulfillment are, in effect, arrested at one of the stages prior to full self-actualization. "Insofar as religious beliefs or practices appear to impart zest or meaning to our lives they rightfully warrant our recognition as valuable 'hypotheses' concerning the ultimate nature of reality. Even though the utility of a belief does not logically prove its truth, it does suggest that the belief in some way corresponds to the structure of reality. . . . In the same way, the fact that common human experience repeatedly verifies the pragmatic truth of religious beliefs alone is sufficient grounds to prompt us to act faithfully upon them even without logical proof. . . . The mystical validation of faith refers to those limit experiences in which individuals somewhat ineluctably find themselves confronted with nonsensory dimensions of reality. Insofar as an individual has direct experience of a presence or power beyond the limits of rational or sensory knowledge, he or she possesses empirical evidence for considering this nonphysical reality as a clue to the nature and meaning of life. Undoubtedly the strong importance that religion places on prayer, meditation, ritual, and various altered states of consciousness is precisely owing to their ability to afford individuals a firsthand experience of a spiritual More beyond the limits of ordinary waking thought" (Fuller 1988, 45–46).

The intellectual or contemplative validation of faith refers to the rational insight that the extrinsic properties of reality are not self-explanatory.

Reason runs up against its own limit when it asks why it is that there is a universe at all . . . although reason can ask the question of its own origin, it is inherently incapable of deriving the answer. . . . This realization that reason is an inherently inadequate tool for relating ourselves to the intrinsic meaning or purpose of life forces us to acknowledge the "validity" of concepts that do not confine themselves to the limits of logical reason. (46)

Gordon W. Allport said that mature faith must be well-differentiated, dynamic, productive of a consistent morality, comprehensive, integral, and heuristic. That means that religious experience must provide us with a firsthand faith, not be eroded by the ossifications of dogmatism or traditionalism, imply coherent ethical principles, afford an integrated meaning for the whole of life, and possess the suasive quality of an appealing belief system and worldview. If it is to provide the foundation for mature identity it must afford us ideological direction for continuing personality development at each stage.

Erikson's stage 6, age twenty to thirty-five, presents us with the crisis of intimacy and our quest for the virtue of true love. Stage 7, age thirty-five to sixty contains the crisis of generativity versus self-absorption and the quest for the realization of care for what we have created and for the world context of that creation. The final stage of old age, from sixty to our death, Fowler calls the universalizing phase in which we expand our capacity for understanding and caring to all truth and all reality, if we mature to this degree. Stages 6 through 8 are dominated by the quest for a profound, warrantable, and durable sense of the meaning of all life and existence, and for an ethical-moral maturity in which we take responsibility for our world and for communicating that caring perspective to those who follow us.

This capacity for a strenuous moral life of authentic and transcendent, that is, supratraditional quality, is a developmental achievement and not an inherited disposition. It implies a type of ultimate individuation in which our socially defined ego gradually gives way to a wider and more universal and transcendent range of potentials, constituting the core of authentic selfhood. This process postulates and reaches out toward the reality and existence that transcends our selves, time, and space. If we possess a notion or theology of ultimate reality that is formatively constituent to our ego structure, and, therefore, authentic to our real inner self—a genuine firsthand religious spirituality—our moral consciousness postulates and reaches out to a "God through whom we can come to feel intimately identified with our fellow living creatures and in terms of whose demands we are prompted to take seriously the requirements of the remote future," indeed, of eternity (Fuller 1988, 66).

In James's words, "When . . . we believe that a God is there, and that he is one of the claimants, the infinite perspective opens out. The scale of the symphony is incalculably prolonged. The more imperative ideals now begin to speak with an altogether new objectivity and significance, and to utter the penetrating, shattering, tragically challenging note of appeal" (1956, 212).

James believed that if the only reason for believing in God were its ethical necessity, the emergence of "religious faith in the fully rational adult is yet justified by its own evolutionary-adaptive functions," that is, by the manner in which it empowers us to successfully negotiate our way through our limit experiences into the next stage of our development and growth and into that broadening of our doctrinal or philosophical framework which makes it possible for us to integrate healthily our ever expanding world of understanding, truth, and experience; thus achieving the resources to be a wholly ethical personality. "Every sort of energy and endurance, of courage and capacity for handling life's evil, is set free in those who have religious faith (and thus for) this reason the strenuous type of character will on the battle-field of human history always outwear the easy-going type, and religion will drive irreligion to the wall" (13).

Alfred North Whitehead's reinforcement of this notion is expressed in the claim that religion emerges out of the "longing of the spirit that the facts of existence should find their justification in the nature of existence" (Fuller 1988, 67).

Fuller connects Viktor E. Frankl's "will to meaning" to this ethical-moral proclivity with its inherent religious dynamics and demonstrates how this process is the vital driver of Fowler's "universalizing" quality of the mature adult. Fuller concludes cogently:

> The claim being staked out here is that insofar as humans regularly and even predictably confront limit experiences, . . . one must also acknowledge that the ego-dominated psychological processes cannot alone fully center the personality. The implication is that the rhythms of the life cycle themselves prompt the individual to search for a Self which in some fundamental way transcends the historical flux. And, surely, this psychological observation must simultaneously have a great deal of ontological and metaphysical import. Among other things, it suggests that humans do inhabit environments that go beyond the physical world mediated by our sensory experience . . . this is precisely the issue raised most poignantly in the prototypical limit experience—the confrontation of death in old age. (1988, 72–73)

> Just as the acquisition of basic trust in life rests upon nonempirical judgments about the basic character of the universe, so does the acquisition of wisdom depend upon accepting life in its totality rather than its specifics. One cannot find integrity in one's own life unless the integrity of the whole of life can be affirmed. It is not the extrinsic utility of this or

that thing we have done that is at stake, but whether there is any intrinsic meaning to the human enterprise itself. This is a religious rather than a scientific or ethical issue. As with all other limit experiences, this final developmental challenge clearly relativizes the scope and significance of human rationality. Logical analysis and scientific observation can guide us through many of the developmental challenges of the middle years, but they can tell us little about the intrinsic character or integrity of existence.

The religiosity of this stage must go well beyond the beliefs and doctrines of the churches because it must accept the doubts and frailties humans have when they so starkly face life's greatest trauma. Wisdom emerges as these doubts have been fully admitted and accepted even while continuing to affirm the intrinsic meaningfulness of life in all of its human ambiguities. (78)

True maturity can finally arrive in old age, in the age sixty to death stage, and transcendent religious insight and conceptualization of our worldview is the crucial maturing dynamic in this stage. This ultimate maturity and self-actualization means the achievement of detachment—"the refusal to confuse the quality of our being with the quantity of our having"; hope—emotional strength and desire to look forward continually, despite the adversities of life, with the confidence "that there is a will or power central to the universe that is receptive toward our efforts and will, in the end, bestow wholeness upon our lives"; humor—the ability to preserve integrity amidst loss; and vision—the ability to see "beyond the limit or boundary of the finite self and disclose a supersensible reality that envelops or surrounds the physical. Vision of this sort shifts the focus of our identity away from the material to the spiritual, from the physical to the metaphysical, and from the finite to the infinite . . . this vision gradually 'invites us to a total, selfless surrender in which the distinction between life and death slowly loses its pain.'"[2]

Fuller here cites Elisabeth Kübler-Ross's discovery

that those rare individuals who have an "intrinsic faith" readily find acceptance of death. Her interviews reveal that some individuals find the wisdom to accept death long before they approach serious illness. Having developed a firsthand faith, they had long ago come to identify themselves not as a body who possesses a soul, but rather as a soul who possesses a body. Acceptance of death, then, is the byproduct of a vision of the light. Insofar as we come to place our primary identity in some spiritual or nonphysical aspect of our being, death need no longer be viewed as a final barrier. Indeed, death can actually be viewed as a type

2. Fuller (1988, 81–82). See also Henri Nouwen and Walter Gaffney (1976, 36).

of healing in that it alone makes possible a release from a no longer useful body. In other words, death confronts individuals in such a way as to
disclose a limit dimension to human life that can best be resolved by
learning to affirm and identify with some supersensible reality beyond
the limits of our finite personalities. (1988, 90–91)

Obviously, it is not possible for us to consider the full scope of our
life span authentically without noting how central is the religious character of life's most crucial and most profound developmental challenges and the spiritual understandings, which empower us to meet
them. The hunger of our hearts is for God.

Conclusion

There is a fairly broad stream of literature in pastoral theology and
Christian education, as well as in transcendental and structuralist psychology which relates directly and deeply with the thesis and argument
of this chapter.

Fuller's understanding of the crucial role of spirituality in human
growth and Fowler's perspective on the nature of faith are among the
most important insights available regarding the function of our relationship with and perception of God in the unfolding of the Christian
self.

Fowler's concept of faith is wider and deeper than just religious content or context. It exceeds the bounds of theological commitment or
belief. "Faith is a person's or group's way of moving into the force field
of life. It is our way of finding coherence in and giving meaning to the
multiple forces and relations that make up our lives. Faith is a person's
way of seeing him- or herself in relation to others against a background of shared meaning and purpose" (Fowler 1981, 4). "Prior to our
being religious or irreligious, before we come to think of ourselves as
Catholics, Protestants, Jews or Muslims, we are already engaged with
issues of faith. Whether we become nonbelievers, agnostics or atheists,
we are concerned with how to put our lives together and with what
will make life worth living. Moreover we look for something to love
that loves us, something to value that gives us value, something to
honor and respect that has the power to sustain our being" (5). With
Wilfred Cantwell Smith (1963), Fowler insists that words such as "religious" or "belief" refer to the cumulative traditions societies collect
from the faith of people of the past. If "religious" and "belief" refers to
the tradition, perhaps the words *spiritual* and *spirituality* might more
correctly be used, therefore, to refer to Fowler's definition of faith or
the capacity and experience in humans from which faith springs. Faith
is the inner human dynamic that reaches for meaning. Religion is the

cumulative fruit of the history of past expressions of that inner dynamic as it was experienced, formulated, and testified to by our antecedents, and which history we recapitulate in traditions of doctrine, liturgy, perspective, and practice.

Without question, the faith perspective of Smith and Fowler can be clearly seen as the backdrop to Fuller's understanding of faith as the meaning insights that modify our worldview and make successful coping and growth possible, especially at those crises points when we stand before the affective and conceptual limits of our experience and need a personal inner vision that leads us beyond ourselves and our world of understanding to the More, to the Beyond: to God. Fowler says that

> faith, at once deeper and more personal than religion, is the person's or group's way of responding to transcendent value and power as perceived and grasped through the forms of the cumulative tradition. Faith and religion, in this view, are reciprocal. Each is dynamic; each grows or is renewed through its interaction with the other. The cumulative tradition is selectively renewed as its contents prove capable of evoking and shaping the faith of new generations. Faith is awakened and nurtured by elements from the tradition. As these elements come to be expressive of the faith of new adherents, the tradition is extended and modified, thus gaining fresh vitality. (1981, 10)

It is in this context that Fuller declares that

> what distinguishes religion from philosophy, psychology, or sociology as a guide toward human betterment is that it views the sacred as the principal sphere to which humans ought to adapt themselves . . . human fulfillment cannot be understood totally in terms of our ability to adapt successfully to the social and economic spheres of life. Insofar as there are various moral and metaphysical contexts within which the life cycle unfolds, it would seem that any comprehensive account of the human enterprise must ultimately take seriously the religious hypothesis that, in the final analysis, wholeness is dependent upon the degree to which we can locate our lives within a wider spiritual environment. (1988, 117, 149)

Religious symbology, in the form of doctrinal systems, confessional documents, or personal formulations of belief, can be empirically demonstrated to enhance human negotiation of the limit experiences of life. Effectiveness in that process is clearly essential to maturation and wholeness.

The Christian community of believers, throughout its history, has called humanity to face the crises of our limit experiences at each stage of life with the faith response of conversion (Ellens 1988). The Bible itself poses the challenge of *metanoia*, conversion, a change of mind. Conversion is still the best term for the remarkable moments, events, or processes we have addressed in this chapter, those significant changes of mind and worldview that occur when we are at the boundary of our growth in any given stage and must enlarge our framework of insight and understanding in order to take in and integrate the expanding volumes of truth that are bearing in upon us as we grow. To mature from one stage to the next we must be converted; that is, we must be awakened to a new dimension of faith in or experience of a transcendent vision which enlarges our paradigm, revises and expands our worldview, and reintegrates our selves and our experience within a new framework of conviction and perspective. When we reach the limit experiences that challenge us to this conversion, and then resist the demands of the new and expanded vision of truth, faith, or perspective, we regress and entrench ourselves in the immature worldview of the previous stage of our development, and then proceed to idealize that outlook or formulation with dogmatism.

One can be converted to Christianity from atheism or some other religion. One can be converted from Christianity to atheism or some other worldview, from Marxism to humanism or Christianity, from humanism to naturalism, or from any ideology to another. The psychodynamics are always the same. The thing that makes any of these psychospiritual processes distinctive or redemptive is the content that shapes the critical transition through our limit experiences into a larger world of insight and faith. Christian conversion is just such a psychological transition in which the content of the process is Christian truth, faith, and understanding: a new and expanded insight, a new relationship with God in Christ, and the new trauma which that demanding change always brings.

It seems clear from the evidence and argument of this chapter that what really happens in such a conversion is this: At a crucial and formative moment in a transition through the psychological stages of structural development, a person experiences the impact of a profound new insight, relationship, or trauma. This impact cuts down through the defensive structures of the personality, through the conceptual framework of our worldview, through the formative coping patterns that have shaped our nature and function, and disturbs, reorders, and reintegrates our values and belief system at our characterological level. This reintegration takes its shape around the new insight, relationship, or traumatic force we have experienced.

As we are cracked open by new insights of truth or relationships, with others and with God, particularly in those times that we are at our wits' end, at the boundaries of our prevailing stage of development, we are vulnerable to the leaps of growth that faith affords and that bring us into our next stage of development.

Those are the moments when we know beyond proof that our souls are restless until they rest in God and in his incomparable grace—that long divine embrace out of which we do not slip.

10

Grace and the Importance of the Self

RONALD H. ROTTSCHAFER

The American way of life, for both the Christian and the non-Christian, embraces individual freedom, materialistic increase, and the development of oneself to the fullest. Yet, despite the expansiveness of this vision of self-fulfillment, many Christians seem uncomfortably aware that these secular goals clash with their spiritual values. Thus, while believing they should love God above all and serve others ahead of self, many Christians do not match spiritual belief and daily practice. The contradiction between putting self last on Sunday while hastening to put it first on Monday raises the central issue of what to do with the self while remaining true to Scripture. The question of whether the self is good or evil, crucial or detrimental to spiritual practice, demands answers.

The purpose of this chapter is to examine the confusion concerning the importance of the self—a confusion most prominently seen in conservative religious circles—and to consider that because of grace the self is encouraged to find what J. Harold Ellens (1982) refers to as its "full-orbed status."

By way of definition, the word *self* has a variety of meanings. The common usage is that the self refers to one's entire being. The word *self* describes the structure of the individual—one that can be understood and analyzed—but "self" also refers to one's own private definition of who she or he is. We thus can love or hate ourselves, and we can have realistic, unrealistic, and pathological notions about ourselves. These self-representations constitute our self-concept and may or may not be realistic. Similarly, others can have observations and opinions about both our inner self and also how it is presented to them for scrutiny. These descriptions also may or may not be accurate—a fact that helps account for the conflicting opinions any two people may have regarding another person.

Mental health professionals view individual attempts to disown the self as clear evidence of intense neurotic conflict. Whether a sign of low self-esteem, identity crisis, fear of separation and individuation, anger turned inward against the self, hostile manipulation of others, or dependent clinging, symptoms of self-negation signal that the individual is in emotional trouble. Nowhere in mental health circles, Christian or not, is a troubled self viewed as either healthy or spiritual. Furthermore, practicing clinicians are dedicated to bringing the self out of the pit of inadequate development and self-negation and into the light of a full expression of its God-given purposes.

Conservative Christianity and the Self

Despite the "good news" of the gospel, there is a long history of the church's tendency to deal harshly with people, much like angry, controlling parents. Even in times of an increasing awareness of God's loving messages to humankind, many church denominations persist in dealing with God not as though they are the redeemed but the condemned, not under grace but under the curse. Self to many religious conservatives is equated with a self-centeredness that includes rebellious questioning of authority, an indulgent preoccupation with self, and a spirit of worldliness that differs from traditional biblical teaching. Self to these believers, then, is a threat to established order and risks open defiance of God himself. To be self-confident for many zealous Christians is to become cocky, self-reliant, selfish, and above any dependence on God. They deeply fear that the development of self outside of strict rule and constant examination will lead to a haughty pride that eventually will overshadow spirituality. They point to the index in their *Thompson New Chain-Reference Bible* under the section called "Bible Helps," to note that the first entry under the topic of "Self-deception" is titled "Self-esteem" (1934).

Conservative religious believers are the most zealous of all when it comes to focusing on the worship of God, service to others, and the downplay (if not the denigration) of self. The most conservative of all, the fundamentalists, seem to thrive on the control of self with themes of guilt and punishment. They bombard the self (theirs as well as others') on all fronts so as to subdue its passions and ambitions. The more conservative and/or charismatic the church, the more likely there will be an emphasis on self-denial, suppression of impulses, and passive obedience. Pastors warn parishioners against self-centered and lustful drives, and they, in turn, attempt to warn the public at large. The more fanatic have bumper stickers that threaten "the wages of sin is death." Some sit in the end zones at nationally televised football games where they can hold up placards with Bible verses on them. These efforts seem destined to convey to the public the very image of God to which the conservative believers themselves hold fast—one of punishment and control rather than of grace.

A number of denominations also employ a control of the mind in the form of an anti-intellectualism. People who think too much or read secular books or attend nonreligious (even nondenominational) colleges are seen as jeopardizing their salvation. There is an obsessive fear of being seduced by anyone outside their specific belief system. To maintain the purity of the faith (that is, to keep their constituents under firm control), various church groups insist on forms of confession and disclosure that border on brainwashing. Some churches threaten excommunication for whatever they decide is fallenness, as if excommunication from the local church is tantamount to exclusion from heaven. Others demand public admission of wrongdoing with guilt, shame, and punishment being necessary prerequisites for reinstatement. In all of these efforts there is a ubiquitous, obsessive preoccupation with fears of individuation. Satisfying one's own personal wishes and ambitions risks embracing another way of life, one that could lead to a falling away from the faith (a euphemism for leaving a particular church). Independent thought is feared lest thinking lead to rebellion. The local pastor is to be obeyed to the letter if God is to be pleased. Submission to his will and to the local church leaders is demanded.

I argue in the next chapter that passive Christians have traditionally thrown out the baby of the self with the bathwater of repentance. If self is the culprit, the source of sin, then eliminating self has seemed to many to be a ritual of purification. Such believers have identified themselves with a message of self-renunciation, impoverishment of the will, and underachievement. In an effort to lose the self, many have focused on its imperfections and have struggled to disown the self with all its attendant needs, wants, urges, schemes, lusts, selfishnesses, ambitions, and pleasures. The impossibility of losing our human characteristics, scriptural intonations notwithstanding, has led to the popular curse for so many religious people: guilt and depression. When belief and practice do not match, guilt-ridden Christians castigate themselves for their temptation to put self first, others second, and God last. When the self is not lost by covering it up with a pious, "other-world" focus or by pretending the self to be unimportant, these well-meaning Christians become depressed and turn against themselves even further. In such a state of mind, they seek parental-like guidance from a religious subgroup that may trade on their vulnerable state. Frightened, passive, depressed, selfless Christians are very easy to control.

It is interesting that in a land of individualism and freedom, people will still seek, or at least tolerate, rigid control systems. These conservative religious systems provide a hiding place where, in the name of righteousness, the "evil" self can be subdued. What is ironic is that those who control these followers are not at all passive, or even obedient, as they demand others to be. The higher up the ladder they are, the more aggressive, self-willed, self-serving behavior they may manifest. If questioned, they can claim divine authority, as Oral Roberts did some years back in explaining why his followers had to send in more money to build a new hospital. God had given him a "vision."

The various denominations and churches that tend to view the self as a threat to the believer's salvation (as well as to the structure of their particular church organization) base their beliefs on selected parts of the Bible. It does not seem to matter to them that reputable theologians with solid academic and spiritual credentials disagree with them. Nor do they seem to care that they are guilty of reading into the Scripture what best serves their own purpose, and that they tend to quote Scripture out of context and selectively disregard all biblical evidence that refutes their points. Their favorite retort when cornered is, "My Bible says . . . ," as if they have some special edition of Scripture that is more valid than others.

Those who see self as a problem tend to emphasize the Old Testament with its hellfire and damnation themes drawn from God's very firm and punitive handling of the wayward Israelites. They select those passages that emphasize control from without, and with an obvious parent-child theme, to illustrate the God-person relationship. Even the New Testament, with its message of love and grace, is carefully culled to select those passages that stress how evil we are. A favorite is 1 John 2:15–16:

> Love not the world, neither the things that are in the world. If any man love the world, the love of the Father is not in him. For all that is in the world, the lust of the flesh, and the lust of the eyes, and the pride of life, is not of the Father, but is of the world (KJV).

Conservative Christians buttress their arguments against the self by reminding others that Christ himself urged his followers to be "meek and lowly" as he was (Matt. 11:29 KJV), and to renounce all earthly signs of power and acclaim. Christ urged a believer to "give up everything" (Luke 14:33 NIV) and to "deny himself" (Mark 8:34). Coupled with this advice for personal discipleship are the suggested religious behaviors for daily living with other people—deference, meekness, humility, sacrifice, gentleness, and self-restraint. In his Sermon on the Mount (Matt. 5–7) Christ, in fact, describes the "blessed" as those who are mournful, poor in spirit, meek, and persecuted. Then there are the scriptural paradoxes that cite the first shall be last (Matt. 19:30); one must be as a child to enter the kingdom (Matt. 18:3–4); and that one must lose self to find it (Mark 8:35). Paul's contribution to the seeming confusion over how to view the self is seen in 2 Corinthians 12:10: "for when I am weak, then I am strong." Taken from this perspective, scriptural evidence seems to be clearly urging humble self-negation as *the* term for spirituality. As I have noted elsewhere, many Christians have responded by identifying themselves with an image of passivity and submission (1984).

Self, then, is seen by many conservative Christians as worldly-minded, as if the self is untouched by grace and unredeemed by the resurrection. Self is at odds with God; enjoyment itself is suspect. Individual autonomy in the form of personal appetite and a drive for achievement is seen as dangerous.

It is not just the humble Amish or the poor Southern Baptist or the hard-working Bible-belt farmer who struggles with what to do with self. Self as culprit is also a popular issue among evangelical biblical scholars who easily become embroiled in heated debates on a number of issues. Recent preoccupations include the role of women in the church, the inerrancy of the Scriptures, and the integration of psychology and theology. What seems to spark controversy, apart from differences in theological interpretation, is the matter of how much freedom one has to both think for oneself and to be oneself while still under the auspices of divine authority. That is, how can one be true to God's plan and at the same time experience a deep sense of autonomy?

Is the self evil? Should we eliminate it? Is the self at war with God? Will becoming myself mean self-deification? When the laity looks to their own leaders for answers, they frequently get contradictory—even misleading—answers. How much credence then can the lay person put in their pronouncements?

Mark A. Noll, who teaches church history at Billy Graham's alma mater, Wheaton College, writes in *The Reformed Journal:*

Evangelicals will be fooling themselves, however, if they assumed that all were well with the study of the Bible today. Serious problems and manifest uncertainties concerning Scripture beset the restricted world of evangelical scholarship. . . . Evangelical Bible scholars live in Christian communities where fidelity to Scripture is both a badge of honor and an excuse for recrimination. "Separatists" lambaste . . . "fundamentalists" who, in turn, decry the wishy-washiness of "conservative evangelicals" who look down their noses at all of the benighted brethren to their right. And each group assumes its posture because of the others' purported mistakes in understanding and interpreting the Bible. (1984)

Noll adds that "tendentiousness, shortsightedness, anti-intellectualism, and a propensity to play to the galleries are sadly all too common . . . [and] we give the impression of being wise as doves and innocent as serpents" (1984, 17). Donald Hagner of Fuller Theological Seminary states that "the results of the present situation in conservative evangelicalism are truly lamentable." He describes a "climate of fear" and pressures to "compromise intellectual integrity" as each person struggles to assert himself (1984).

David F. Wells, professor of historical and systematic theology at Gordon–Conwell Theological Seminary, calls our society's preoccupation with self-esteem "the new confusion" (1983). Perhaps it is more accurate to say that confusion about the self is not new but that the self is under new consideration today. Believers have always had trouble deciding what to do with the self. In the past self was smothered under denial and submission; in modern times self is more prevalent and assertive. Wells calls self-love "the essence of sin" and asserts that true self-esteem results from Christian salvation. Apparently, what is sinful for Wells is the love of selfish goals apart from the requirements of divine and human responsibility. Wells, I am sure, knows the difference between healthy and unhealthy self-love, and some readers may too, but the rank-and-file believer only reads into these statements the same unfortunate meanings so many have always heard: Thou shalt not love thyself; it is sin.

The confusion of what to do with self is reiterated by John R. W. Stott, director of the London Institute for Contemporary Christianity, an organization designed to help the clergy and the laity interpret the Bible. He writes in *Christianity Today* an article titled, "Am I Supposed to Love Myself or Hate Myself?" (1984). The question suggests that this is a confusion in the hearts of Christians everywhere. Stott proposes a reasonable answer to his own question, as we will see shortly, but before he does he highlights the negative light in which the self is often cast by religious writers. He maintains that "Christ calls us to self-denial," which he defines as follows:

To deny ourselves is to behave toward ourselves as Peter did toward Jesus when he denied him three times. The verb is the same. He disowned him, repudiated him, turned his back on him. So must we do to ourselves. Self-denial is not denying ourselves luxuries like candies, cakes, cigarettes, and cocktails (though it may include this); it is actually denying and disowning *ourselves,* renouncing our supposed right to go our own way. (1984, 26; italics added)

To his credit Stott does not let the issue rest there. He goes on to indicate that Christ also calls people to self-affirmation and that therefore we are to value (although not to love) ourselves because there is good in the self. He refers, of course, to the biblical teachings about being created in God's own image, about being loved and redeemed by God at great cost. It is the redeemed side that we are to love. What we are to deny is our sinful, fallen self: "our irrationality; our moral perversity; our loss of sexual distinctiveness; our fascination with the ugly . . . our selfishness . . . our proud autonomy" (1984, 28).

Stott, like Wells, may not intend to denigrate the self, but his particular choice of words, coupled with those from a thousand pulpits, speak loudly to the contrary. The typical believer has been taught to interpret any form of self-love as synonymous with being sinful. From the pulpit and the religious periodical, the self is castigated in a futile attempt to put it aside. However, the self-flagellations of medieval monks and the self-recriminations of modern believers must be repeated again and again, for the self will simply not go away, evil or not.

The Self under Grace

It is a basic misunderstanding of Scripture to equate passive self-denial with spirituality. First of all, God is defined clearly throughout the Bible as a God of power (Heb. 11:33–34) who actively uses people to work his plans. Not only does he give them dignity and worth by creating them in his own image (Gen. 1:26), he also gives them power through his Holy Spirit (Acts 1:8). The New Testament confirms that this Spirit in us is there for power. Paul confirms that in Ephesians 6:10 when he implores the believers to "be strong in the Lord and in his mighty power" (NIV). Although the Lord's work can be done by the pale and pasty, the history lessons of the Bible show God chooses to deal with those people who are strong enough to rise up and get the job done. Scripture also consistently shows God dignifies the person (self) through his lovingkindness, patience, and forgiveness. He not only gives us the right to think and decide for ourselves, as he did for Adam and Eve, he also gives divine direction to aid in the accomplishing of the fullness of life (John 1:16). The Bible seems to clearly show that God wants people to succeed, to use the skills he gives them, to struggle and thereby grow—much the same as loving parents want for their own children. Christ's redemptive work in his death and resurrection seems to be certain evidence for a definition of self as valuable—so valuable that all three members of the Trinity work together constantly for the benefit of humankind. That ceaseless love, that grace freely given, when claimed, allows people to be their full selves. Paul best summarizes God's true plan in 2 Timothy 1:7, "God does not give us a spirit of timidity but of power and love, and self-control."

This affirmation of the worth and dignity of the human being makes the believer a cocreator with God, free to get off his or her knees and walk with God. Christ confirms the believer's value by saying, "I no longer call you servants . . . instead I have called you *friends*" (John 15:15 NIV, italics added). He teaches that we must internalize divine strength to become truly strong. Christ uses the metaphor of the person as a branch being grafted into him as the trunk (John 15:5). The power to be oneself flows from God the "trunk" to the person as "branch" with such potential force that the believer can do work equal to or even greater than Christ's (John 14:12). Such power was given to believers as they "subdued kingdoms, wrought righteousness, obtained promises, and stopped the mouths of lions" (Heb. 11:33 KJV).

The powerful evidence of Scripture regarding God's intention for us to be strong is not amply summarized in the traditional definition of grace as "God's favor to the undeserving." This definition implies that the person as recipient has no real status in God's eyes. Traditional explanations have thus focused on grace as an unearned gift—which indeed it is—and have ignored the whole purpose of that gift, to wit, God's plan to restore us to an elevated status where he can converse with us as friends. God longs not only to reunite with us, but to empower us to rise to our fullness—the ultimate purpose of grace. Grace theology, therefore, is a shift from the traditional emphasis of human as evil to human as cocreators, to use Ellens's terms. Such a shift makes sense as we compare how we as loving parents prefer to deal with our own precious children. Certainly we do not dwell on an authoritarian punitiveness as a preferred way to be parents. Assuredly God knows what we know, namely, that children raised with love, patience, and forgiveness grow to greater heights of creativity, maturity, and health than do those who are primarily the recipients of the rod. Our status under grace shifts from inadequate, dependent children to mature confident adults, from the bondage of fear to the freedom to grow, from rejection to unconditional acceptance, from anxiety to peace. The central thrust, therefore, of grace is to provide freedom to be our genuine selves. As we grow to our fullness, we have much more substance with which to glorify God and serve others.

Finding One's Self

If we glorify God best with our fully developed selves, how can we account for scriptural advice that we must first *lose* ourselves (Matt. 16:25)?

The teachings of Scripture make it clear that the self is valuable. But what is meant by losing the self if it has such worth and power? The answer seems best understood as one of perspective, of not losing *self* but *self-centeredness*. The problem of the self is one of self-deification where preoccupation with self is at the cost of concern and care for God and others. When we lose self-absorption we are freed from a myopic, limited perspective of self as the end-all and be-all of life. All through Scripture that kind of self-deification has been condemned and punished forcefully. "Sin" has been defined in that very context of the haughty self that needs no one else including God. God urges us therefore to lose our self-centeredness but not ourselves. He requires us to develop ourselves so that his purposes can be manifested through us.

When the theologian says that self-denial leads to self-discovery, we must remember what that means—that we find our peace and perspective as we lose our preoccupation with saving our own existential necks. It makes a person very nervous to think that he or she must be savior, that one's life is totally in the hands of the individual, and that the hereafter has to be earned on one's own merit. That puts us in inescapable despair, for we sooner or later have to know and admit that we cannot manage our own destiny totally by ourselves. Our generic neediness binds us to helplessness and fear. The poets, philosophers, theologians, and thinkers of all ages have attested to this truth. What most legitimate religions offer is the suggestion that looking upward to God for help begins a dialogue with God. We are *then* beginning to lose self-consciousness and to gain our selfhood.

The appeal of religion is that it offers relief from the stress of both our helplessness and our neediness. A perspective that includes God and others promotes a readiness to live life more fully because we finally look beyond the limits of self. Such a God-centered and other-directed perspective, it must be reiterated, emanates from a *strong* sense of self rather than from the self-negating, sin-centered preoccupations of many denominations. A self still under the curse is a self outside the realm of grace. A self negated out of confusion and misinterpretation leaves the person out of the covenant.

We must avoid praying like helpless, hungry children who are looking for relief from El Shaddai (the "Breasted One") who will "feed us till we want no more." We also must rise above the childlike need for the punitive, angry Father to erase guilt through suffering. There is no grace in either of these immature concepts of the divine-human relationship because neither represents us as mature adults.

When people do not grow up by letting go of their naiveté, they make innocence seem like a virtue, says Rollo May in *Power and Innocence* (1972). May points out that the word *innocence* is from the Latin *in* and *nocens,* that is, *not harmful.* Conservative believers easily seize upon this means of avoiding the imagined harmfulness implicit in mature self-

care and thus avoid the risks inherent in disagreeing, rebelling, breaking free, and thinking for themselves. May calls such a perspective "a
childhood that is never outgrown," one that results in a "utopianism"
where real dangers are not seen (49). He concludes: "It is this innocence
that cannot come to terms with the destructiveness in one's self or others . . . and hence it actually becomes self-destructive. Innocence that
cannot include the daimonic becomes evil" (50). "Violence comes from
powerlessness . . . it is the explosion of impotence" (53).

The denial of self for many religious persons is not at all the honest
self-negation they claim it to be. Rather than becoming a true search
for humility and service to God and others, this self-denial is only a
pseudo self-denial, a cover-up for hidden desires. Thus pious believers
who play the role of sweet, innocent, obedient children are not denying
self as much as they are maneuvering God (and others) to provide even
more care for self. At this point, self is not strong enough to be put into
the background; it remains weak and demands more attention. Similarly, those who pretend to hate or avoid hostility, sexuality, and all the
carnal lusts, are not as innocent as they pretend to be. Since they are
all too preoccupied with their forbidden urges, such believers hardly
can claim either self-denial or a reduction in self-consciousness. These
people are very aware of their inner, hidden urges, even if they are constantly guarding against their expression. The frequent public displays
of scandal and impropriety among the clergy and the laity attest to a
hidden truth that a pious pretense cannot cover indefinitely.

Innocence is an ungodly attempt to be more spiritual because immaturity leaves us too weak to be counted on to do God's work. It
bears repeating that, although the Almighty does not need anyone or
anything to help him out, God works through the vehicle of the person
nonetheless. When the self is puny that work is compromised. The self-
denying believer becomes the object of some of Christ's most condem-
natory words; such a believer is salt that has lost its savor; a light
under a basket; a house built upon sand; a tree bringing forth corrupt
fruit (Matt. 5–7). The passive, pseudoinnocent believer with his or her
ubiquitous "niceness" may be one of Christ's worst witnesses.

The self is not found when its unacceptable parts are disowned in a
furtive attempt at self-improvement. Spiritual platitudes and religious
rituals do not eliminate the need for the person to take responsibility
for his or her own personal characteristics and the troubles they therefore get into. A twenty-six-year-old Pentecostal woman, referred for
abusing one of her four children, dropped out of therapy with me
when I questioned her statement, "I don't need birth control; my Bible
says the Lord opens and closes the womb." To deny our own hand in
our personal problems is to stay uninformed both about who we are
and how we must change. Insight does not come by merely mouthing

Bible verses. Relief does not come from merely saying we are relieved, nor does it come from denial and pretense. As we struggle to become the kind of person we want to be, we must first understand more fully how we are stuck and must own up to the deeper qualities of our inner makeup, including the forbidden urge. Religious believers suffer a great deal by pretending they have struggled with their inner material and have arrived at meaningful answers. To ignore our lustful, greedy, hostile, self-serving characteristics is to remain unaware of how prevalent there urges are, and how powerful. Defenses based on denial and avoidance are weaker than those based on informed decision.

Bringing the self under control does not result from pitting good (God) against evil (the devil); there is no final victory as long as there is a clash. One can never subdue the other in an in-the-mind battle. Conscience (rule) never subdues impulse (urge) by sheer power without risking serious (if not psychotic) consequences. This is captured in the old adage, "The man convinced against his will, is of the same opinion still." We cannot force ourselves to be good. There will always be the counter-will that springs forth and defeats good intention. Neither the will to improve nor the counter-will to stay the same can win against each other.

Finding relief from our struggles involves our own personal willingness to take whatever realistic steps are necessary to solve the problem at hand. God is there to help us, but he does not solve our mental problems for us any more than he drills our teeth or removes a ruptured appendix. We find ourselves as we gather evidence of our self-worth and internalize this evidence in order to form an enduring self-concept. To love ourselves is to appreciate who and what we are. The cruciality of self-love is seen in the fact that it is out of this accrued valuing of the self that we set the stage for loving each other.

To love ourselves is not to embrace our sin; rather, it is to acknowledge sin's role and pry deeper to understand its meaning so we can then decide to stop its practice. What so many believers fear about examining their evil is the risk that they will face the truth Augustine and Paul had to face—that we do not necessarily want to be good. When a seminary student once called me in misery over his compulsive rebellion against authority figures, he was not at all ready to set up an appointment either with me or with a sensitive professor on campus to help him.

Part of self-love is to lovingly tend to one's troubled parts, not at first to punish them or condemn them, but to inquire into both what fulfillment one is looking for in the behavior, and what one can do to be finished with the problem. The goal of insight, whether via introspection or psychotherapy, is to arrive at the "Ah ha" of inner enlightenment. Then we can seek out new alternatives or at least end the inner struggle.

To accept oneself "as is" encourages an inner mood that maintains self-esteem while working to understand and correct one's behavior. This self-esteem precludes worry about deeper issues of worthlessness or rejection. Freed from fear of our unloveability, the mind can then shift to the question, "What am I doing wrong?" In such an atmosphere it is far easier to understand and to change oneself.

In summary, as we understand more clearly the clinical as well as the spiritual importance of a strong self, we must acknowledge that, in his grace, God chooses to deal with us as adults, not dependent children, and that he takes pleasure in our growth toward fullness—as any good "friend" would. Those who denigrate the self are minimizing God's finest handiwork and are thus weakening the very Creator-creature tie that he intended for our self-development.

11

The Passive Christian and the Mature Self

RONALD H. ROTTSCHAFER

J. Harold Ellens, in his book, *God's Grace and Human Health* (1982), most eloquently traces our history and nature as "God-compatriots" (those destined to commune with God) who are suffering not because we *are* lost, that is, sick, weak, estranged, but because we perceive ourselves as such. In other words, we seem to persist needlessly in maintaining a sense of inadequacy with all its resulting symptoms and sorrows despite the overwhelming good news of God's grace for us, freely given and copiously applied.

Why is this so? Why do we continue to manipulate God for the very hope and goodness he has already so generously supplied? We do not fully claim the benefits God has made available for the taking, described by Ellens as "the relief of grace, the affirmation of our real selves, the unconditional acceptance of God's unconditional acceptance, and the celebration of our generic freedom."

This chapter considers passivity as one aspect of the Christian's persistent ineffectualness both in the strengthening of the self and in the celebrating of our lives as God's friends (John 15:15). Passive behavior will be examined in terms of weakness of personality development; the role-playing of passive behavior will be described not only as unscriptural, but also as a liability rather than an asset, as a denigration of the self as image bearer, as an offensive witness to a world seeking effective leadership, and as an insult to a God of power who, in love, no longer calls us servants.

The focus on passivity asks two questions. First, do persons either within the church or seeking religion as an answer exhibit more passive behavior than non-Christians? and second, are Christians urged to adopt a passive role model within the system? Put more succinctly, do the weak seek out the system or, to paraphrase what the conquered Germans pleaded after World War II, is it the system that makes us weak?

Passivity as Personality Disorder

Passivity must be distinguished from a well-chosen quietness, a careful withdrawal to gather strength. It also must be separated from acts of deference, gentleness, and cost-to-self where in reality it is strength, not weakness, that leads to such charity. Passivity as a strategy or as generousness to others is truly virtuous. Our human condition is indeed made easier by having the strength to choose such behaviors.

It also must be understood that passivity does not just refer to meek, unassertive behavior. That is only the popular, narrow conception. In the broader sense passivity is reflected whenever we do not fully use our personal-emotional-spiritual assets that God gave us not only to survive but to accomplish and to transcend.

Passivity is born of anxiety; it is a fear of utilizing our energies lest we endanger our approval by others or risk experiencing failure at our own hands. Passivity is a failure to mobilize our resources, a cowering due to fear of consequences that we do not think we could handle. It is a disowning of our nobler parts, our self-reliance, our courage under fire, our resolve to win, our determination to inspire others to greater heights. Passivity is an abandonment of our learned skills, our inherent or acquired abilities that could be brought to bear upon our problems. When passive, we ignore our collected accomplishments and virtues, our carefully garnered past triumphs that are worthy of credit and capable of encouraging us to press on had they not been forgotten. Passivity is an avoidance of our will, a problem called by Rollo May (1969) "an endemic disease in the middle of the twentieth century . . . that saps us of our ability to make decisions, undermines our experience of ourselves as being responsible, and renders us as ethically impotent" (183–84).

At worst, passivity stems from what Theodore Millon (1969) refers to as "mild pathological personality patterns." He divides these disorders into four groups:

1. Detached—the asocial personality
2. Dependent—the submissive (inadequate) personality

3. Independent—the narcissistic personality
4. Ambivalent—the conforming (obsessive-compulsive) personality

Each of these groups will be discussed briefly.

The Detached (Asocial) Personality

This group is noted for the avoidance of close interpersonal relationships because of emotional and cognitive deficits. Passive, detached persons are insensitive to the full range of emotional reactions and retain a passive posture not from hostility but out of what Millon calls "a fundamental incapacity to sense the moods and needs which others experience." They lack spontaneity, warmth, and responsiveness and in fact appear dull, awkward, and lacking in enthusiasm. Detached people absorb little from social interaction; consequently they focus on things, objects, and solitary projects. They stay on the fringes of group discussion, with peripheral interest and impersonal reactions. Avoiding both feelings and ideations, they are easily ignored by others, thus reinforcing their detachment.

The Dependent (Submissive) Personality

These persons are essentially characterized by their clinging neediness, their search for acceptance, support, and reassurance. They foster this personal dependency by denying their own strengths and hence by feeling inferior. As a result they feel justified to seek this reassurance from others, most all of whom are seen as stronger. Often the dependent personality will submit to abuse by others in hopes of gaining approval and avoiding loneliness. He or she would rather suffer abuse than feel the anxiety implicit in fears of rejection.

Passive-dependent people look for authority figures and others to whom they can attribute magical, helping qualities. Typically they do not internalize whatever goodness is given to them and hence they feel empty and ready to seek more in an endless cycle. They love to get more for themselves but not absorb their gains internally (Rottschafer 1980).

The passive-dependent person limits his world of awareness to remain unperceptive, naive, and uncritical. He attempts to look for the "good" in situations even when suffering or losing.

The Independent (Narcissistic) Personality

Independent people who are basically passive in orientation look inward for gratification rather than to others. They avoid inferiority and seek adequacy, power, and status. However, narcissists base their self-esteem on a blind and naive assumption of personal worth and superiority, says Millon. They feel more than mere egocentricity, expecting others will recognize and reward them as if the self-aggrandizement were true. Their benign arrogance allows them to feel they are above the conventions and ethics that govern others. Their exalted self-images also allow a denial of responsibility of social norm-keeping and an expectation that, in fact, others should defer to their wishes. Narcissists actually believe it is their inalienable right to receive special consideration; they rarely question whether this is unwarranted or irrational.

The Ambivalent (Conforming) Personality

Conformists must balance carefully between trying to break free and be individuals while also trying obediently to please the feared authority figures in their lives. They create an enormous existential dilemma for themselves for they must carefully stay at the halfway mark, somewhat like a calf whose head and forelegs are out of the womb but whose torso and hind legs are stuck within. Conformists do not want to be fully alive.

To avoid rejection and punishment from others, conformists apprehensively control their impulses, opinions, and feelings. They work hard, long hours to be as perfect as possible. They live rigid, controlled lives with obsessive-compulsive defenses that guard against doing what is "wrong." Tender, loving emotions are guarded against and human relations are proper or mechanical. They do not give of themselves.

Conformists are strong "law-and-order" people who live by control and have no tolerance for diversity. When thwarted they become inappropriately angry and cold.

The Passive Christian

Many Christians are passive upon occasion but do not use passivity as an escape from risk and confrontation or as an expression of anxiety or fear. Those whose character structure is reasonably intact and who occasionally take a passive posture cannot be called pathological. But there are Christians who *do* fit into one of Millon's four categories and whose behavior reflects a disorder of personality requiring professional help in order to change. Each group is considered in the following:

1. Some Christians are *detached* interpersonally, avoiding close relationships because of insensitivity, under-responsiveness, low energy, and fear of their feelings. They have deficits in emotional and cognitive development. A thousand sermons are not going to inspire, let alone change, them because they do not involve themselves internally with God, Scripture, or other Christians any more than they do their families or coworkers outside the church. This is not a sign of being an unbeliever or of being resistant to grace. This is personal deficit. These are very difficult people to get along with.

2. There are far more passive-*dependent* personalities within the church than there are detached or narcissistic persons. The dependent Christian is a lovable soul, quietly and unassertively following along, smiling and chatting amicably for fear of alienating others. Dependent Christians are "nice" people who try to get along and contribute in their own quiet ways. Dependent Christians, to many leaders, may seem like the best kind because their submissiveness makes them good workers who do as they are asked (or told). They love to please the minister who, as the chief authority figure, is to be looked up to, believed at face value, and not rebelled against.

These believers are also good at tugging at the pastoral cloak, confessing eagerly to doubts, fears, and sins, especially small ones they already know are safe to confess. They love to call the pastor for help and are reassured of their acceptability by being so needy. Many are secretly pleased when they have a problem. When one is needy, especially by having fears, doubts, and "legitimate" physical and emotional ailments, it is only right that the pastor be called to shepherd his or her needy sheep with sympathy. After all, isn't that what he or she is for?

The submissive, dependent personality disorder leaves one with a limited awareness; the person remains naive, unperceptive, and uncritical. These are not the aggressive-dependent Christians who love to ferret out evil both real and imagined and seek punishment for the "bad" people. Instead, passive dependents don't even know evil exists. They love to hear about sin and will ask for details from anyone who will talk about the details, but always with that wide-eyed disbelief, that sense of innocent wonderment of how it all could happen.

Passive-dependent persons love to join prayer circles, not for strength, but to have it all out in the open so as to await nurturing from God, the pastor, and each other. This is not to say that all Christians who seek out prayer groups are unduly dependent nor that seeking help is weakness; it is not. I am instead referring to those who are unconsciously afraid of healthy, assertive self-care and who base their self-worth on the approval of others.

3. The *narcissist*, as you will recall, is a person who overvalues his or her opinions, beliefs, and practices and expects others will eventually come around to his or her way of thinking. The narcissist's deep sense of inner worthlessness is hence covered by the apparent interest in power, adequacy, and status. Narcissistic Christians like to look better than they really are, to sound important and cover their ignorance, to tell others how they have solved their problems and risen above it all. Their arrogance may be rationalized as happiness over how well God has treated them or answered their prayers. They want others to know this. Their needs for attention are never fully met. They love to

come late to church and parade down to the front row to show off new outfits.

Narcissistic Christians are demanding and do not like to be denied or deprived. Their self-centeredness is a request for others to minister to them, but they do not really make friends and get close in the process. Narcissists are very manipulative, sometimes in very subtle and even superficially loving ways, to maneuver others to do what they want.

Many church committees are inhabited by one or more narcissistic Christians who want things done their way and are quite unbending. There is little empathy or patience with others' needs; there is no genuine love. The more intelligent ones will manipulate skillfully; the less intelligent will demand and even throw tantrums. They just can't understand why others don't see things their way. Often they threaten to leave the committee, feeling very wounded and unappreciated. The minister's help has to be refused; how could he or she understand. They do not want comforting, just gratification.

4. Finally, there are the *conforming* Christians, those who use obsessive-compulsive ways of balancing their inner ambivalence between being themselves or seeking others' approval. Conformists can be very strict conservatives who form committees to improve others, to purify the doctrine, and to keep everything ship-shape. These are the good law-and-order people; they fit so well into the church because there is so much wrong that needs righting, not angrily or aggressively as the active ambivalent persons do, but grimly and with dedicated austerity. These people love to say, "Oh no, we just couldn't do that" when asked to cut through red tape and change the rules a little to expedite things, or even to initiate some action with authorities so as to be helpful. Their answer of no is formed before the question is even fully spoken. Rules must never be broken.

Conformists have been having a terribly hard time lately what with all this liberality and self-gratification in the world at large. Sometimes they are amazed that the church tolerates such frivolity and unscriptural goings on. They love to recall "the good old days" when sins were rooted out and made public, when ministers were more somber and punitive, and when there was modesty and decency.

Obsessive-compulsive Christians want that "old-time religion" where they made you sweat a little and told you what to do. New books on theology, new social interests in the church, and even changes in the order for worship bother them. Dialogue in church is abhorrent because talk leaves them unguarded, exposed for everyone to see, especially if their hidden anger should come out.

Teaching Christians to Be Passive

We can examine three areas within Christianity that suggest a definite leaning toward passivity both as a philosophy and a way of behaving.

Biblical Teaching

Although the Bible is replete with action verbs such as to subdue the earth, to fight the good fight, to win others to Christ, to shine forth as a light in darkness, and to abound in love toward one another, Scripture also reiterates a seemingly paradoxical message of passivity that has confused and immobilized Christians for centuries. There seems to be a double standard in Christian teachings when it comes to the use of strength. One is urged to be strong in the Lord in overcoming sin, temptation, and turmoil, but in interpersonal relations one is to defer, put self last, and pray for one's enemies. It has never been clear to many believers how much personal strength is inherent in putting self last or in turning the other cheek.

At the center of the confusion over how strong we must be is the example of Christ himself who described himself as "meek and lowly in heart" (Matt. 11:29 KJV) and who refused all signs of kingly power and acclaim (in earthly terms) despite being hailed as the Messiah, the one celebrated, exalted, and fervently looked for throughout the ages. It is not at all surprising that he was rejected by all the people who were disappointed in him and who mockingly called him "the king of the Jews" as he died a criminal's death. They, and perhaps we, did not understand the true nature of his strength. They as well as we have refused to identify with Christ's power due to fears of giving up to face life maturely.

Christians have identified themselves with a message of self-renunciation, impoverishment of the will, and underachievement. They have found scriptural backing to justify, if not to take pride in, being weak. Some believers play weak while in reality remaining strong; others live a double life with power in secular, workaday issues and passivity in spiritual matters. Many with personality disorders have found the Christian standard of deference and humility to be an excellent camouflage. The news media have abounded with sickening examples of religious asininity masquerading as humility and piety.

The teachings of Scripture have included many examples of self-denial, submission, and self-sacrifice as exemplifying the Christian way. These have included meekness, humility, contrition, gentleness, and self-restraint. Christ seems to have summarized it all in Luke 14:33 when he said, "So likewise, whosoever he be of you that forsaketh not all that he hath cannot be my disciple." Likewise, the "blessed" are those described in the Sermon on the Mount (Matt. 5–7) as the poor in spirit, the mournful, the meek, the merciful, the persecuted, and so on. To add to this are the Bible's frequent paradoxes: the first shall be last, one must lose his life to find it, the flesh should be denied, suffering is a mark of virtue, and, unless one receives the kingdom of God as a little child, he or she cannot enter in (Luke 18:17). The Bible truly can lead one to believe that passivity is virtuous. Perhaps the most exemplary of all in context here are Paul's statements found in 2 Corinthians 12:10, "for when I am weak, then I am strong," and 1 Corinthians 1:27, "for God hath chosen the weak things of the world to confound the things which are mighty" (KJV).

Prayer Life

I for one have trouble believing that God the Father enjoys what he hears from his children here below. How many of us as parents would like to have our children constantly telling us what miserable failures they are, how weak, unworthy, and bad they are, and how needy and dependent they are on us for their very life's breath? We also might be chagrined, if not annoyed, with a child of ours who disregarded our eagerness to be with that child, who avoided our desire to love and to share by his or her sniveling, breast-beating, and constant protestations of unworthiness. And then to hear the endless stream of begging, the helplessness, and dependency—would it not make us believe we had failed as parents?

I wonder how God feels, having made us in his image, having promised us his full presence, having given us his Spirit for power and told us we are his friends, not his servants (John 15:15)? Where are the happy prayers, the celebration of how good he is and we are, the frank discussions of a problem with the solutions reasoned out right there on the spot before the "amen" is spoken?

The Christian's prayer life may be more indicative of how deep passivity is at our roots than any other aspect of our daily religious behavior. We seem to believe Christianity demands this kind of obedience, that God himself would have us devoid of confidence. We have been taught to honor him, to look up to him for guidance, and not to ever consider ourselves as strong enough in our own right; but where does this teaching imply that we must adopt an attitude of personal inability to take action and feel strong?

Our prayers too often degenerate into a childlike supplication replete with expectations of magical, superparent intervention. We passively wait "for the Lord's good time" to arrive and finally deliver us. We confess "our heavenly Father knows we have need of all these things" (Matt. 6:32, paraphrased); do we believe, as do our children, that if we nag him long enough he will finally change his mind and give in? If we, being evil, know how to give good gifts to our children, how much more does God in heaven give good things to them that ask him (Matt. 7:11)? Begging, whining, and manipulating are not what the apostle James had in mind when he said, "The effectual fervent prayer of a righteous man availeth much" (James 5:16 KJV). God says, Ask, I already know. Being God's sons and daughters does not necessarily make us children. Our prayers need to reflect a dialog free from helpless whining and self-degradation. God deserves better honor than that, and so do we.

Church Structure

A third area in Christian belief and practice that reinforces passivity is found in how the organization sets itself up structurally. This religious "caste system" may be most easily identified in those religious organizations that demand blind obedience to its leaders. We think of the demands made not too long ago by the Roman Catholic Church that the laity remain uninformed by denying them freedom to read and interpret their own Bibles. We are reminded too how Catholics are punished for disobeying papal decree. Protestants feel somewhat self-righteous about that because we have no powerful hierarchy dictating religious policy.

It was mentioned earlier that Christianity presents a number of paradoxes to the believer that often results in confusion. Is it not indeed puzzling that Christians are taught meekness, humility, patience, gentleness, and obedience and yet all through Scripture God's favorite people were aggressive, dominating, headstrong people who argued with, ran away from, disobeyed, and openly conned the Lord into getting what they wanted? They often had to be prodded into shape before they could be used more effectively, but men like Moses, Abraham, Jacob, David, Elijah, Daniel, Jonah, Paul, and Peter were hardly passive people. Nor were Saint Augustine, Martin Luther, or, currently, Billy Graham. The Lord used their own native assertiveness to get the job done. Passive people are not assertive.

Christians currently may be lulled into a spiritual sleep knowing the preacher and the board run the church, that all the parishioner has to do is reasonably perform his or her duties and let Reverend George handle things.

This problem has been admitted openly by one denomination, the Christian Reformed Church, and has been looked into by its ruling body, the synod. In the 1980 Acts of Synod, a committee was established to identify barriers to the use of the various talents of the constituency. The report to synod admitted that the way the church is organized has been a major barrier, that "the notion is quite prevalent that only ministers, elders, deacons, teachers . . . are gifted ones within the church . . . [and that] many congregations are largely *passive* and silent" (561). The report states, "Barring a few exceptions the minister is expected to do it all 'because he knows it all, and after all, he is getting paid for it'" (561).

A second barrier, says the synodical report, is the attitude of the members in ignoring or denying their own talents. Because of a negative self-evaluation and self-image, they lack awareness of their gifts, they deprecate their gifts with false humility, they possess a fear of failure and rejection, they often have fear of change, they have stereotyped ideas, they have other priorities and hence are apathetic, and they are oriented to passivity. The committee notes that, as passive members, they hide comfortably under the flag of piety and humility, follow a culturally expected mode of behavior, and are caught up in a "consumer mentality."

The report's stated remedy is manyfold, but regarding passivity the recommendation is to "challenge the [members'] initiative and imagination so as to wean them away from passivity" (566). It may or may not have been intentional for the synod to use the term *wean*; nevertheless, the word is most descriptive.

In general, it seems evident that the system does indeed make its members weak, that this seems to be man's intention despite scriptural proof that passivity is not God's intention. Both leaders and followers within organized religions reinforce passivity, to the detriment of all.

The question remains whether those who seek out the system in the first place are weak; that is, do passive people gravitate to religious institutions?

Do the Weak Seek Out the System?

Sigmund Freud originally called religious people "obsessive neurotics" who sought out substitute parent figures to satisfy their dependency needs and to avoid the fears of growing up. "To these charges," says May (1940), "there is no answer I believe except the frank admission that for some people religion *is* precisely that" (148).

There is evidence that some religious people act in disturbed ways and may be considered mentally weak. As this chapter was being written the news headlines in one week featured members of a religious group in Memphis that claimed the police were satanic and thus shot a policeman (the police subsequently shot them all to death). In another instance a Texas minister personally destroyed one million dollars worth of art relics from ancient Mexico because he claimed they were idols.

There is no doubt that religious cults have traditionally given

Christianity bad press and fixed a stereotype in the public's eye that many religious people are indeed disturbed. I suspect the public would admit in the majority of the outlandish cases (Jim Jones in Guayana, for example), it was sick people who sought out the system rather than the system that made otherwise good people sick. Nevertheless, it may not be often clear to the public why so many religious leaders with questionable reputations and practices (most recently, Moon) draw thousands and thousands of followers who become their literal slaves. In many instances the weak do seek out the system but gravitate more to cults and splinter groups than to the organized church.

Two research articles have been reviewed that refute the claim in psychoanalytic theory that mentally ill people are more religious. The first, by R. C. Armstrong, G. L. Larsen, and S. A. Mourer (1962), concludes that mental illness and religious commitment are negatively correlated; the second, by W. E. Reifsnyder and E. I. Campbell (1960), states that there were no significant differences between neuropsychiatric patients and normal persons on religious commitment. In fact, the authors found a tendency toward less interest in religion for patients compared to nonpatients.

Since this is not a research paper, no statement will be made regarding the validity of these conclusions by the authors quoted. Also it should be understood that I did not carry out an exhaustive review of the literature on mental illness and religion, despite the intriguing potentials of the topic. I have not found empirical evidence that suggests that persons who are passive because of personality disorders seek out organized religion. It goes without saying that some passive Christians are indeed suffering from personality disturbances while others are basically normal, albeit passive. How many of each are in organized religion is an unknown. At this time it cannot be said that Christians are more passive than non-Christians.

My purpose is to point to the uncomfortable relationship between passivity and religious commitment and to stimulate discussion and further research into the topic. Regardless of whether Christians are more passive than non-Christians, the demeaning of the self as an image-bearer, plus the denial of the power implicitly available via God's grace, is, in my estimation, of sufficient importance to expose the problem for subsequent discussion. Christians should not be weak and passive. As Paul writes in 2 Timothy 1:7, "For God hath not given us the spirit of fear; but of power, and of love, and of a sound mind" (KJV).

The Assumption of Power

To be a strong, independent male or female does not rule out deference or gentleness. Many would agree it takes great strength to show such behaviors. The uninformed might also erroneously assume that to turn the other cheek is weakness and that Scripture demands the terrible price of denying our own personal power. This is not true.

The Bible is replete with examples of a powerful God leading his own who "subdued kingdoms, wrought righteousness, obtained promises, stopped the mouths of lions" (Heb. 11:33 KJV). To emphasize only those parts of Scripture that speak of the meek and mild, passive and gentle believer is to do a disservice to a powerful God who will have his way and who does so also by working through people—his image-bearers. This is not to deny that Christians suffer from a permanent sense of inadequacy and fearfulness, as do *all* people as a matter of being alive; I am arguing that we are scripturally enjoined to use our strength to accomplish all the goals God has set for us to do.

When the Bible says that "the race is not to the swift, nor the battle to the strong" (Eccles. 9:11), and "God hath chosen the weak things of the world to confound the things which are mighty" (1 Cor. 1:27 KJV), Scripture is *not* saying that it is spiritual to be slow, weak, and passive. The meaning seems best found in Paul's statement in 2 Corinthians 12:10, where he says "for when I am weak, then I am strong." Paul is saying that we must minimize self-preoccupation and solitary self-reliance. When we admit we are not the ultimate origin of our strength, then the glorious image of God can shine through to inspire us toward action. Then we are strong. We are to set aside self-consciousness, not self.

God works through humans' strengths, talents, and efforts—hardly an act accomplished by passive, doubtful, and selfless believers. Paul is not, I believe, urging us to be puny; weakness here is not a lack of strength but a statement of priorities, of putting God first to glorify him and draw upon him for power. He is our strength but that only as prelude to our subsequently taking action with our Christ-ordained power.

The whole concept of self-denial has never been a statement regarding our worthlessness or to advocate dependency. Instead, self-denial urges less preoccupation with self-functions, less myopia, so that we can see God's purpose and can attend better to serving others. The Sermon on the Mount, in essence, is Christ's encouragement to be *so* strong that one can stop being preoccupied with oneself (weakness) and can truly joy in giving to God and others. This message has traditionally been misunderstood by Christians. To put self last is not an invitation to ignore self, but is an encouragement to be strong enough to forget about self with ease. What we enjoy about the so-called Christmas spirit is that for once it does not matter what I get, I just want to see you happy.

A second argument against passivity relates to the work of the Holy Spirit. Before Christ ascended he promised, "You will receive power when the Holy Spirit comes on you" (Acts 1:8 NIV). Since the Holy Spirit is our way of knowing that God dwells in us, to have the Spirit is to have power. The New Testament is very clear about this. When Paul writes, "Finally, my brethren, be strong in the Lord and in the power of his might" (Eph. 6:10 KJV), he is not advocating passive, dependent personality structure; Paul himself was never anything but an aggressive achiever. Paul knew it took courage to be gentle, peaceful, loving, and forgiving. As passive Christians do their gentle, peaceful things from fear and avoidance, not from inner confidence, they hide in God not for strength but for comfort, not to win but to flee. This is a denial of their having been empowered by the Spirit.

Thirdly, passivity is a denial of God's grace, grace which, when internalized, allows us finally to be our full selves, to give up security for productivity, comfort for growth, innocence for power. Christians who refuse to be strong fear being "strengthened with might by his Spirit in the inner man" (Eph. 3:16). They avoid Saint Augustine's dictum, "Ora et labora"—pray *and* work. They also avoid God's desire for us to be cocreators with him, to walk with him as friends and experience our true freedom. They love to hear about strength and may even pray for such power, but deep within lies one of two problems; first, their personality structure is weak and not built for accomplishment; or, second, they have the native character but are lazy, afraid, or indifferent.

The passive Christian may be suffering from the separation anxiety so commonly found as a cause of personality disorder. Their self-image as God's little children encourages the fantasy of the benevolent parent who will never leave them. Their power is projected onto God and is therefore unavailable, not because God does not give power but because anything projected is unwanted, disowned. What is left for them is the profound characterological emptiness that always accompanies the renouncing of strength, the avoidance of self, the denial of the grace which, as Ellens states, allows us to assume our rightful posture as the "God-compatriot."

We perhaps best assume our fullness in Christ when we utilize the strength given to us by God and claim our worth and power. When we avoid the passivity that denies our native and acquired talents, we get right with God and with ourselves. Refuting passivity demands a reevaluation of our use of Scripture, of the religious language we speak (especially in our prayers), and of the roles we play based on what our own denominations model for us. To get right with ourselves may require professional assistance as we work on our personality functions and a resolve to put away the childish things implicit in our avoidance of being strong. Our goal is to accept God's wish for us, "power, love and a sound mind" (2 Tim. 1:7 KJV).

12

Spirituality in Personality and Psychotherapy

DAVID G. BENNER

In spite of a long-standing antipathy on the part of psychology for religion, some sort of a rapprochement seems to be occurring between psychology and spirituality. Recent conferences and publications focusing on this relationship attest to the interest in spirituality on the part of not just Christian or other religious psychologists but also psychologists not identifying themselves with any traditional religious positions.

As used in these and other contemporary contexts, the term *spirituality* has a variety of meanings. Sometimes it is used as a synonym for religion. More often it is used to refer to nontraditional, noninstitutional religiousness, an interiorized religiosity that Lucy Bregman (1982) has described as "psychological religiousness." Others use the term to refer to Eastern or mystical experiences, explicitly eliminating Christian understandings of spirituality.

The ambiguity surrounding the concept of spirituality is so great as to make the term almost meaningless. Zen Buddhists and Protestant Pentecostals share an interest in spirituality but the differences in understanding of the concept are so great that dialogue would be extremely difficult. Even when we narrow the field to Christian spirituality we discover differences of such magnitude that while many Roman Catholic and Eastern Orthodox Christians would understand growth in spirituality to lie at the very heart of the Christian life, Protestants have usually avoided the term altogether and have most frequently proposed an understanding of the Christian life without reference to spirituality.

Some of this ambiguity is semantic and could be eliminated by careful definition and use of language. However, much of the ambiguity is an unavoidable consequence of the topic. Spirituality brings us up against some of the most complex mysteries of our being. In the words of Gerald May, "Spirit and mystery are closely related . . . mystery may not always be spiritual but there is no doubt that spirituality is always mysterious" (1982, 32). This being the case, it would appear to be self-defeating to attempt to formulate a psychology of spirituality that eliminates all mystery. Such psychologies already exist, perhaps none being neater than Sigmund Freud's reduction of spirituality to biological instincts. However, in this and a number of other contemporary psychological views of persons, we end up with a truncated view of persons which fails to adequately account for the self-transcending and integrating experience of genuine spirituality.

In attempting to avoid the dangers of reductionistic explanations of spirituality we are, however, liable to fall into an equally perilous trap of making spirituality an appendage of persons that is not well integrated into the rest of the fabric of personality. Here we relate to God, and he to us, through our spirit, a part of persons judged to be separate from other more natural psychological mechanisms and structures (e.g., Minirth 1970). Spiritual problems are then judged to reside in the spiritual part of personality while psychological problems have their locus in a separate psychological part. But such efforts to reintroduce the spirit back into psychology tend to trivialize spirituality by completely divorcing it from the rest of personality. Spirituality becomes the activity of some relatively independent part of personality outside the mainstream of other psychological mechanisms and processes. While a personality theory of such an added-on, nonintegrated spirit may superficially look more Christian than one which ignores spirit or reduces it to some more basic psychological or physiological mechanisms, the result should be recognized to be poor psychology. It fails to account for the richness of genuine Christian spirituality which flows up out of the depths of our being and transfuses and integrates all of personality. It also fragments personality into a spiritual and nonspiritual sphere and limits psychology to the nonspiritual sphere.

In an attempt to walk a middle path between these two equally unsatisfactory extremes let us first consider a view of spirituality that situates our spiritual life in the heart of our psychological being. We will then examine the role of spirituality in psychotherapy.

What Is Spirituality?

Contemporary definitions of spirituality are often so broad as to be almost meaningless. A good example is C. T. Tart (1975), one of the leading proponents of transpersonal psychology, who uses the word to apply to "that vast realm of human potential dealing with ultimate purposes, with higher entities, with God, with life, with compassion, with purpose" (4). U. T. Holmes (1982) defines spirituality as "the human capacity for relationship with that which transcends sense phenomena," this relationship being perceived as a state of heightened consciousness that exhibits itself in creative actions (12). Even more focused is B. J. Groeschel's (1984) definition of spirituality as "the sum total of responses which one makes to what is perceived as the inner call of God" (4). What these three definitions share in common is the notion that at the heart of the spiritual experience is something that pulls us out of and beyond ourselves, something that we might call self-transcendence.

Following Groeschel's lead, I suggest that spirituality is the human response to God's gracious call to a relationship with him. Thus understood, spirituality has its origin, meaning, and fulfillment in God's grace. It is grounded in our having been created in God's image, designed for deep and intimate union with him. In the words of Saint Augustine's famous prayer, "Thou hast made us for thyself and our hearts are restless until they find their rest in thee." Although this restlessness is not always, or even usually, experienced as a spiritual longing, it is in fact the core of our spiritual quest.

From a slightly more psychological perspective, spirituality might be defined as our response to a deep and mysterious human yearning for self-transcendence and surrender, a yearning to find our place. Such a definition incorporates the elements of self-transcendence and yearning for integration common to many uses of the term. Within this understanding, human spiritual longing is an unconscious searching for our roots, not the roots of family or even of race, but our roots as human creatures. Spiritual longing is an awareness that we have forgotten who we are and where we belong. We seem, however, to have an archetypal memory of the shape of the place where we belong and it seems to be something other than self, something transcendent to self. It also seems to be a place of surrender. We seem to need to be in the service of some cause much bigger than ourselves, and when we experience this kind of self-transcendent surrender we suddenly recognize that we have found our place. Like a tool seized by a strong hand or a piece of a jigsaw puzzle placed in proper arrangement with the rest of the puzzle, we suddenly discover who we are and where we belong.

While the quest to find our place through self-transcendence and surrender is the primary element of human spirituality, the quest for integration of our being and for the discovery of our true self are important secondary components. It might be thought that these are merely useful psychological by-products of spirituality. However, more correctly understood, we yearn to bring together the diverse aspects of our being, this as a part of a deep longing for the discovery of our true self. We seek the integration of action and thought, interior life and external behavior, affect and cognition, conscious and unconscious, self and ego, animus and anima, shadow and persona, the material and the immaterial, body and soul. But the reference point for this integration must be something outside ourselves. While any self-transcendent point of reference provides some opportunity for this needed integration, the most complete integration of personality is found only when our spirit is grounded in God's spirit. Then, and only then, do we find our true self. False selves are transcended and the self we find is our self-in-God.

As Adrian van Kaam (1972) points out, in speaking of the spiritual quest as a quest for self-discovery, we must be careful to distinguish this from a quest for mere self-fulfillment. Our search should not be for self in isolation from God but rather a search for self-in-God. This is the crucial difference between selfism as idolatry and Christian spiritual growth. Self-fulfillment quickly deteriorates into mere ego-enhancement unless we discover the paradoxical truth of Christ's words that to find our life we must first lose it. To live, we must first die. To discover our true self, we must first die to our old self, that is, to our ego. Dying to this idolatrous self-as-God, we are then able to discover our true self, our self-in-God.

All persons are created spiritual beings. To describe someone as spiritual and someone else as not is to describe their differing awareness of, and response to, these deep strivings for self-transcendence, surrender, integration, and identity. The spiritual person is one who listens to the messages from the innermost self and seeks to respond to them. This is what it means to describe spiritual persons as inner directed. The inner world, although unseen, is very real and of great importance to such a person. Spirituality is not, however, merely a life of interiority. The spiritual person responds to the inner call by turning not simply outside of self to others, but beyond self and others to some higher Being.

However, not all spirituality is religious and not all religious spirituality is Christian. May notes that the spiritual quest becomes religious only when the individual begins to experience his or her self in relationship with some higher power and responds to this relationship with prayer or worship (1982, 33). Christian spirituality, a subset of religious spiritualities, is a state of deep relationship with God made possible through faith in Jesus Christ and the life of the indwelling Holy Spirit. The relationship of these various spiritualities is represented in figure 12.1.

Figure 12.1
Three Kinds of Spirituality

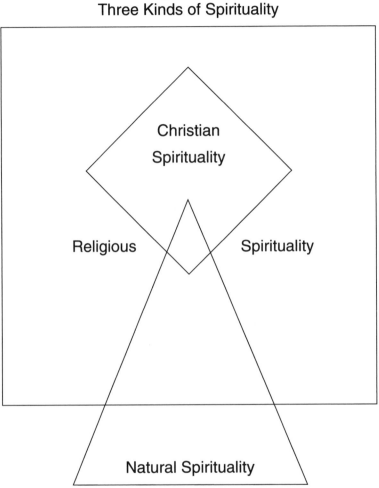

The ground of all religious spirituality is what I call *natural spirituality*. This is the quest for self-transcendence and surrender, a quest which is a fundamental part of our being creatures made in the image of God. It is quite possible to become aware of these longings and yet fail to recognize their ultimate significance, that they represent the voice of God within calling us back to relationship with him. Persons who are aware of these longings and who are responsive to them are undoubtedly more alive, more fully human, and better off psychologically than persons who have no such awareness. From a Christian point of view, however, such persons are still outside the intimate relationship with God to which their longings were intended to direct them.

Religious spirituality involves a relationship with the Power of Being, which serves as the focus of self-transcendence and meaning for life. This may be a movement toward the one true God or it may be a movement toward some other god. Spirituality here explicitly includes prayer or meditation, and worship. Contrary to their claims, much of what occurs within groups such as Alcoholics Anonymous appears not merely to support a natural spirituality but also to nurture a religious spirituality. Those seeking help are encouraged to turn over control of their lives to a higher power and then to develop a relationship with this power through meditation and prayer. While it is possible to encourage a nonreligious spirituality, and some applications of the Alcoholics Anonymous concept may in fact be doing this, it appears that no spiritual quest can progress very far without becoming religious.

In *Christian spirituality*, the probings and responses to the deep spiritual longings are carried out within the context of Christian faith and community. For the Christian who is growing spiritually, life is being lived in the Spirit of God with an ever deeper and more present awareness of being in the presence of God. The integration of personality and direction toward life that flows from this are discovered in the light of God's presence.

The essence of Christian spirituality is the experience of God made possible by the indwelling presence of the Holy Spirit. Spirituality which is not rooted in the Holy Spirit is not Christian. This is consistent with the biblical use of the term *spirituality* which implies life in and of the Spirit. Natural, or even religious spirituality, where the human spirit is not grounded in the Spirit of God, is therefore not identical with Christian spirituality. It may be related to it as it reflects humans awakening to the realization that they are created as spirit and intended to transcend self in surrender to something beyond themselves. However, unless this self-transcendence is through surrender to, and life in, the Spirit of God, the spirituality that is experienced falls short of Christian spirituality.

There are many forms in which such Christian spirituality may develop and express itself. The spiritual pilgrimage of each person must be a personal response to the deep inner call for self-transcendent surrender and service. Prescribed spirituality is not spirituality but authoritarian religion and it is quite clear that not all religion is spiritual in the sense we are using the word here. Spirituality may be guided, nourished, and supported. It may not be externally manufactured or controlled. To attempt to do so is to produce a sham spirituality which does not grow out of the heart. It can also destroy more genuine spirituality, which may in fact have been developing.

Christian spirituality begins in and grows out of a life of interiority. True, the reference point for the self is not itself but God, who is outside and beyond the self. However, God meets us within the depths of our selves and it is here that we relate to God and are changed by this relationship. This is the difference between spiritual transformation and religiosity. Spiritual growth starts from within, in the heart, and spreads outward. Religious changes are much more exterior and superficial. Unfortunately they are also more common. They represent mere behavioral compliance with some exterior standard. Spiritual transformation in the Christian is not unrelated to exterior reference points. God's revelation of his will for us as presented in Scripture is the supreme reference point for our spiritual growth. However, the transformation must be empowered and directed by a change within; the person now behaves differently because of a new spirit within. God desires more than changed behavior; he desires a changed heart, a changed spirit.

Note that this understanding of spirituality does not require the addition of some new extra part of personality through which we relate to God or experience him. The totality of our being yearns for and responds to such a relationship. Furthermore, our relationship with God is mediated by the same psychological processes and mechanisms as those involved in relationships with other people. The spiritual quest is, at one level, a psychological quest, and every psychological quest can be understood to be in some way reflective of our basic spiritual quest. Human personality is such that we are psychospiritual beings; no problem is purely spiritual nor purely psychological. Similarly, no step of psychological development is devoid of spiritual significance nor is spiritual development ever devoid of psychological significance. Psychological and spiritual aspects of human functioning are inextricably interconnected and any segregation of spirituality and psychology is, therefore, both artificial and destructive to the true understanding of either.

Psychotherapy and Spirituality

History of Psychotherapy

The confusion surrounding the understanding of psychotherapy is almost as great as that surrounding spirituality. While this confusion in the psychotherapeutic arena has been generally well hidden from the consumers of psychotherapy, it has been painfully apparent to its practitioners and critics. Consider the enormous differences in the understanding of psychotherapy among the several hundred approaches which can be found in any recent catalogue of current therapies (e.g., Herink 1980). These differences are not just variations of standard techniques or goals but are frequently differences of understanding of the fundamental nature of psychotherapy.

What is psychotherapy? The answer to this question has changed frequently and radically since the term was first used near the end of the nineteenth century. According to *The Oxford English Dictionary* (1933), the term *psychotherapy* was a derivative of the term *psychotherapeutist*, which referred to one who treated disease by psychic methods. Originally these methods were understood to be primarily sleep, hypnosis, and suggestion. But note that this earliest understanding of the term viewed the goal as changes in bodily states; only the method was psychological. Early psychotherapy was, therefore, psychosomatic medicine, this forming the basis for latter attempts to define psychotherapy as a medical act.

While this earliest definition of psychotherapy focused on healing through the psyche, it was not long before a second understanding emerged, that is, psychotherapy as healing of the psyche (Ellenberger 1970). Here one encounters concepts such as "mind cure" or "mental healing" and during the first several decades of the twentieth century definitions of psychotherapy more and more frequently emphasized both psychological methods and psychological goals—the use of psychological methods to bring about the cure of the mind.

But the confusion over what psychotherapy is has not been limited to the competing claims of psychology and medicine. Practitioners of psychotherapy within the Emmanuel Movement of early twentieth-century New England argued that psychotherapy should be understood to involve healing through the use of mental, moral, and spiritual methods. This view was also espoused in the *Journal of Psychotherapy as a Religious Process*, a publication of the Institute for Rankian Psychoanalysis in the mid-1950s. William Rickel, the journal's editor, wrote in the first issue that the bold assertion of the journal's title was justified in terms of the etymology of psychotherapy. He argued that with *psyche* meaning *soul* and *therapist* meaning *servant*, the psychotherapist was a servant of the soul (Rickel 1954, 97).

It may be difficult to resolve these competing claims over the essential nature of psychotherapy on the basis of etymological arguments. However, the history of the practice of healing by means of conversation does yield some important clues to the essence of psychotherapy. In spite of the frequently held assumption on the part of contemporary therapists that psychotherapy is a relatively new craft developed within the past century, it is quite clear that the roots of psychotherapy go back much further. Tracing these roots leads us back to the long-standing religious tradition of the care of souls. Viewing modern-day psychotherapy as continuous with this ancient tradition provides strong support for the argument that psychotherapy is in essence a spiritual process.

Cure of Souls or Cure of Minds?

A detailed examination of the history of psychotherapy, documenting its roots in the religious tradition of the care of souls, has been well done by others (e.g., Entralgo 1970; Szasz 1978; Ehrenwald 1966) and would take us too far from our focus to be appropriate at present. What is quite clear is that since earliest times most civilizations in history have, until the present, made the care and cure of souls a religious specialization. Each culture and each religion has understood and implemented this care in slightly different ways. However, in each case it has involved the use of conversation and instruction for the edification and healing of the soul.

The movement from the cure of souls to the cure of minds was primarily a consequence of the seventeenth- and eighteenth-century growth of science and the subsequent nineteenth-century decline of religion. Historian of psychotherapy Jan Ehrenwald (1966) describes the demise of religious soul cure as occurring "when magic has been eroded by critical reason, and religion, emptied of its meaning, has become a formalized institution, a repository of magic rituals and observances" (10). He goes on to argue that psychotherapy arose as a stopgap effort to fill the spiritual void left by the demise of religion, its challenge being "to meet unmet metaphysical needs . . . without recourse to mythical ideologies or magic ritual" (16).

The great hope of science, particularly the social sciences, was for new solutions to old problems without the old trappings of religion. With face toward the future, nineteenth-century science strode ahead with the confidence that myth and ritual were forever left behind in the pre-scientific era. However, what actually happened was the replacement of old myths with new ones. Twentieth-century psychotherapists have now replaced clerics as healers of the soul, and psychotherapists, packaging this healing as cure of sick minds rather than cure of sinful souls, have sought to distance themselves as much as possible from their religious heritage.

But how well has psychotherapy done in its attempts to distance itself from soul cure? J. Neaman (1975) notes that mental health professionals have moved away from the treatment of the mentally ill, the primary focus of early twentieth-century psychiatry, back to the aid of people with spiritual struggles. Similarly, Carl G. Jung (1933) notes that "patients force the psychotherapist into the role of the priest. . . . That is why we psychotherapists must occupy ourselves with problems which strictly speaking belong to the theologian" (178). Psychotherapists have been asked to tackle an impossible task, the cure and care of the soul without reference to spiritual aspects of being. But spirituality does, in fact, have a legitimate place within psychotherapy.

With the exception of the rare technical and very focused intervention, such as the behavioral treatment of a tic, psychotherapy inevitably deals with a broad enough slice of personality that spiritual considerations are necessarily involved. Struggles associated with the search for meaning to life, or with the quest for identity, wholeness, or even fulfillment, are all spiritual struggles. People do not have to be talking about God to be expressing a problem that is at core a spiritual one. Once we begin to understand the diverse ways in which people mask their experience of and response to the spiritual quest, we come to be more discerning of the presence of this quest behind the seemingly more psychological struggles our patients present to us in therapy (Benner 1988).

We are always either growing spiritually, that is, becoming more sensitive and responsive to the spiritual call in our life, or we are becoming more spiritually dead. At times of crisis or transition in our lives the opportunity for spiritual movement in one direction or another is particularly great. This is even more the case when we face these times with the assistance of a psychotherapist and begin to listen to messages from our inner selves. Psychotherapy has, therefore, great potential as a spiritual influence. But this potential is a two-edged sword.

Spiritual Hazards of Psychotherapy

There are several potential spiritual dangers in psychotherapy. The first and most obvious one is associated with psychotherapists who have a spiritual or religious axe to grind. Such persons may view religiosity as either a symptom, or possibly a cause, of neuroses. They may, therefore, see it as their responsibility to rid their patients of their religious convictions. Although most who would hold such a view might attempt to exercise restraint out of a respect for the patient's personal values, their own personal belief is often subtly but powerfully communicated. Such a situation does in fact represent a serious spiritual hazard given what we know about the powerful influence therapist values have on patients in an intensive psychotherapy experience (Rosenthal 1955).

The second spiritual hazard of psychotherapy is much more subtle. Moreover, it is a danger that is not eliminated by merely seeing a Christian therapist because this is a trap into which some such therapists have fallen. This is the danger of adopting a psychological spirituality and confusing this with a genuine Christian spirituality. Here, insight, listening to the voices of your inner self, and integration of personality around the deepest aspects of what you perceive to be your true self all become primary, and self-transcendence through surrender to God is either lost or missed. Listening to your dreams, understanding and being responsible to your feelings, learning to discern the messages of your anxieties, or cultivating an inner quietness or composure, all potentially most significant tools in genuine Christian spiritual growth, become the end in and of themselves and the voice of the transcendent God becomes more and more faint. Psychotherapy has then become a religion, not a tool.

But psychotherapy also has great potential as a tool of genuine spiritual growth. If the therapist avoids defining the focus of therapy too narrowly and gives permission, either implicitly or explicitly, for the patient to raise spiritual issues and questions, the therapeutic encounter can be a place where psychospiritual matters can be addressed and spiritual as well as psychological growth experienced.

One way in which the therapist can give permission for the raising of spiritual matters is to inquire about the patient's religious history in the course of the assessment or history taking. It is amazing how therapists who routinely inquire about developmental, medical, interpersonal, academic, and vocational aspects of their patient's history never once ask about their religious upbringing and current state. Quite clearly, religion has replaced sex as the great taboo subject of our age.

Therapists can open the door to spiritual considerations in therapy in an even more direct way by simply telling the patient in one of the early sessions that they view spiritual issues as inseparable from psychological ones and are glad, therefore, to have such considerations raised at any point. My experience with such a statement has been that patients respond to it by raising issues that they judge to be spiritual in nature. Sometimes these may be explicitly religious, other times more broadly existential, and sometimes esoterically mystical. Always, however, it has served to enrich and broaden therapy.

Inviting the inclusion of spiritual considerations in psychotherapy is not the same as inviting religious or theological discussion. Psychotherapy is not a good place to talk about God, prayer, scriptural interpretation, or theology. It is, however, an excellent place for a person to raise for therapeutic consideration their experience of God or the meaning and experience of other aspects of their spiritual life. Although psychotherapy does share much common ground with other soul-care professions it is not the same as any of them. Psychotherapy approaches soul care in a unique manner. The unique way in which the psychotherapist treats spirituality is that it, along with everything else that is considered, is addressed psychologically.

If you discuss prayer with your spiritual guide you should expect help in the development of personal prayer life through advice. However, if you discuss prayer with your psychotherapist, you should expect help through increased understanding of your experience in prayer. This is the essential contribution of psychotherapy. Whatever it considers, it does so by means of exploration of the meaning and experience of that topic to the person. Thus your experience of prayer, your uses and abuses of it, and the dynamics and significance of it in your life are all appropriate areas of psychotherapeutic exploration. However, specific suggestions as to how to pray are probably more appropriately the focus of a relationship of spiritual guidance.

Similarly, the topic of God should be handled in a different manner in therapy from that which is appropriate in spiritual guidance. The psychotherapist should primarily be focused on the patient's experience of God. How is God understood? What are the images of God and how do these relate to the internal representations of others? How does the person relate to God? Is God seen as a harsh and punitive father and can this be meaningfully understood in terms of his or her earthly father? Or perhaps is God benevolent but basically impotent, again quite clearly revealing something of the person's experience of his or her self and the world? This is not to suggest that God is merely a creation of the mind. However, because persons are unified psychospiritual beings, relationships with God, self, and others are all mediated by the same internal psychological processes. It is these processes that psychotherapists are best trained to understand. It is this, therefore, with which psychotherapists should occupy themselves.

In addition to the exploration of the meaning of one's spiritual experience, psychotherapy is also an excellent place to explore blocks in spiritual growth. Why is my prayer life so dead? Why do I have such trouble trusting God, or why am I so angry at him? Why do I continue in sinful behavior which I wish to stop? While these and many other questions can also be addressed by spiritual guidance, psychotherapy is in a position to address them in a unique and equally legitimate manner. It is a manner that often complements rather than competes with that of the spiritual guidance.

A clear understanding of the unique way in which psychotherapy addresses spirituality allows us to be able to pronounce it a legitimate soul-care service. If psychotherapy fails to approach soul care in a manner different from that of spiritual guidance, then it is an illegitimate profession. However, while psychotherapy is closely related to spiritual guidance, it is unique. It is this uniqueness which must be clear for both patients and therapists alike.

The therapist who views psychotherapy primarily as a place to work evangelistic purposes or to make spiritual disciples has missed his or her calling. Such a person should not be a psychotherapist but should pursue some more explicitly religious vocation. The psychotherapist should be someone who affirms the value of alleviating human emotional suffering and of promoting growth through the removal of blocks to such growth. Such a therapist would see how this is both valid and significant as preparation for spiritual growth. Therapeutic work has spiritual implications of immense proportion. However, to attempt to make it what it is not, that is, a relationship primarily of spiritual guidance, is to be dishonest. The dishonesty involves the act of placing the mantle of the psychotherapist over the clothing of the spiritual guide in the hope of capturing a market that might not otherwise be available to the religious worker.

Understanding the differences between psychotherapy and other soul-care approaches must also include the awareness of the limitations of psychotherapy. Psychotherapy may lead persons into a place of readiness for spiritual growth and may even help them take significant steps toward God. However, this is not salvation. The Christian gospel proclaims that the mechanism of the new birth is trust in the redemptive work of Christ, not insight or increased emotional health. Hendrika Vande Kemp (1983) notes that while psychotherapy does often "have the effect of leading the person to awareness of transcendence and ultimacy . . . it does not identify the person's ultimate need as a relationship with God nor confront the person with the need for confession or the acceptance of Christ's redemptive work" (119).

Psychotherapists are in a unique position to help those who struggle with psychospiritual problems, even when these are experienced purely in psychological terms. For many people, no one else will ever get as close to the spiritual issues in their lives. The psychotherapist who is sensitive to the fact that the interior world is not neatly divided into psychological and spiritual compartments is therefore a person who may have the unique opportunity to provide help, not merely for the psychological or structural aspects of personality, but also for the spiritual or directional aspects of personality.

The Person and Spirituality of the Therapist

One of the most significant implications of Christian theology for the practice of psychotherapy seems to grow out of an understanding of the way in which God communicates his grace to us. God does not communicate his grace to us by means of some impersonal mechanism. Rather, it is incarnated into a person. Christ is the good news. He does not merely bring the good news. The good news is communicated in the form of a person. And so it must be in therapy.

Psychotherapy is a personal process. When healing occurs within it, such healing cannot be adequately explained in terms of techniques or impersonal forces and mechanisms. Psychotherapy is an intimate and deeply personal encounter of two or more people, regardless of whether this encounter is carried out within the framework of psychoanalysis, behavior therapy, or an encounter group. An incarnational style wherein the therapist comes to the patient on the patient's terms and makes himself or herself available to be used and even abused by the patient is the style of relationship that most closely matches the way in which God relates to us (Benner 1983). While it is so much easier to relate from the safety of anonymity, distance, and superiority, we must recognize that transformation occurs in others only as we make ourselves available to them and allow ourselves to incarnate God's gracious acceptance of them.

But obviously, I must first experience God's grace in my own life if I am to be able to communicate that grace to others. Similarly, if I wish to serve as a facilitator of spiritual growth in others, I must be not merely religious, I must be deeply spiritual. That is, I must have responded to the deep inner call to self-transcendence and surrender by grounding my spirit in God's Spirit and I must be daily living more and more fully in the awareness of his presence and my relationship with him. This relationship must be central to my being, in reality and not just in word. My ever deepening union with God must be the center around which the rest of my personality is being progressively integrated if I am to be a person who is to give spiritual as well as psychological help to those who come to me with psychospiritual problems.

The person of the therapist is a much more important ingredient in the therapy process than has usually been realized. I believe we tend to de-emphasize this obvious fact, trusting in technique and theory, in order to escape the immense demands that it places upon us therapists. We want to believe that we can help people regardless of whether we are tired or even sick on any given day, whether we have faced and courageously dealt with our own issues, or whether or not we are honestly facing our own relationships or inner realities. Believing this, we often are tempted to feel that we can cheat in therapy and get away with it. We feel that we can help others face things from which we have run. But this is a lie.

We cannot lead others where we have never been. Whether it is into the freedom of self-forgiveness, the courageous entry of and reemergence from a personal abyss, or the experience of self-transcendence through genuine and deep Christian spiritual growth, we cannot lead another where we have not been. The personal psychospiritual health of the psychotherapist is a crucial ingredient in the therapy process and there are no shortcuts to this health for therapists or for patients.

The Christian therapist who is alive and growing spiritually is able to give to others from his or her depths and not be depleted. The alternatives to this are burnout or giving to others only from the exterior or periphery of our life. If we are to respond to the challenge of therapy, that is, to the call of deep onto deep, we must be living our lives out of our own depths. This is the spiritual life. It is in the depths of our being where Christ meets us and this is the point from which he wishes to do his work of restoration in us and in those with whom we work in psychotherapy.

13

The Self as Gift
and Promise

LYMAN T. LUNDEEN

Fascination with the self has been a mark of our era. Prescriptions for self-development are legion. They show up in books, newspapers, and magazines. They pervade the public media of movies, plays, and television. They even get center stage in the religious marketplace, appearing in sermons and religious literature as ways to succeed and be happy in life.

Critiques of individualism and privatism emerge periodically, encouraging us to see the self in its context of interdependent relationships. We might even be led to ask, "What kind of society do we want?" "What strategies should we pursue to create a better world?" The questions are cast in a social mode, but the importance of the individual as the irreducible constituent of every group still lingers underneath. Individual dreams and decisions mold both the questions and the answers.

For all its problems, fascination with the self has a positive (and promising) side. It introduces us to a consideration of the problems of choice and consequence. It opens up diverse possibilities for the imagination by implying that individuals are not yet what they will become. It carries with it a future orientation where development and direction become key issues. In a word, emphasis on self-development raises philosophical and religious issues that might otherwise be neglected.

Christian theology has a keen interest in the self and its development. It is concerned about the self in relation to itself, to others, and, above all, to God. In its eschatological domain, it has considered what changes are possible and what routes are available for full and final human development. At this point, it touches directly on the contemporary preoccupation with self-development and gives its own perspective on the problems and the possibilities of self-fulfillment.[1]

As a Christian theologian, I think it is necessary to bring this faith perspective into conversation with the self-development craze. I believe that the Christian faith provides a better perspective on self-fulfillment than contemporary self-development theories do. Instead of relying merely on human diagnoses and human resources (methods), it addresses the self from a transcendent perspective and turns the self-development quest into a preliminary (penultimate) endeavor alongside God's empowering initiative. It is this thesis that I want to explore and develop here.

Precarious Paths to Self-Fulfillment

When self-development and a Christian perspective on development are brought into dialogue, the risk is that ideas that actually conflict with the Christian faith will be mixed indiscriminately with authentic Christian proposals or will be substituted for them. This is possible because the competing alternatives all pick up pieces of Christian truth and package them in ways that lose the content and power of the gospel. It is appropriate to give at least brief attention to some of these divergent alternatives.

I will identify and discuss four alternatives. Each one is not the Christian faith at its best but is a truncated, or even a superficial, version of the faith that distorts it features. Some of them sail under Christian colors; others sail under secular flags or labels. In either case, all of them stand as alternatives to the Christian faith and its deeper proposal for self-fulfillment. The four alternatives can be labeled self-affirmation, self-assertion, positive thinking, and twelve-step programs.

Self-Affirmation

Theories that promote self-affirmation maintain that the way to a healthy self is the celebration of the inner person. We are encouraged to find within ourselves all the resources that we need for fulfillment. We do not need to rely on other people. What is needed is a good self-image, and only the individual can produce that. When one has a good self-image, one's interior life will yield all that life needs or offers.[2]

---

1. Paul Tillich's treatment of ultimate concern leading to fulfillment or disappointment opens up this connection with religion. See Tillich (1957, 1–4).

2. Much of the New Age literature, with its search for cosmic connections in the interior of consciousness, goes in this direction. More blatant "self-love" proposals can be heard in the preaching of some successful televangelists such as one called Brother Ike.

When brought into conversation with the Christian faith, this approach makes contact with the mystical tradition. It assumes an identity of truth and self-awareness that translates into an internal unity of the self with all that matters, even with God. In modern garb, it stands behind every proposal to get one's personal act together, first, before one comes to terms with others.

Programs of self-affirmation are present in contemporary expectations for homogeneous support groups. If it is assumed that only people with similar experiences can understand one another, we are not very far from the affirmations of isolated selves.

The classic Christian criticisms of certain kinds of mysticism are relevant here. The Christian claim is that selves need some kind of intervention from outside their experience. They need to hear a message that both calls into question their own inner resources and sets those resources free for new directions. God's message supplies something new from the outside and thus needs to be part of the prescription for authentic self-development.

Self-Assertion

A second orientation is found in programs or schemes that appeal to self-assertion. The focus here is not toward the inner self but the active expression of the self in relation to others. Assertiveness training evokes an appropriate image where we are encouraged to express our wills and thereby to develop the self. Any group that encourages one always to stand up for one's rights fits the same pattern. It is thought that the willful assertion of rights not only will gain freedom for the person's full potential but also will yield consequences that are even better for society.[3]

Like the first orientation, this one has a long history and contains an element of truth. It is often assumed that the self achieves its greatest potential by assertive—active—striving in the power complexes of the situation, and as a matter of fact this kind of assertion can and does yield a certain degree of development of the self.

From a Christian point of view, the limitations of this approach have been noted. On one level, willful self-assertion can do damage in terms of blind self-righteousness and the oppressive exercise of power. On an even deeper level, the attempt to earn God's favor is active, making partisan and compulsive egos of us all. In this sense, self-assertion as a prescription for self-development runs head-on into the Christian claim that human worth is established by grace, and not just by victories won or by opponents vanquished.

---

3. Such exercise for the will gets support from some modes of therapy and is summed up in the popular assertiveness book by Manuel J. Smith (1975).

There are diverse versions of the self-assertion orientation. Promoting one's rights against all oppositive injustice is not too different than the pursuit of self-interest in capitalistic schemes. Both approaches stress self-assertion and make our hopes for social and individual satisfaction hinge on persistent determination. Both of them are criticized when put in touch with the Christian claim that there is more to life than either rights or competition. This criticism warns us of the dangers of selves alert only to the rights of special groups. It also calls into question the self-interest that ignores and exploits the needs of others. By putting God in the picture, the Christian faith shapes a very different image of the self in society. It points beyond mere self-assertion to a self that is in life-giving relationships of interdependent and mutual concern.

Positive Thinking

Perhaps a more attractive prescription for self-development comes under the label *positive thinking*. This approach touches the inner life of the self and also its external relationships. It shapes both the image and the expression of the self, asking that everything be seen in a rosy light. Christian pulpits often reflect this orientation when they put forward a "gospel" that is focused not on problems but only on possibilities.[4]

While this approach can lay claim to certain connections with the Christian faith, its exclusive concern with possibilities distorts the truth. The classic Christian faith stresses both negative and positive thinking with very precise development of each. The negative reality is sin; the positive reality is faith, which, by grasping onto God's promise, creates redemptive possibilities. One without the other is a distortion of both.

Every proposal for self-development, including positive thinking, involves a critical rejection of inappropriate, harmful behaviors. The Christian proposal is very direct and specific in its description of destructive alternatives. Sin recognizes that people trust in gods that cannot save.[5] It points out an inappropriate positive understanding of the self and the illusions and distortions that accompany it.

Also, the promise on which the Christian faith depends is not merely positive thinking about the human situation. It is the announcement of God's intervention in the struggle with evil. It is a clear recognition of the battle that is underway and an announcement of God's decisive way of dealing with it. Thus human fulfillment is not obtained merely by celebrating human capabilities, not even the capacity to think positively. Rather fulfillment comes from acknowledging human depen-

4. See Robert Schuller (1977).
5. See Tillich (1957, 35) for ultimate concerns that are not focused on the truly ultimate.

dence on God's initiative, and a willingness to turn away from all narcissistic solutions that make the self its own solution.

Twelve-Step Programs

Twelve-step programs like Alcoholics Anonymous offer an approach to self-development that moves closer to the Christian view. This is precisely because they take the complexity of human problems seriously and recognize that recovery and growth is not simply the result of one factor but the convergence of several different ones.

Specifically, twelve-step programs call for honesty about personal difficulties, reliance on some higher power, dependence on other people, and work at specific tasks. This approach recognizes the persistent power of self-deception, so that simple forms of self-affirmation and self-assertion are not sufficient. In addition, surrender to a higher power and dependence on other people form the context in which strenuous effort toward developing the self takes place.

Twelve-step programs resemble the Christian way of dealing with self-development. They manifest a sin-and-grace pattern in terms of their understanding of human problems and in terms of their agenda for change. They also have a dynamic and future-oriented view of recovery. "I'm a recovering alcoholic" is a vision of growth and achievement that many self-development proposals lack. This vision recognizes that growth is a continuing struggle, not a simple clear-cut achievement.

In spite of these important points of contact with the Christian faith, there is still potential conflict between the twelve-step programs and the Christian vision of growth. The conflict occurs primarily on two levels.

First, the programs' use of the broad, undeveloped notion of a higher power tends to hide the need for a specific view of God. They often imply that any higher power will do and therefore the resources for growth in terms of a specific revelation of God are minimized. The Christian faith takes the opposite tack. It proposes that the God we know in Jesus contributes to wholeness and healing precisely because he has made himself known in a specific and historical way.

Second, the programs' emphasis on working at the twelve steps can imply that the person's own efforts are the primary basis for recovery or growth. The intervention of God in grace and forgiveness slips into the background and is replaced by a secular salvation (working at it).

In these two ways twelve-step programs compete against a Christian understanding of self-development, even while in other ways they can serve as a partner with the Christian faith.[6]

---

6. The importance of this conversation was made clear by the focus of Union Theological Seminary's "Union Day '90" on "Twelve-Step Theologies: The Social and Spiritual Implications of Addiction and Recovery."

A Critique of Growth and Measurement

Some issues run through all self-development proposals. Two assumptions often emerge without being criticized. The first is the notion that growth of the self progresses like steps up a ladder. Growth is portrayed as a discernable upward movement that reflects consistent achievement. The danger inherent in this assumption is the expectation of achievable perfection and the self-justifying illusions that accompany it. The second assumption is that growth can be clearly tested and measured. This assumption takes a modern scientific attitude toward the development of the self and says in effect that if growth is real it is measurable.

The expectation of consistent upward movement runs counter to the Christian understanding of growth as increased awareness of deviation from God's will. Growth for the Christian is not simply "doing better" but "seeing deeper." Thus the Christian faith does not encourage claims like "Look how much I have grown" but recognizes that there is increased struggle, ambiguity, and surprising contradictions in the Christian life, and consequently it encourages increased dependence on God's love and forgiveness.

While the Christian faith allows for growth in faith and in performance, it challenges the assumption that experience will manifest consistent and measurable growth, even for the so-called best Christian. Instead it maintains that the mature Christian self is one who is more involved in struggle and more aware of its depth and persistence.[7] In terms of behavior, the concern for consistency and precise measurement becomes even more problematic. It rules out the complexity and ambiguity of dynamic situations. It tends to make the life of Christians look like a straight line toward perfect performance. Over against this notion stands the faith claim that Christians are both saints and sinners at the same time. Saint Paul, for instance, stands as a permanent warning to any easy confidence in consistency, progress, and measurement. God functions to free us for greater honesty and renewed effort in our struggles.

For Christians, any assessment of the mature self involves risk and forgiveness as cornerstones of mature faith and selfhood. Factors that can be measured play a secondary role at best in any image of a desired self. We must be careful, then, lest the models of development are set by commitment to progress, consistency, and neat measurability.

The Self in Christian Perspective

In a Christian framework, focus on the self runs into trouble in two other ways. First, it tends toward ego worship. Preoccupation with the

---

7. Paul in Romans 7:15–20 offers the relevant image of increased Christian awareness as both saint and sinner at the same time.

self runs into direct conflict with the gospel's emphasis on a love that "seeketh not its own." The Christian faith includes the promise of salvation, but it also makes it clear that such fulfillment can be lost by seeking it too directly. A fulfilled self is a by-product of participating in God's love for others. It is not an end unto itself, something that is enjoyed over against other human beings whose needs and worth are ignored. In Scripture, there are calls for self-denial and even self-hatred, indicating that loving the self directly is not a biblical prescription.

Second, focus on the self tempts us to put our confidence in techniques. It encourages a "pull-yourself-up-by-your-own-bootstraps" understanding of faith in which the meaning is the method. It makes no difference whether the method rests on secular credibility or on some biblical reference, it is basically a preoccupation with teaching a method rather than a proclaiming of the gospel message.

The classical biblical tension between faith and works can help us assess the self-development emphasis. As the apostle Paul has it, God's law demands works from human selves but those works are not the main event. They rest on the possibility of transformed hearts that are moved by faith. Focus on self, growth, technique, and measurement can have their day as long as they are kept in subordinate roles. This gives priority to God's initiative while allowing for the possibility that all efforts of self-development may be ways that God uses to lead us to better and deeper things. If our priorities are straight, fascination with the self may end up serving the gospel rather than replacing it.

The Self as God's Gift

The encounter between the Christian faith and self-development can be clarified by addressing faith's concern with the relationship between God and the human self. Here, in fact, self-development concerns can help clarify faith's posture and prepare us to deal with the conflicting proposals. How humans are seen in relation to God provides the stage on which Christian utilization of self-development themes will have to be played out.

Christians have often stressed the radical difference between God and the human. In that perspective, self-love is a perverse form of idolatry, and self-affirmation and self-assertion are heavily criticized. If the focus on self is self-worship, it should be challenged, but if self-love stems from God's love for us, it is a totally different thing. It can be both appropriate and God-centered.

The difference or distance between God and the human is not the chief teaching of the Christian faith. A more fundamental theme is the difference between a destructive and a fulfilling relationship to God. All humans are in close connection with God by virtue of creation, but the way they are related to him has direct consequences for their sense of self and the way that sense gets played out in the world.

What we need to affirm is that focus on the human is not necessarily an idolatrous turn away from God. Christian talk often sounds that way. In the twentieth century, neo-orthodoxy made the difference between anthropocentric religion and theocentric faith its central concern. Modern, or even postmodern, Christian theologies tend to assume that anthropomorphic interpretations of God are a clear sign of idolatry.[8] In this sense both neo-orthodoxy and postmodern interpretations obscure the radical affirmation of humans in the gospel.

If we take the Christian focus on God in Jesus and treat it seriously as a way of affirming the human, then God as known in Jesus is not a call to turn away from the human. Instead it enables us to see two different ways of relating to God. The issue is self-affirmation against God's will or self-affirmation in accord with it.

The Self as Gift

Christ reminds us of the relational aspect of the self. He also gives us a perspective on authentic selfhood. The incarnation of God in the flesh of Jesus is the effective revelation of God's will for people. In other words, God corrects our misconceptions of both divinity and selfhood. The intimate involvement of a loving God dignifies the human situation at the same time that it calls into question destructive human tendencies. The doctrine of justification by faith, where human identity is firmly established only when ultimate dependence on God's mercy is acknowledged, expresses and protects both truths.

Salvation by grace through faith has often been accompanied by the denial of anything good in human selves. The necessity of grace stands out against a background of human depravity. The depravity touches every aspect of our lives, but it peaks in our effort to establish the significance of our existence on our own terms.[9] Recognition of this cutting edge of grace was crucial in Reformation times, and it continues to be a needed theological emphasis. Grace cuts both ways, denying the self as ground for its own worth but affirming the self as the focus and channel of God's care.

---

8. Christianity can be understood as radically anthropomorphic in certain respects. God is personal and has will and purpose, for example. These features that God shares with human beings are not merely human projections but understood as based on God's own revelation. In the Christian frame, therefore, not all imaging of God in human form (anthropomorphism) is idolatrous.

9. The term *total depravity*, even in the heat of the sixteenth-century Reformation, referred to the inability of humans to save themselves and their persistent efforts to do so. It was not a blanket condemnation of everything that was human but zeroed in on the central deviation of the will, which then colored all aspects of human life to some degree.

This second side of grace gives a primary thrust to our theological expression. The gospel is fundamentally the elevation of the human on the grounds of God's love, not the denial of human worth for the sake of an exalted and distant deity. This gives human identity a different twist. The self, and its worth, are God's gift. Authentic selfhood is denied those who insist that it is a personal achievement or possession. Christians have expressed this truth by making a careful distinction between works of the law and the power of God's grace. Grace is the only sufficient basis for selfhood, even though God's hand can also be seen in the stirrings that move people to strive for selfhood on their own terms.[10]

The broad interest in self-development, then, is the arena that God creates for the fruitful recognition of the self as a gift of God's saving work. Moreover, Christ gives us a view of authentic selfhood. Our selfhood derives from, and is dependent on, God's gift of love and forgiveness. Human dignity is not something inherent in us. It is not a rational necessity or something earned by conformity to some law of performance. It is conferred by the Creator and makes every individual special beyond any rationalistic and legalistic consideration.

Authentic selfhood is to be accepted with gratitude. God's affirmation in grace is a new basis for self-identity and a new dynamic for action. It calls us from the quest for isolated personal satisfaction, delivers us from a prideful or masochistic estimate of our private capabilities, and grasps us in the flow of radical Christ-like love toward the whole of God's creation. The gift of self produces a task within the ambiguities of a still unloving society. The struggle against unauthentic selfhood goes on. Human dignity in Christ is a gift to be celebrated, but more so it is a gift to be used against all tempting alternatives. It thereby frees us for more responsible exercise of our human capabilities.

There are ways of speaking of self-acceptance, self-affirmation, and self-development in the context of the gospel. Self-acceptance in Christ is a special kind of self-acceptance. It is the acceptance of the human on account of Jesus Christ, taking sin and forgiveness seriously as a way of deepening psychological perspectives. This kind of self-acceptance is grounded in a God who shoulders the pain and shame of our struggle, changing our present experience and our future expectations. It carries with it an exclusive thrust. Based on radical love for people, it exposes the negative features of selfhood as sought by other approaches, it sets the terms for authentic human identity, and it initiates a particular direction in life.

---

10. Although the law in this sense cannot ultimately save, nevertheless, efforts to obey the law, even when pressed to the recognition of impossibility, make a positive contribution to salvation and also to relative justice along life's way.

In spite of the need to be critical of the isolated, technique-oriented self often promoted by self-development approaches, we should have a positive appreciation of their affirmation of the human self. There are hints of God's affirmation even in the distorted attempts of self-development approaches to free people to be their authentic selves. We can share the concern and recognize that God can work through secular structures to move people toward authentic selfhood. The power of God's love may be seen in very ordinary human relationships. The acceptance of family, friends, therapists, and neighbors not only affirms us but also suggests our need for cosmic resources. It tells us that we need to be affirmed by One whose dependability and resources go far beyond human relations.

God's word of affirmation in Jesus Christ makes all the difference at precisely this point. The proclamation that the very Creator of the universe cares about us can set loose a sense of identity so fresh that Christians speak of a "new birth." Proclamation of Christ as God's gift of authentic selfhood changes the direction of life and the basis of self-understanding.

The Self as Promise

Because the self as God's gift is not a static, finished identity, the self is also promise, a directed and anticipatory acceptance of what is yet to be. This truth may be recognized in all self-development approaches. The Christian faith adds the anticipation of a loving God who goes with us into the future. Humans as authentic selves, then, are sustained not only by a once-given identity but also by the giver who leads and beckons toward a hopeful future.

The horizon of the future, impinging on present reality, provides a perspective in which God's promise of fulfillment in Christ has some intelligibility and relevance. Selves are not just what present circumstances or past behavior indicate. They are also what they are becoming. In this sense, a promise that we can live by is essential for every claim of selfhood, and the Christian promise stands in direct competition with alternative claims about the future. The future unfolds very differently when Jesus rather than any other vision maps the road ahead.

Being a Christian self initiates an internal conflict between the old and the new identity. In this creative tension, the authentic self emerges ultimately as promise while at the same time it is a present task. Our identity is established by the gift of faith, but that very identity includes the energetic application of all our talents to serve in the world. When this happens, we celebrate God's grace. When it does not occur, we require the same discipline as those who have not heard the promise or who have not acknowledged God's gift. God must keep the struggle alive, reminding us that self is promise as much as gift. In this sense, authentic selfhood reflects persistent ambiguity, even as gift and promise are claimed anew.

The self as gift and promise has direct consequences for the way we see identity developing. We are free to be ourselves in a deep sense because at every stage of life gifts of dignity and responsibility from the hand of God are ours. In a continuous way our lives are free from success or failure. The Christian faith speaks of this freedom in terms of forgiveness of sins. The term is not a morbid phrase that focuses on how bad we are, but a phrase that points to God as the continued dynamic for self-development in a pattern that does not frustrate or disappoint. That pattern is growth, seen in continual reference to justification by grace. Forgiveness of sins is received as a declaration of a derivative human worth in the face of increased awareness of rebellion and failure. God's love frees us to begin again and again in the perennial struggle to show love to others. It also frees us to love ourselves, to admit our perversions and know that they are serious but not so serious that we cannot afford criticism and correction. We are free to know that measurement is not the meaning of our existence, and therefore we are turned loose to engage in activity of finite proportions rather than of unattainable perfection. In words reminiscent of twelve-step programs, we are nothing more or less than "recovering sinners" and are free to admit it because of God's gift and promise.

The Christian faith has a definite stake in all talk of self-affirmation and self-development. Faith in Christ gives us ways of identifying commitments and practices that can be ultimately destructive to selfhood. It also asserts a positive claim about authentic selfhood. It holds up the fundamental relationship on which identity can rest without becoming totally and finally engaged in self-destructive competition and isolation. It puts forward a derivative sense of the self that makes dependence positive when coupled with penultimate responsibility. It promises fulfillment in spite of contradictory evidence. Such Christian selfhood includes a confidence that is not based on our own capabilities but is rooted in God's reaching down to touch our lonely competition with a totally new possibility. "We love, because he first loved us" (1 John 4:19 RSV). Our love derives from being loved, and it embraces a self that is given by God as both gift and promise.

Part **3**

Developmental Theory in Specific Situations

14

Women and
Mid-Life Crises

F. COLLEEN ZABRISKIE

Mid-life or middle age as a period of significant growth
and development is beginning to get long-denied attention. It was
neglected as a significant area of research and theory development
long after old age began to receive much attention from both practitioners and investigators. In addition, when adult growth and development has been examined it has been done primarily by studying the
lives of men. The recent monumental work by Daniel Levinson (1978)
is a prime example of this. As we will see, there are some major differences in the sequence and the type of tasks through which men and
women move. Thus, it is essential that we study the developmental
cycles in both sexes and draw comparisons and contrasts. These normal developmental processes must be understood before we can begin
to deal with anticipated or common crises that occur, as well as the
reaction and hoped-for resolutions.

Definition

The task of defining mid-life brings us face to face with the differences between men and women. If an objective definition is advanced
by an investigator it often corresponds closely to that person's own age.
If subjects are asked to define middle age or mid-life the disparity
between men and women becomes apparent. The Levinson (1978)

study established eras to divide the life cycle, which for men were principally determined by work and career concerns. For women, the organizing theme is the family and its cycle (Neugarten 1975). It is easy to recognize the similarity here to the archaic "biology is destiny" approach to feminine psychology. The tendency to stereotype caused the biological or reproductive function to be seen as constricting and limiting, rather than as an organizing theme producing a myriad of possibilities to women.

The most consistently used definition of middle age in women does relate to this biological timetable. B. L. Neugarten (1968) and A. Rossi (1973) both propose that for a woman middle age begins when she launches children into the adult world and ends when she finishes the parental role. This definition seems to be a difficult one to apply with decreasing family size and increasing age when the first child is born. However, even with this, and the option of not having children at all, there are just so many finite years during which the issue of pregnancy must be faced.

Gail Sheehy (1976) found age thirty-five to be the crisis point for childless women. At this time the yet childless woman usually senses that "it's now or never," meaning the decision about bearing a child now takes on a note of finality. While the family experiences as a whole are highly significant as determinants of the developmental sequence, they do not set the entire stage. Rather it is more accurate to describe the developmental changes that occur within as the result of an interplay of experiences: intellectual growth and the relationship to work, establishment of personal identity through separation and autonomy, and finally family development propelled by childbirth and parenting.

Theories of Growth and Development

The stage most central to middle age is that of generativity. With the task of establishing intimacy more or less accomplished one can move on to the process of establishing and guiding the next generation and in general being productive and creative. The concern here is with production in every sense of that word and the virtue is that of care. In the process of "caring for," mature persons get their dependency needs met by being needed by the younger generation (Erikson 1963). If the previous tasks have not been successfully mastered, and especially the task of establishing an intimate relationship, a regression takes place to a sense of stagnation and pseudointimacy. These individuals indulge themselves as if they were their own child and this self-concern is reflected through physical or psychological disabilities.

Erik Erikson (1975) has been soundly criticized by liberationists for his descriptions of women that focus on the inner space while his masculine descriptions accentuate the outer space with protrusions and use of height. This resulted from his observations of boys and girls playing with blocks. He reduced these spatial and narrative themes to the basic differentiating genital elements in boys and girls. Herein again lies the "anatomy is destiny" theme, a frequent focus of criticism. It is sufficient to note that Erikson does make an attempt to defend himself by shifting his emphasis. He points out that men have as many negative identity problems to resolve as women and that society should foster choices, and these choices are free only when made with a "minimum of denial and guilt and with a maximum of insight and conviction" (243). He reiterates his choice of the word *generativity* over "procreativity" or "productivity" to signify a variety of activities beside parenthood or making money; any activities which "contribute to the life of the generations" (243).

Sheehy discovered an interesting discrepancy between men and women in the area of generativity. About the time women turn to productivity through things and career, men often realize the lack of generative functions in the affiliative realm. As the family becomes of less importance to women, men just begin to realize that being president of a company is meaningless unless he has a family or at least a philanthropic cause.

As a person adapts herself to take care of things and people she moves toward ego integrity. If this ego integrity is lacking one has an acute fear of death, which is heightened by the sense of having little time left. This time awareness is a significant characteristic, not only of the elderly, but of many mid-life individuals as well and often results in significant readjustments of priorities.

Carl G. Jung also focused on the ego and the need for it to be well integrated in order to confront the demands of the self in mid-life (Corsini 1977). Jung differentiates between the individuating processes of infancy and childhood and the individuation proper, which occurs in middle age and is related typically to life crises. He is actually a forerunner of Erikson and the first theorist to study older adults and their personality development. He postulates the normalcy of a mid-life crisis, which leads to greater self-actualization from an active struggle for increased psychic differentiation and synthesis. It is necessary here to understand the relationship between the ego and the self. The self refers to the totality of personality while the ego is one's sense of self-identity. The conscious portion of the ego assists in the integration and manifestation of the total self. In later life a dialogue between the ego and the self occurs, which is the psychodynamic process of individuation. While in early adulthood the concern is with gaining freedom from mother and childhood, in the second half of life the concern is to let go of the internal ego strivings and more youthful defenses.

One additional conceptualization of Jung's is especially pertinent to our concern for mid-life women. He believed both men and women are basically androgynous and therefore able to experience both masculine and feminine aspects of their personalities. He spoke of the anima (potential to experience the image of woman) in man, and the animus (potential to experience the image of man) in woman. Growth is limited by the repression of the animus in women and is realized only with an increasing consciousness of their masculine (animus) component.

The Crises in Mid-Life Women

The family is the organizing theme for a woman's life, no matter what her actual life experiences and relationships are. It has been argued that there are two distinct classes of women: the wife and mother and the professional woman. The two are merging more and more in our present world. The fact remains that love is the essential driving force for women. Women always need some person to do things for and this personal love is the secret of women's success in any field (de Castillejo 1973).

We can observe this in an interesting clinical phenomenon. Depression of pathological proportions is often seen in a woman who experiences the loss of her husband at about the same time her children are leaving home and no longer needing her to do things for them. It is easy to see the connection here between the depression, the perceived losses, and the resulting paucity of meaning. What is more difficult to explain is the depression of similar magnitude which we see in the woman who has a long-standing professional career who has experienced similar losses. As therapy uncovers the dynamics and the grieving process it becomes apparent that to the same degree both classes of women have their self-identity centered on the roles of wife and mother.

Current evangelical church dogma emphasizes the value of the maternal and marital roles for women. Woman's most sacred purpose is fulfilled as she becomes a mother and her entire life is to be spent helping her husband become what he should be. A balance regarding other significant roles was long ago lost, as was the value of the paternal and marital role for men. This explains why the described phenomenon is apparently more of a problem for Christian women, although the potential danger exists for any woman who marries. To the degree that marriage is looked at as the source of total satisfaction (Harding 1970), a danger exists that the end of a marriage will mean an end of meaning. Even single women sometimes point to the absence of a marriage partner as the reason for their unhappiness. They also view marriage as a potential panacea. Women need to believe throughout their lives in their ability to make contributions other than those channeled through their children and husband.

Erikson emphasized a wide range of generative activities but there seems to exist a value hierarchy within our society which greatly limits the meaning given to care-taking functions outside the family. Intrapsychically, women accordingly deny other parts of themselves. The anima woman attempts to act, think, and feel only as a feminine (eros) being. This requires a denial and repression of the animus or masculine principle (logos), which Jung associates with factual knowledge and wisdom (Harding 1970). It would seem that some women allow themselves to use the masculine or logos only as long as they are attached to a man. This is an unconscious process. When they are confronted at the time of their spouse's death with the obvious necessity to produce from the animus, they are not aware of the possibility. They projected the animus totally onto their mate and they lack consciousness of an animus that lies within.

From this understanding the goal for therapy with these women evolves quite naturally. We will not be concerned here with grief work. That must precede the bringing to consciousness of the other part of the self. With women who have been functioning in the world of work it is usually not difficult to point out the strengths they are already using, and then help clients consciously accept this as a part of themselves. However, women who have the logos more deeply buried are resistant to accepting and expressing this part consciously. These women need to do some uncovering of the unconscious process to become aware of their strengths. It is necessary to interpret the projective process in relation to the husband so the woman can reintegrate those projected characteristics. Once she begins to acknowledge the strengths, the woman must give herself permission to use them. This may call for an examination of her sex role stereotypes and the realization that she can be feminine at the same time as she is making mature, adult decisions as part of the process of caring for herself and others.

Women who are able to move through this transition and then able to be alone comfortably, rechannel their creative energy and use their inner resources to pursue their own aims. This is the process of individuation, through which a person becomes more uniquely an individual (Levinson 1978). This task of separation is confronted as children move out of the family, a process which revives old memories and earlier conflicts from the woman's own adolescent separation. This is in turn compounded by the death of the woman's parents or at least the recognition that they will eventually die. Women are more dependent than men on these relationships as affecting what happens developmentally. As the specific childbearing functions near an end, the development of occupational skill may begin, along with more potential for self-expression and autonomy. But these real losses must be reckoned with to facilitate working through the meaning of each separation.

There is new-found freedom here as a person reduces the demands of society as well as the repressed inner demands. This permits self-definition and self-satisfaction, an uncovering of what is often termed the authentic self. Obviously if a woman is living her life through another or feels she is living out someone else's life (her own parents), she will never experience life with this kind of personal meaning and awareness. This totally changes one's perspective (and is at least consistent with the description in Colossians 3:9–10: "You have taken off your old self with its practices and have put on the new self, which is being renewed in knowledge in the image of its Creator" [NIV]) of what it means to become a new person, with our focus only on the Lord rather than any other person.

A comment is needed concerning those women who do not marry and/or do not raise a family. The crisis points are experienced differently and yet there are parallels. The single woman reaches a point where she realizes she will never have children, often about the time children are becoming more independent in a mother's life. Thus, she experiences the loss of potential if she has conversely not developed (the expression of the more feminine eros) in ways other than procreation. She does have the advantage often of having a greater sense of her personal competence and worth. In a study which compared married professional women with equally gifted homemakers who were not working, I. K. Broverman (1975) found that professional women had more positive self-images and a higher level of satisfaction and feeling of competence. So there may be advantages centering around self-esteem for the woman who is not a mother.

The menopause is probably the most consistent mid-life event in the lives of women. This event is now understood as a simplistic explanation for depression. If depression occurs it is usually a response to the loss of the reproductive capacity and the transition to aging. As such it more frequently occurs in women who have invested heavily in the childbearing role (Notman 1978). The reaction to menopause can best be understood in the context of an entire life and more specifically the reaction to puberty. The woman who sees herself as primarily, if not solely, a mother has the most to lose with menopause.

The curve of men rises to the height of power, as a gradual incline followed by a decline. However, woman blossoms in the spring but the summer plateau is a period of slow ripening and the giving of much nourishment. As she approaches autumn she is filled with fruit ready to be picked and used. A conscious woman realizes all the ways in which her life is beginning at fifty rather than ending. However, for every crisis period there is the possibility of growth being retarded and interrupted.

It is important not only to consider effective therapy for women in mid-life crisis, but to think about prevention as well. As Erikson pointed out, we know that insufficiently mastered tasks at any stage of development will present problems during future periods. We seem to be dealing with two primary hurdles in the mid-life woman. The first has to do with a sense of autonomy based on a sense of being "all right" as oneself (Erikson 1950). This paves the way for all the future separations, which can be successfully handled only with a sense of individual integrity and competence. If a girl is encouraged to be totally dependent she will encounter difficulty as she loses those people close to her. Young women often go directly from parents who make all the decisions to a husband who makes all the decisions. The solution to this lies in encouraging women to make independent decisions before marriage, followed by the establishment of an egalitarian marriage relationship. This brings us to the second hurdle, one having to do with sex-role stereotypes. In general, dichotomous concepts of sex-role are not adaptive or facilitative if one has a clear sense of gender identity (Lerner 1978). Stereotyped notions about femininity have a constricting effect at any age. If a girl has been raised this way she will undoubtedly carry the constriction of her personhood into middle adulthood. For many Christian women this takes on the quality of being Christ-like. Many recent publications have said the role of a Christian woman should be a submissive one, reflecting a sweet, feminine countenance. The goal of this submission is to win the protection of the "stronger" man (Zabriskie 1976). This makes it difficult for a woman to develop a sense of self with its accompanying strengths. However, in a relationship of mutual submission (Eph. 5:21) and mutual vulnerability, both people experience and exercise their unique gifts and develop a sense of being worthwhile. This will be true whether their personalities are predominantly masculine or feminine according to our present cultural stereotypes. Thus, the mid-life crisis will be less traumatic to women who already have established a feeling of individuality based on their created uniqueness and a sense of intrinsic worth.

The challenge to psychotherapists is to work with women effectively, regardless of age. Certain guidelines need to be followed, as clearly elucidated by the American Psychological Association (*American Psychologist* [1978]: 1122–23). The main theme in these "Guidelines for Therapy with Women" seems to be freedom. The therapist needs to be free of misconceptions and stereotypes in order to facilitate the woman's freedom to grow and make free choices. These choices will be truly free only when they are made with a "minimum of denial and guilt and with a maximum of insight and conviction" (Erikson 1975, 243).

15

Religious Ritual and the Excommunication of Ann Hibbens

DONALD CAPPS

Psychologists of religion have paid less attention to religious rituals than almost any other form or expression of religion (Capps, Ransohoff, and Rambo 1976). William James and his followers have never had much to do with religious ritual. James identified two basic forms of religion, the personal and the institutional, and suggested that personal religion involves people's direct and immediate transactions with the divine, while institutional religion depends on external ritual acts: "Worship and sacrifice, procedures for working on the dispositions of the deity, theology and ceremony and ecclesiastical organization, are the essentials of religion in the institutional branch. Were we to limit our view to it, we should have to define religion as an external art, the art of winning the favor of the gods." He is far more favorable toward religion whose acts of devotion "are personal not ritual acts, the individual transacts the business by himself alone, and the ecclesiastical organization, with its priest and sacraments and other go-betweens, sinks to an altogether secondary place. The relation goes direct from heart to heart, from soul to soul, between man and his maker" (1958, 41).

Gordon W. Allport, who stands more or less in the Jamesian tradition, concurred with James's view of ritual, saying that "the first apparently religious responses of the child are not religious at all, but wholly social in character. They consist at first of trifling habits such as bowing the head or folding the hands, and soon after of learning to repeat simple prayers or hymns" (1950, 28–29).

These comments by James and Allport concerning religious ritual indicate that they have avoided the study of ritual not merely because rituals are social and therefore fall in the province of sociology rather than psychology of religion, but because ritual acts are external and inherently inferior to direct and immediate religious experience.

In contrast to the Jamesians, Freudians have paid much more attention to religious rituals. However, most of their studies have been based on Sigmund Freud's view (1953, 1959) that religious rituals are similar to neurotic obsessions. This reliance on Freud's theory of religious ritual persists even though his theory has been shown to have serious flaws (Gay 1975) and in spite of the fact that religious rituals lend themselves to comparison with other repeated behaviors that are not inherently neurotic but adaptive. In the psychoanalytic tradition itself, concepts are available for comparing religious rituals to repeated behaviors that are genuinely adaptive. Heinz Hartmann's notion of the automatism (1958), Ernest J. Schachtel's concept of the focal object (1959) and Donald W. Winnicott's concept of the transitional object (1958) are but a few examples. Paul N. Pruyser's application of Winnicott's concept of the transitional object to religious rituals (1974) and Gay's analysis of the public recitation of the Lord's Prayer by means of Hartmann's theory of adaptation (Gay 1978) show that psychoanalytic concepts can be successfully employed in this fashion. It is also noteworthy that these concepts are derived largely from observation of children's ritual behaviors. Thus, application of these concepts to religious ritual involves comparing religious rituals to the ritual behavior that occurs in the normal adaptive growth of the child.

Another approach to the psychology of religious ritual that draws on child development is Erik Erikson's theory. Other psychoanalytic theorists developed concepts of repeated behaviors applicable to religious ritual, while Erikson applied his developmental theory. Moreover, though Freudian in general orientation, his studies of the rituals of Native Americans (1963), his theoretical essays on ritual (1966, 1977b), and his discussions of ritual and political leadership (1968, 1969, 1977b) add up to a major reformulation of the traditional psychoanalytic view of religious ritual.

Central to this reformulation is the view that human ritual behavior is rooted in the life cycle. More precisely, the first four life stages are the "ontological sources" of the major elements of human ritualization. The major elements of all social ritualizations, including religious rituals, are experienced in infancy and early childhood. Thus, the ritual element of the numinous is rooted in the trust versus mistrust stage;

the judicial in the autonomy versus shame and self-doubt stage; the dramatic in the initiative versus guilt stage; and the formal in the industry versus inferiority stage (1977a, 85–106).

In locating ritual behavior in the life stages, especially the earliest four, Erikson provides a conceptual basis for viewing all societal forms of ritual as continuous with normal human growth. These four ritual elements enable a person to cope with certain life problems, and they also help the society cope with these same problems. On the other hand, Erikson recognizes that rituals, whether those of childhood or adulthood, individual or social, can be used to excess. They can become ends in themselves rather than means of coping with enduring problems. When this happens, rituals assume the obsessive character that Freud observed when comparing religious rituals to neurotic obsessions.

Table 15.1 schematizes Erikson's theory of ritual by identifying its basic components. Column A lists the four life stages. Column B indicates the ritual elements corresponding to each of these stages. Column C identifies the basic life problem that each ritual element addresses. Column D indicates the ritual excess to which each ritual element is subject.[1]

Unfortunately, this highly suggestive theory of ritual has not generated much research. Erikson's own analysis of the Sun Dance of the

Table 15.1

Correlation of Life Stages and Ritual Elements

Life Stages	Ritual Elements	Life Problem	Ritual Excess
Trust vs. mistrust	Numinous	Separation and abandonment	Idolism[1]
Autonomy vs. shame and self-doubt	Judicial	Approval and disapproval	Legalism[2]
Initiative vs. guilt	Dramatic	Self-image and patterns of emulation	Impersonation[3]
Industry vs. inferiority	Formal	Work and cooperation	Formalism[4]

[1] Manipulation of object of devotion

[2] Victory of letter over spirit

[3] Pretending to possess personal qualities of personage represented

[4] Excessive reliance on techniques and methods

1. Besides these four ritual elements, Erikson proposes the graduational, generational, and integrational elements to correspond to the stages of adolescence, adulthood, and old age. They have not been included in the chart because it is unclear whether they are additional ritual elements or simply new ways of appropriating the four basic ritual elements established in childhood.

Dakota Sioux (1977a, 147–53) illustrates the theory's potential for research on religious rituals; it supports his view that the numinous element of ritual is rooted dynamically in the trust versus mistrust stage. But this is only one study, and Erikson carried it out prior to his systematic formulation of the theory.

The present study applies Erikson's theory to another religious ritual, the excommunication of Ann Hibbens from the First Church of Boston in 1640–41. This church trial enables us to explore the correlation of the judicial form of ritualization with the autonomy versus shame and self-doubt stage. As a judicial-type ritual, the trial focused on the problems of approval and disapproval and succumbed to the excess of legalism.

The Trial of Ann Hibbens

The proceedings against Ann Hibbens were recorded verbatim by one of the members of the First Church of Boston (Keaynes 1972). I summarize this material before applying Erikson's theory of ritual to it.

What precipitated the trial was Ann Hibbens's quarrel with a carpenter she had hired to make furniture in her house. The carpenter had agreed to do the work for a certain price, but she asked him to do some additional work for which she agreed to pay extra. When he presented the total bill, she complained that it was excessive. Another carpenter, a member of First Church of Boston where Mrs. Hibbens was also a member, was called in to arbitrate, and he arrived at a negotiated figure. This figure satisfied the original carpenter and Mr. Hibbens, a wealthy merchant, but was unsatisfactory to Mrs. Hibbens. She contended that the two carpenters had acted in collusion, that the negotiator had arrived at the figure the two carpenters had agreed on in advance. The negotiator vigorously denied this accusation and brought charges of defamation of character against her before the whole church body. If sustained, these charges would result in her excommunication.

The Censure Phase

The excommunication proceedings began with these charges being formally lodged against Mrs. Hibbens by the carpenter. The minister, Rev. John Cotton, asked her to respond to the charges, and when she refused to answer, the focus of the proceedings shifted from the original charge against her to this act of impertinence. A supporter argued that she remained silent because it was unlawful for women to speak in the church, but Rev. Cotton replied that "it is lawful for a woman to speak when she is asked a question." He noted the lateness of the hour, however, and terminated the meeting.

When the proceedings resumed the following Lord's Day, Mr.

Hibbens apologized for calling a brother "sir" during the previous week's trial. Pastor Cotton said he hoped Mr. Hibbens's contrition in a small matter would prompt Mrs. Hibbens to demonstrate the same contrition for her much larger sin. When she rose to speak, she did confess to impropriety in her failure to respond to the charges lodged against her the previous week. But she contended that she was not guilty of the original charges and asked to be allowed to respond to these charges in writing. Her request was rejected by Rev. Cotton on the grounds that it lacked scriptural precedent, and the pastor strongly admonished her to proceed immediately with her response to the charges because the church had other pressing business to attend to and this trial had already taken longer than planned.

Ann Hibbens proceeded with her defense, arguing that she had not acted out of self-interest but was protesting the high prices charged by the village craftsmen. This defense angered the congregational leaders. As the pastor put it, "All this you now relate is only to excuse yourself, and lessen your own fault, and lay blame upon others." An elder said that everything she had spoken "tends not to any measure of repentance or sorrow for her sin." Another said that her worst crime was to take the issue in her own hands and not allow her husband to handle the dispute with the carpenters, "as if she were able to manage it better than her husband, which is a plain breach of the rule of Christ." After a number of similar speeches, the pastor proceeded with his charge against her. The decision was to censure rather than formally excommunicate her. This decision was intended to give her opportunity to repent in the weeks ahead.

The Excommunication Phase

Five months after being censured, Ann Hibbens was again brought before the church because her subsequent behavior reflected an unrepentant spirit. The major evidence introduced to support this latest charge was her public criticism of the church's handling of the earlier trial against her. The pastor and elders decided no useful purpose would be served by allowing her more time to repent because "all her speeches hath tended to excuse herself and to lay all blame upon others—as upon our honored Magistrate Mr. Winthrop, upon our Elders and the revered elders of other churches. . . ." It was again pointed out by one parishioner that Mrs. Hibbens had usurped her husband's authority. When the pastor observed that she had claimed that her husband consented to her dealing with the carpenters Mr. Hibbens said that he had initially given her permission to deal with the carpenters but when the dispute with the negotiator developed, he tried to get her to accept the negotiated price and "had some exercise of spirit with her, that she hath not done so." This confession from Mr. Hibbens, prompted by his desire to defend himself against charges that she had made a "wisp of her husband," was the last straw. The elders immediately called for excommunication. The pastor, without further delay, delivered a lengthy and vitriolic excommunication pronouncement. The proceedings ended with Mr. Hibbens expressing the hope that his wife would someday be restored to the church.

While our analysis focuses only on the trial itself, it should be noted that when Mr. Hibbens died in 1654, Mrs. Hibbens lost the protection his influence in the community had provided for her. Two years after his death, she was convicted in the courts on a charge of witchcraft and was sentenced to death. The evidence presented in court in support of the witchcraft charge was that she had an uncanny ability to hear what her neighbors were saying when they were out of normal hearing range. She was one of only five or six persons executed for witchcraft in New England prior to the witchcraft hysteria that broke out in Salem in 1692, thirty-six years later (K. T. Erikson 1966, 154).

The Judicial-Type Ritual

The task now is to show how the trial against Ann Hibbens fits Erikson's theory of ritual. Since my argument is that the trial is a judicial-type ritual, dynamically rooted in the autonomy versus shame and self-doubt stage, a brief description of this stage and its corresponding ritual element precedes my analysis of the trial.

The Autonomy Versus Shame and Self-Doubt Stage

In this stage of the life cycle, the still highly dependent child acquires a range of cognitive, muscular, and locomotor capacities. These capacities, together with readiness for increased interaction with other people, give the child greater pleasure in exerting his autonomous will. The child's relationship to parents is likely to manifest itself in periods of "guerilla warfare of unequal wills" (Erikson [1959] 1980, 66). But this "test of wills" need not result in an unhealthy stalemate if parents steer a middle course between breaking the child's will and capitulating to it. Through firmness, parents protect the child against "the potential anarchy of his as yet untrained sense of discrimination . . . and against meaningless and arbitrary experiences of shame and of early doubt" (Erikson 1963, 252). Thus, autonomy means the freedom to express one's will within certain necessary boundaries and constraints.

Of the two meaningless and arbitrary experiences in this stage, self-doubt is best known to us because it takes quite observable forms of self-manipulation and obsessive behavior. Shame is more difficult to identify because it tends to be absorbed by guilt. Nonetheless, one distinguishing feature of shame is that, like self-doubt, it is directed against oneself. The impulse to bury one's face or sink into the ground is essentially rage turned against the self. The child who is ashamed wishes the world would look away and not notice his exposure. But when this does not happen, the child turns against himself in a desire for invisibility.

On the other hand, this rage turned against oneself undergoes a reversal when the child has been shamed beyond endurance. The child then becomes stubbornly defiant. To illustrate this defiance, Erikson cites the traditional ballad in which a murderer about to be hanged before the whole community begins to berate his onlookers, ending every salvo of defiance with the words, "God damn your eyes" (1963, 253). Here, rage is expressed outwardly in the form of hostile defiance.

The Judicial Form of Ritual

Erikson contends that the judicial type of ritual has its "ontological source" in this autonomy versus shame and self-doubt stage. If parental firmness is necessary to protect the child against the potential anarchy of his untrained will, the judicial form of ritual defines and maintains the boundaries within which individuals are free to exercise their will. These socially sanctioned boundaries are most dramatically reaffirmed in the trial.

The trial is also a dramatic example of how the judicial-type ritual may fail in its adaptive function of transmitting workable boundaries from generation to generation. Such failures occur when the trial employs inappropriate or ineffective shaming tactics, and when it encourages in the citizenry the excessive self-manipulation and obsessive compliance of self-doubt. In the case of shaming, the trial's use of sensational voyeurism and moralistic sadism is likely to increase "the hopeless isolation of the culprit and can aggravate an impotent rage which will only make him more 'shameless.'" In the case of self-doubt, the trial's tendency toward legalism, the victory of the letter over the spirit of the law, encourages a "vain display of righteousness or empty contrition or . . . a moralistic insistence on exposing and isolating the culprit whether or not this will be good for him or anybody else" (1977b, 96–97). Thus the adaptive function of the judicial-type ritual is its reaffirmation of workable boundaries within which the will has sanction to operate. But this adaptive function is threatened when rituals based on the judicial model use shaming devices that encourage defiance, or when they encourage compliance that is self-manipulative and obsessive instead of autonomous.

The Use of Shame in the Trial of Ann Hibbens

Our analysis of the trial against Ann Hibbens begins with the matter of shame, because the most dramatic feature of the trial was its shift from the dynamics of guilt to those of shame as the trial progressed. Issues of sin, guilt, and repentance were prominent at the formal level of deliberation throughout the proceedings. But when it became obvious that Mrs. Hibbens would not repent and lay herself on the mercy of the church, the underlying dynamics of shame began to dominate. In the proceedings that led up to her censure, some parishioners expressed the desire to "help on the work of humiliation upon her heart," and one added that he did so because she sought to "hide" her sin. Also, the pastor preached his sermon just prior to beginning the trial on "hypocritical humiliation" and in his opening statements encouraged her to "take shame to your own face" and "abase yourself." But it was not until the excommunication phase of the trial, five months later, that the pastor and elders took upon themselves the task of shaming her. One parishioner, for example, compared her to Moses' sister Miriam,

> who rose up against Moses and Aaron [and] whose leprosy appeared in the face of the congregation. And there was a law for lepers that the priest should search and view them; and if upon the search they found leprosy appearing, the priest was to pronounce them lepers, and then they were healed of that disease for the [sake of the] congregation and the society of God's people. As this Sister hath been diligently searched and viewed and upon the search she is found leprous and diverse spots are risen and do manifestly appear to the congregation, therefore, according to the law of God, I think she ought to be pronounced unclean and as a leprous person to be put out from amongst us.

Rev. Cotton joined in shaming her when, in his final excommunication pronouncement, he concluded:

> I do here . . . pronounce you to be a leprous and unclean person. . . . You have scorned counsel and refused instruction and have like a filthy swine trampled those pearls under your feet. . . . And so as an unclean beast and unfit for the society of God's people, I do from this time forward pronounce you an excommunicated person from God and His people.

The fact that there were various statements of this sort during the excommunication phase of the trial indicates that shaming had come to dominate a judicial process that was ostensibly concerned to determine her guilt.

The major reason for the shaming is not difficult to identify. In the first phase of the trial, the congregational leaders were impatient with Ann Hibbens's efforts to defend herself against the carpenter's charges, but they held their anger in check. However, when the trial resumed five months later, they were in no mood to exhibit restraint. This change in attitude can be attributed to the fact that she had subsequently criticized the church's treatment of her in the earlier proceedings, and had done so publicly. Thus, in his excommunication pronouncement, Rev. Cotton observed that "the wise providence of God" had seen to it that persons from other churches were witnesses of the proceedings and "are gone home fully satisfied, being very sorry . . . that they were so inclinable to harken to [Mrs. Hibbens] and to entertain the least thought of jealousy against our church or any member in it."

Clearly, the pastor and elders were extremely sensitive about her criticism of their disciplinary procedures. The shame they heaped on her was for her temerity in criticizing the church's disciplinary actions in censuring her. One elder complained that her attack on the church's handling of her case indicates that she presumes to sit "in the throne of God Himself" and "hath usurped authority over her guide and head," namely, the pastor. Another said that her attack against the church was indicative of "the great obdurateness of her heart."

Why was the church so sensitive about her criticisms of its disciplinary actions? Why did these criticisms make them heap shame on her? An answer that relates directly to the issue of autonomy versus shame and self-doubt can be found in Puritan child-rearing practices. As John Demos points out (1970), in Puritan families the infant was treated indulgently for a period of roughly a year. Then, in the second year (during the autonomy versus shame and self-doubt stage), the child was subjected to weaning, the arrival of a younger sibling, and, most important of all, a radical shift toward a harsh and restrictive style of discipline having one primary object, that is, to curb and even break the child's "willfulness" as soon as it first began to appear. In these disciplinary procedures, shame and humiliation, rather than severe physical punishment, were employed to curb and break the child's will.

In a similar way, the pastor and elders were content in the first phase of the trial to curb Ann Hibbens's will by means of censorship. When this did not work, the second phase of the trial focused on breaking her will. As Demos shows, the prescribed method for doing this was shaming the child into submission. But whether the parents attempted to break or merely curb the child's will, it was essential that they maintain authority over the child. It was precisely this authority, especially as vested in the pastor, that Ann Hibbens chose to resist. In challenging the validity of the church's disciplinary methods, she threatened the very core of its authority. In retaliation, the pastor and elders heaped verbal shame on her and, in so doing, employed the most severe disciplinary measure available to Puritan parents. The trial had become a reenactment of early parent-child conflicts.

While Ann Hibbens was undoubtedly concerned about the excessive prices charged by Boston craftsmen, her delaying tactics in the early phase of the trial (refusing to speak when called on, requesting permission to put her response to the charges in writing) indicate that she, too, was being drawn into a "test of wills" between parent and child. Participants in the trial were no longer concerned with a dispute between a carpenter and a housewife, but rather they were engaged in a dramatic reenactment of the test of wills between parent and child. While most parishioners seem to have accepted Pastor Cotton's initial decision merely to "curb" her will, perhaps because they secretly identified with her refusal to put on a display of false contrition, this relatively benevolent mood quickly wore thin when they realized that her public criticism of the censorship proceedings meant that she would have the child sitting on the throne, deciding which parental sanctions to honor and which to ignore. In effect, Ann Hibbens was challenging the society's prescribed resolution of the "guerilla warfare" between the wills of parents and children, that the child's will must be subdued and, if necessary, crushed. But this effort to shame her into submission did not succeed. It merely reinforced her determination to remain in silent defiance of the church leaders' authority.

The Effects of Self-Doubt in the Trial of Ann Hibbens

Could the trial have been handled more effectively by Rev. Cotton? Could there have been a different resolution of the conflict, one that would honor the society's concern to place appropriate limits on the individual wills of its citizenry but at the same time insure the autonomy of persons like Ann Hibbens? The original account of the trial indicates that Rev. Cotton was not unkindly disposed toward Mrs. Hibbens, that he hoped for her sake as well as the church's that a quick and positive resolution of the issue could be reached. Moreover, his original decision to censure rather than excommunicate her indicates that he preferred to follow a course of moderation. Yet, at the end of the trial, he was thundering at her in a diatribe, comparing her to lepers and swine.

In asking how the ritual might have gone differently, I am not attempting to rewrite history in a more positive vein. My concern is to ascertain whether Erikson's theory helps determine why the ritual failed to carry out its adaptive function. Why was the trial maladaptive for the individuals involved? The theory would suggest that it failed because it succumbed to legalism, the victory of the letter over the spirit, in matters pertaining to the conflict of autonomy versus shame and self-doubt. In exploring this suggestion, I will focus especially on the role that Rev. Cotton played in the trial.

How could Rev. Cotton have retained his original intention of dealing fairly with Mrs. Hibbens in spite of her own resistance to his authority and the hostility of many of the church elders toward her? The key to an alternative resolution of the conflict is the fact that this was a judicial-type ritual, and Rev. Cotton's prescribed role was that of judge. His formal task as judge was to determine Mrs. Hibbens's guilt in defaming the carpenter's character. Given his role as judge, it could be argued that the whole affair would have gone differently had he not allowed a dispute of relatively small magnitude (an argument over furniture) develop into a situation in which the axiomatic values of the society were at stake. Undoubtedly, there are occasions in every society's history when these values need to be tested, challenged, and reaffirmed. But it is questionable whether the dispute between the carpenters and Mrs. Hibbens ought to have been one of those occasions. It seems plausible to suggest, therefore, that Rev. Cotton erred in allowing the dynamics of shame, always subliminally present in these types of proceedings, to become explicit, overloading a simple test of guilt with the more volatile and, for this society, more fundamental overtones of shame.

If allowing the matter of shame to dominate the trial was unfortunate from a tactical standpoint, it is also the case that shame and guilt were so deeply intertwined in Puritan social relationships and worldview that it would have been virtually impossible to maintain a clear demarcation of shame and guilt throughout the proceedings. For example, Rev. Cotton frequently confounded these two dynamics when he pleaded with Mrs. Hibbens to confess her guilt. He called on her to "abase yourself, and take shame to your own face, and freely and openly and readily confess the faults and sins and offences." The implication here is that shame is the outward sign of a true confession of guilt. How was the church to determine whether Mrs. Hibbens was genuinely repentant? The most reliable means of determining this was external evidence that she was ashamed of what she had done. Repentance should have shown on her face. It should have been possible for onlookers to witness, in her demeanor, a desire to bury her face or sink into the ground. In trying to defend his wife, Mr. Hibbens pointed out that she had made a partial confession of guilt to the offended carpenter, "confessing her error with tears." Tears are one means of taking shame on one's face in an outward expression of inward repentance. Thus it seems unrealistic to expect that Rev. Cotton could have ruled all references to shame out of order.

On the other hand, the trial could have taken a different direction if Rev. Cotton had insisted on a more discriminating use of the language and imagery of shame. The trial appears to manifest such discrimination in that the trial account reflects the penchant for splitting hairs typical of Puritan trial narratives (K. T. Erikson 1966, 103). But this is merely an illusion of precision and discrimination of thought that is not there in fact. As we saw earlier, Erikson suggests that self-doubt is reflected in a tendency to overmanipulate oneself, to become obsessive in thought and behavior. Without suggesting that Puritan theology and polity are inherently obsessive, we can say that in the context of a trial, legalistic or obsessive thinking is likely to be accorded a certain prestige it might not command in other contexts. Hence, the ritual proved susceptible to the excess of legalistic thinking.

An example of such legalistic thinking that results directly in the use of shaming is one parishioner's attempt to relate the case of Mrs. Hibbens to the early Hebrews' handling of the problem of leprosy. This essentially spurious connection between biblical ideas and the present experience was accomplished by means of an allegorical interpretation of the story of Miriam. Metaphors portraying Ann Hibbens as a leper or as a filthy swine before whom the church's pearls had been cast indicate the congregation's anxiety to gain mastery over the ambiguity this case had aroused, and metaphors were valuable means of doing just that. But these particular metaphors grossly oversimplified the complexity of the situation and therefore were poor and imprecise efforts to give the situation meaning. In addition, they demeaned the trial by introducing an element of "moralistic sadism" that could only intensify the defendant's determination to defy her accusers.

An extended metaphor that would have been more reflective of the situation, and more appropriate to the pastor's desire to resolve the conflict in a positive manner, is Jesus' parable of the unscrupulous judge and the importunate widow. In this parable, the judge continues to refuse the widow's request for money owed to her and then finally relents, saying, "Maybe I have neither fear of God nor respect for man, but since she keeps pestering me I must give this widow her just rights, or she will persist in coming and worry me to death" (Luke 18:4–5 JB). This parable has application to Mrs. Hibbens's behavior both toward the carpenters and in the trial itself. Like the widow in the parable, she was a persistent woman who would not let Rev. Cotton off the hook by being appropriately penitent so that the congregation could settle the issue and go home. But the judge in the parable eventually concluded that it would do neither himself nor the widow any good to continue this "test of wills." By insisting on demonstrating his greater determination, the judge will lose in the long run because the woman will "worry him to death."

Suppose that Rev. Cotton had told the congregation that he often felt placed in the position of a judge whose suppliants would persist, if he permitted it, in worrying him to death. Suppose he then refused to censure or excommunicate Mrs. Hibbens not because her innocence had been established but simply because he is not her parental judge but her pastor. As pastor, his responsibility is not to engage in the task of breaking the will of this persistent woman but to help her learn to deal more effectively with the frustrations of life in a small town.

From this refusal to be her parental judge, he might propose a number of alternative courses of action. He and Mrs. Hibbens could discuss the problem privately (a pastoral counseling approach). He could arrange a conference between the carpenters, Mr. and Mrs. Hibbens, and himself (an administrative approach). He and the elders, together with Mrs. Hibbens, might discuss the matter of the local carpenters' price structures with a representative group of craftsmen and businessmen in the community (a social action approach). He might even propose the formation of a discussion group for husbands of wives who, as one male parishioner put it, think they are "able to manage better" than their husbands (an institutional approach). The pastor's refusal to be "worried to death" by contentiousness of this sort makes these approaches possible. Moreover, these alternative courses of action would express the pastor's conviction that the church's and his own authority are firmly enough established that they need not crush the will of one of the church's members to prove it. They would not need to act from self-doubt.

In terms of Erikson's life cycle theory and its corresponding ritual elements, this resolution of the problem can be schematized as follows: The trial began as an attempt to determine guilt (the third stage of the life cycle) but instead regressed to the level of shame (the second stage). The alternative resolution proposed here would involve terminating this regressive move before it began to shape the outcome of the trial by introducing a progressive movement. This would take the form of the fourth stage of the life cycle (industry versus inferiority) with its ritual element of the "formal" or "methodical performance." The various courses of action, I have proposed (pastoral counseling, administrative action, social action, and institutional programming) would fall under the heading of "methodical performance."

This alternative resolution of the Hibbens controversy does not mean merely replacing ritual with other types of social activity, but it means shifting at a critical juncture in the dispute from judicial to formal ritual, which issues in the "methodical performance." The formal ritual and the religious role that enacts it—the pastoral role—may not be as emotionally cathartic to participants as the judicial ritual and its corresponding role of the parental judge. But, in being farther along in the developmental cycle, it is better adapted to life beyond the family circle, that is, in the neighborhood, which is the pastor's more appropriate locus of influence and authority.

Does this alternative resolution of the problem obscure the real differences between the Puritan and modern minister? Do the specific proposals made here require a more sophisticated understanding of the ministry and its various functions than was available to Rev. Cotton in the Puritan period? Perhaps. Yet, it should be noted that Rev. Cotton was confronted with challenges that differ only in degree, not in kind, from the challenges of ministry today. This case threatened his personal authority, the church's harmonious functioning and normal operating procedures, and its relations in the community. These threats are not peculiar to the Puritan period. Moreover, the courses of action were available to him at some time in his ministry. It simply did not occur to him, or to the church elders, that these actions would be appropriate to the case at hand. I am suggesting that the reason for this is that, when threatened, the minister and church leaders allowed obsessional thought processes to overwhelm a judicial ritual with legalistic excess.

Ritual Elements and Types of Religious Authority

The foregoing analysis of the trial of Ann Hibbens invites recognition of the relationship between Erikson's ritual elements and types of religious authority. I alluded to this relationship in contrasting the roles of judge and pastor. In my view, each of Erikson's four types of ritual has a parallel type of religious authority: certain types of religious authority encourage certain types of ritual, and certain types of ritual encourage their corresponding authority structures. Correspondences between ritual elements and types of religious authority are represented in table 15.2. The types of authority are derived from various classifications of authority types (Wach 1944, Weber 1963, Eliade 1967, Schoeps 1968). The types corresponding to each of the ritual elements are not exhaustive, merely illustrative. Moreover, space does not allow for a rationale for each of these proposed correspondences. Still, the table helps to identify the authority structures that occur in rituals based on each of the four ritual elements. The chart can also be viewed in relation to table 15.1 in order to determine the life problems (col-

Table 15.2

Ritual Elements and Types of Religious Authority

Life Stages	Ritual Elements	Authority Types
Trust vs. mistrust	Numinous	Mystic, seer, shaman, magician
Autonomy vs. shame and self-doubt	Judicial	Saint, martyr, judge, sage
Initiative vs. guilt	Dramatic	Prophet, evangelist, reformer
Industry vs. inferiority	Formal	Pastor, priest, rabbi, teacher

umn C) with which each type of religious authority is particularly concerned, and the ritual excesses to which each is most likely to succumb (column D).

However, the major value of these proposed correspondences between ritual elements and types of religious authority is that they demonstrate how religious rituals can be used to explore the interrelationships between psychological dynamics and social structures in religious life. Erikson's major criticism of Freud's view of religious ritual is that Freud's comparison of religious ritual and neurotic obsession failed to see that the latter is a private ritual with highly idiosyncratic meanings (1966). By contrast, Erikson's theory of ritual takes special account of the social nature of religious ritual. Thus, these correlations of ritual elements and types of religious authority provide a means of bridging the gap between the psychologist's concern for psychological dynamics and the sociologist's interest in larger social structures. Erikson's theory of ritual indicates that the place of religious ritual in the scientific study of religion may prove analogous to the role of family studies in the social sciences inasmuch as both stand at the intersection of psychological dynamics and social structures.

In concluding, I would note that in his recognition of four ritual elements, Erikson takes seriously the variety of ways that religious rituals contribute to adaptation. While Erikson stands in the psychoanalytic tradition, this emphasis on the variety of ways that religious rituals serve the adaptive requirements of persons and groups should be welcome to Jamesians, since James consistently affirmed the importance of pluralism in religious matters. Perhaps, like his work on personal religious experience (1958, 41), Erikson has moved the psychology of ritual in a direction that is congruent with the epistemological assumptions of James's psychology of religion (Capps 1974).

16

Life Cycle Theory and the Dismissal of Jonathan Edwards

GARY S. ELLER

History and psychology make uneasy partners. Both disciplines, however, can contribute substantially to our understanding of religious experience. The historian may search the diaries, letters, published writings and accounts of an ancient personality to derive an insightful biography. The story will remain incomplete, though, if the historian fails to weigh and incorporate evidence concerning the psychological contours of the subject. The psychologist may diagnose the same personality, noting characteristic strengths and weaknesses; but lacking the historian's diligent research methods or a sufficiently broad contextual lens, will fail to place the case in its proper perspective. Erik Erikson's life cycle theory offers both the historian and psychologist a conceptual framework for making assessments of the religious experiences, both individual and collective, of historical personalities. Erikson's *Young Man Luther* (1958) and *Gandhi's Truth* (1969) are examples of life cycle theory presenting history as psychobiography.

In the years since Erikson's pioneering works, he has continued to refine and extend his theory. Notably, he has proposed a series of rituals attendant to each stage of the life cycle that impinge upon every life narrative (1977).[1] Here I will attempt to demonstrate that Erikson's theory of ritual can illumine case reflection on clergy and ministry. The

1. See also Erikson (1982).

subject of the case is Jonathan Edwards (1703–58), the defender of the
Great Awakening. The exerpts from Edwards's life are the events of his
dismissal from Northampton Church in 1750. I maintain that Edwards's
dismissal was a maladaptive ritual based upon the dynamics of shame
and guilt activated in his life story and the community of Northampton. In addition, I believe that Edwards's case is far more than a remote example from colonial America; instead, the multiple dimensions
of Edwards's conflict can assist clergy and congregations in coming to
terms with the vital impact of ritual upon faith communities.[2]

The Final Events

The public issue, which resulted in Edwards's dismissal, concerned
the basis for admission to the Lord's Supper. Edwards's refusal to
admit the unregenerate to the table contradicted views of his
predecessor Solomon Stoddard. Stoddard was a very practical patriarch. He had seized the opportunities of 1700 to become champion of
an expanded Half-Way Covenant which opened all of the ordinances of
the Northampton church, including the Lord's Supper, to everyone pro-
fessing a "historical faith" (an intellectual knowledge of the essentials
of Christianity). Stoddard urged even young teenagers to become full
participants in the church and to receive communion as a "converting"
ordinance. The result of Stoddard's reforms was the virtual eradication
of the original Puritan conception of a "gathered" community of regen-
erate saints constituting the church.

By mid-century, the covenant was a dead issue for almost everyone
but Edwards. Even Edwards had followed Stoddard's way for almost
his entire ministry at Northampton. Now, just before the end, he was
reversing his position. Certain to alienate and confuse his parishioners,
Edwards's decision was devoid of political wisdom. Raising an old controversy as a public issue was tactless and pastorally unwise. Character-
istically, Edwards did not let the almost sure prospect of a losing battle
deter his relentless search for truth.

Edwards's opposition to "Mr. Stoddard's Way" came after long deliberation. For years he resisted making his decision and did so only
when he was firmly convinced that theory and practice did not agree in
the Half-Way Covenant. As Ola E. Winslow (1940, 248) reports, "Grandfather Stoddard had been a kind of demigod to the Edwards children,
and acceptance of his ideas came naturally." To demur from Stoddard's
views was to reject the considerable pastoral authority that Edwards
still granted his maternal grandfather. Stoddard contributed greatly to

---

2. Capps (1979, 48–53) offers a psychosocial interpretation of Edwards and
Northampton parish focused on the theme of identity versus identity diffusion.

the development of Edwards's religious sensibilities. He invited Edwards to assist him in ministry at Northampton when other, more experienced clergy, might well have been chosen. Stoddard shepherded Edwards, respecting his intellect and providing well for him, so that Edwards's first real pulpit was a prominent one. Now with Stoddard dead and Edwards occupying his mentor's position, many critics would view his opposition to the covenant as ungrateful and unnecessary. Stoddard still represented for many the Puritan ideal of the authoritative patriarch. Yet Edwards's determination to be right in the defense of doctrine overrode his deference toward Stoddard or his justified concerns about public censure.

The result of Edwards's decision was his treatise entitled *An Humble Inquiry into the Rules of the Word of God, concerning the Qualifications Requisite to a Complete Standing and Full Communion with the Visible Christian Church*, published in the early autumn of 1749. In his own words, Edwards engaged the controversy "with the greatest reluctance that ever I undertook any public service in my life" (Tracy 1980, 167). His words *public service* show precisely his sense of the debate's importance. He knew that most of New England would oppose him; yet, he jeopardized everything for the sake of truth and freedom from what he believed to be an unwise doctrine.

There was great risk in taking up such an unpopular issue. Edwards was not an adventuresome risk taker. He was a measured, extraordinarily cautious person inclined to introspection and muted affect. Exceptionally devoted to Sarah and their children, Edwards was very hesitant to do anything that might imperil their well-being. Northampton could not equal Boston, but the town was still a desirable location for a landed minister. There were no guaranteed pulpits awaiting Edwards if the issue became so intense that he was removed from his church.

Why did Edwards take on the Half-Way Covenant in view of these risks? In one way, it was his chance finally to establish his pastoral authority in Northampton. Stoddard was dead, but his theology endured. Edwards could see the deficiencies in Stoddard's views and the problems created for the church by unregenerate members. Edwards realized that if commitment was to be strengthened in Northampton parish, then the value of regeneration had to be reestablished. If he could make his case convincingly, then he would be removing an old stumbling block to vital churchmanship in his parish. This accomplishment would finally legitimate him as Northampton's pastor and not simply Stoddard's grandson.

The issue was crucial to Edwards because it exposed his vulnerabilities and deepened his ego needs. He recognized his intellectual superiority to Stoddard, which even his grandfather did not deny; but he lacked comparable authority and respect from his parishioners. The Half-Way Covenant was an abiding theological thorn in his ego. He firmly believed that the covenant was theologically improper. Moreover, it represented for him the continuing spiritual influence of Stoddard upon Northampton. To be rid of the covenant would also sweep away one of Stoddard's main legacies. For Edwards's pastoral identity to be fulfilled, he needed his parishioners' respect. Stoddard's practices diminished Edwards's authority and consequently injured his self-esteem. To defeat the covenant would allow Edwards finally to lay his grandfather to rest and assume his rightful place in the hearts, as well as the minds, of his parishioners.

Edwards would not relent even if he could have done so. To withdraw his written public statements about the covenant would discredit his theological views—an ideology in which his identity was heavily invested—and violate his obsession with true religion. Edwards could not fail to sense the passion of his opponents. Those who had waited hoping for a chance to bring him down would not leave any possibility unexplored. The covenant dispute became an enactment of Edwards's childhood essay "Of Spiders" in which he expressed a dread of rising to a pinnacle then falling suddenly.

A stormy controversy arose almost immediately when Edwards expressed his views on the covenant. He offered to resign on April 13, 1749, if the members of the standing committee of his church would consent to read his treatise and issue a verdict on its merits. However, the hour was already passed for reasoned debate. The weight of rumors against Edwards had grown so great that the majority of Northampton did not want reconciliation. He had embarrassed them in the "bad books" affair (when Edwards mistakenly named all of the parish children as guilty of secretly reading dubious volumes on midwifery) and now he challenged the estimable Stoddard's memory and a theology that they generally approved. They wanted to be rid of "Mr. Edwards, root and branch, name and remnant." The people of Northampton did not wish to assess the truth or error of Edwards's refined theological arguments. They intended to reject the author without reading his treatise.

With Edwards and the church deadlocked, a council was formed. The nomination of council members was bitterly contested. After weeks of argument, a settlement was reached. The committee would consist of nineteen men from the town and fifteen from the church. Edwards knew that he had been defeated by the choice of committee members. Using his own word, he was made a "cipher." His choice of terms reveals the hollowness he felt. The trial would effectively strip him of his vocation, at least for a while, and his views would be publicly ridiculed by the same people whom he had nurtured for years as a pastor. He would become a nothing in their eyes and in his own heart feel the ominous threats of self-doubt and nonbeing. Edwards's identity conflicts were adequately resolved by his conversion; now old psychic wounds would be reopened as he searched for a new role in late mid-life. His dismissal would leave him grief-stricken and nearly abandoned. Leaving Northampton by compulsion would be a mini-death for him. His family, dependent upon him for their necessities, would suffer for his political, if not theological, mistakes. He worried deeply about their physical and spiritual wellbeing during the dismissal process. Still, his needs to claim his pastoral authority, to prove himself right, and to depose Stoddard's patriarchal memory meant he could not seriously reconsider his position. Fidelity to his ideology required that he pursue the issue.

During the months of contention communion was not served at Northampton. Anger and resentment welled up on both sides of the controversy. Dismissal was, of course, a certain outcome. It was only a matter of procedure. Still, Edwards would not resign.

The select council met on June 19, 1750. Their number was incomplete as the church of Cold Spring refused to attend. A motion to postpone the case was defeated. There were final vain attempts to reconcile the church and pastor. Those efforts failing, the council voted, by a majority of one, to immediately dissolve the pastoral relation between Edwards and the Northampton church. By June 22, after three days of deliberation and a 200 to 30 vote of male church members against Edwards, the council was ready to conclude the process of dissolution as "passed in the affirmative." The minority united in a published protest.

According to the diary of David Hall, one of his few close friends, Edwards received the verdict calmly. Hall's entry reads:

> that faithful Witness received ye Shock, unshaken: I never saw ye lest Symptoms of displeasure in his Countenance, the whole week, but he appeared like a man of God, whose Happiness was out of ye reach of his Enemies, and whose treasure was not only a future but a present good: overbalancing all Imaginable Ills of Life, even to the Astonishment of man, who could not be at rest without his Dismission: it manifestly appeared to me. (Tracy 1980, 185)

Edwards's journal chronicles the dismission without a sign of affect. As Winslow surmises, Edwards's ninety pages of entries have all "the impersonality of an official record" (Winslow 1940, 265). Even in defeat, Edwards could not admit that he had made a serious mistake in taking public issue with the Half-Way Covenant. Had he kept his reservations to himself or shared them confidentially, then the Northampton furor might have been delayed or avoided. But Edwards was willing to risk everything, if necessary, to make his point.

Edwards's final sermon as pastor of Northampton church was on July 1, 1750. As autobiography it is a telling message. Edwards had only ten days to decide what to say. The recent ordeal was fresh in his mind. The future was uncertain. He had fought tenaciously against dismissal and lost decisively. Now the dramatic moment was his. He could assume the martyr's mantle, castigate the congregation, indulge in some sentimental reflections, or continue to debate from the pulpit. Instead he chose 2 Corinthians 1:14: "As also ye have acknowledged us in part, that we are your rejoicing, even as ye are ours, in the day of the Lord Jesus" (KJV).

In spite of the inner pain Edwards must have felt, the sermon is devoid of recrimination. He preached with the courage and conviction of a person possessing an unqualified assurance that he is in the right. The resultant sermon is one of the clearest statements from the colonial era describing the minister's preaching office. The preacher, Edwards concludes, is called to be one of God's chosen messengers.

Edwards refers to the "unhappy debate and controversy managed with much prejudice and want of candor" without dwelling on his position (Winslow 1966, 174). He accepts the unpleasant affair as an event in the remote past. He puts the quarrel behind him until that day when God would be the final arbiter of all disputes. He named no villains. Instead, Edwards urged his congregation to beware of Armenian encroachments. He warned: "If these principles should greatly prevail in this town, . . . it will threaten the spiritual and eternal ruin of this people, in the present and future generations" (170). The sermon ends with the affirmation that the "righteous judgment of God" will see justice done, "either in receiving and wearing a crown of eternal joy and glory, or in suffering everlasting shame and pain" (Faust and Johnson 1962, 202).

Outwardly, Edwards would not allow himself to display any shame. That the "Farewell Sermon" does not begin to tell the whole story of his true sentiments can be established from his contemporaneous private writings. In the manuscript rough draft of his farewell letter to his congregation, the last sentence reads: "I am dear Brethren He who was your once affectionate and I hope through grace faithful pastor and devoted servant for Jesus' sake. J.E." (Winslow 1966, 268). The word *affectionate* is carefully crossed out. Edwards could not sacrifice the truth of his feelings for the sake of polite appearances.

Edwards was unsure of his future. Old fears, self-doubts, and anger nagged at him. Writing to a friend on July 5, 1750, he confessed that he felt "thrown upon the wide ocean of the world, and know not what will become of me, and my numerous and chargeable family" (268). Though some options were open, the Edwards family remained in Northampton for another unhappy year with Edwards serving as the supply pastor of his former church. It was disconcerting for the congregation to see Edwards in the pulpit from which they had so recently deposed him. They shared guilt for the shame they had inflicted upon him. Though Edwards never mentioned the controversy during any of his sermons that year, the leaders of the church could not abide his presence. Even though there were no other local ministers to invite to preach, the church voted not to permit Edwards to return. They had shamed him in the dismissal; but without speaking a word, Edwards made them feel deeply guilty for what they had done. He finally settled on a call as a missionary to the Indians in Stockbridge, where he would pastor a small church formed under rude conditions by Indians and a few white settlers. There, in a frontier exile, Edwards produced his most influential theological works.

The Role of Shame and Self-Doubt in the Dismissal

Edwards was brilliant in defending the doctrinal basis for the Northampton revivals and identifying the attendant dangers of religious enthusiasm. He became so confident of the experiential validity and the analytical precision of his theological views that his definition of conversion gradually became fixed in his mind as the norm for judging all religious conversions. Edwards's intellectual certainty was paralleled by his vocational insecurity. The Second Awakening in Northampton, 1740–42, threatened Edwards's pastoral identity. As revival enthusiasm dissipated, he faced again the familiar challenges to church discipline and ministerial authority. He never gave up attempting to recapture the joyous success of the first revival of 1735. But the doctrines that had once terrorized his flock now only bored them. The young people of Northampton, such as Joseph Hawley, his chief antagonist, had grown up. Edwards was no longer young. His charisma had faded. As Edwards aged, his evangelistic zeal began to wane. By trying to claim the same pastoral authority as Stoddard, he tried to hold on to the past too long. The 1740s were a different era than 1700. Stoddard assumed pastoral prerogatives and commanded obedience; Edwards searched for pastoral authority and met with stern resistance. Through the mid-1740s, Edwards's identification with his grandfather was a strategic disaster and a mark of his uncertain self-image.[3] In his controversy with Northampton church, Edwards could not prevail by emulating Stoddard. He lacked the interpersonal skills necessary to survive the conflict. Ironically, Edwards was much more like Stoddard than the Northampton of 1750 resembled the parish of 1700. As much

---

3. See Erikson (1969, 440). He offers an account of the relationship between historical and personal regression.

as he wanted to retain his pastorate, the rift between Edwards and the majority of the congregation was far too wide.

This spirit of contentiousness became increasingly manifest in Northampton during the 1740s. As Patricia J. Tracy comments, the town had become more worldly. The citizens of Northampton were settling into the patterns of a normal eighteenth-century American town (1980, 193). In their early years they were united by the daily sacrifices required to overcome the wilderness and Indians. But by the 1740s, what had been a united, rather homogeneous community had evolved into a competitive, commercial enterprise dominated by the will of authoritative individuals. The new leadership of Northampton refused to submit passively to traditional authority figures. Morality and piety were shunted aside by expediency and commercial interests. When Edwards discovered that several of his formerly pious young people were rebelling, he was certain that they must be made ashamed of their sins and repent. Yet after 1742, he found the young people increasingly resistant to confessing their sin, whether the offense was sexual license or a lack of piety. To his amazement, they seemed to lack a sense of social shame. Edwards internalized their rebellion as personal rejection of his ministerial authority, thus magnifying his self-doubts.

From the beginning of Edward's conflict with Northampton, sin, guilt, and repentance were important themes. The council's task was not so much to establish Edwards's guilt in the fracturing of the pastoral bond as to discern whether his dismissal could be handled with grace. If the dissenters demanded Edwards suffer public humiliation and shame, the council's task would be far more difficult. A score of Edwards's parishioners objected to his overconfident, prideful stand. They were equally determined, with Hawley, to break Edwards's perceived arrogance and to heap public censure upon him.

Why was the church of Northampton so intent upon shaming Edwards? He had served them well for more than two decades. A response may be found in the role of autonomy versus shame and self-doubt in Puritan child-rearing practices (Demos 1970).

Edwards's opponents were single-minded in their determination to shame and humiliate him. He had resisted their offers of compromise by insisting that his views on the moral behavior of young people and the practice of the Lord's Supper were in absolute conformity with Scripture. The townspeople resented both Edwards's use of pastoral authority and his recourse to biblical authority against them. In retaliation, the dissenters heaped verbal shame on Edwards charging him with every manner of gossip. By so doing, the dissenters reenacted the most extreme disciplinary measures available to Puritan parents in conflict with their children. The process of Edwards's removal became a reenactment of early parent-child conflicts in which approval and disapproval are conferred.

Their efforts were not lost on Edwards. He felt "like a Cipher." He lost the dismissal drama. He suffered the shame of public disapproval. He sensed that his defeat meant more than a setback for his theological views; it underscored the community's rejection of his ministry. The issue that mattered most to his opponents was his removal from Northampton church; the theological issues were secondary.

How might Edwards's difficulties been handled in a more ritually adaptive manner? How could his personal sense of defeat been assuaged or the intense opposition he faced been defused? Why was the process so maladaptive that Edwards could never accept Hawley's belated appeal for forgiveness? Erikson's theory of ritual suggests that the process was maladaptive primarily because of the ritual excess of legalism present, the victory of the letter over the spirit, in issues pertaining to the conflict of autonomy versus shame and self-doubt.

The special council erred when they gave up too soon on efforts to reconcile Edwards with his antagonists. The council allowed the dynamics of shame to become explicit in the dissenters' condemnations. A thorough and informed disputation of the issues on their theological and pastoral merits might have produced enlightenment on all sides. In the emotionally charged dismissal, Edwards became the "culprit." A culprit must be either exonerated or condemned. No middle ground remained where judiciousness might prevail over legalism. Edwards was compelled, like the infant, to look at himself while being isolated from other adults. Erikson describes such legalism as a "vain display of righteousness or empty contrition" in which there is the "moralistic insistence on exposing and isolating the culprit whether or not this will be good for him or anybody else" (1977, 97).

Shame and guilt were deeply rooted in Puritan society. It would have been very difficult for the council to separate the two. Edwards would admit no wrong. His adversaries were equally obstinate. The council had to make a choice in a win-lose situation. Had shame and guilt played less pivotal roles in the conflict, more potentially adaptive alternatives might have been pursued:

1. The council charging Edwards to moderate his theological positions in the interest of the "peace and harmony" of the church if he wished to maintain his ordination.
2. The council acting as arbitrators, perhaps in concert with other clergy, requiring Edwards and the Hawley-led group to abide by their decision.
3. The council taking the time to assess the deep, long-standing differences between Edwards and his opponents so that if he

were dismissed, it would be for the deeper reason that remained unvoiced.

4. The council requiring Edwards to take an extended leave of
absence from the church after which time the case could be
reviewed when emotions were less volatile.

5. Edwards recognizing that the outcome of the process would be
more injurious to all concerned if he were forced out of the
parish, so he might have resigned voluntarily without conditions.

6. Edwards choosing a position other than that of absolute moral
superiority to his parishioners, so that those sympathetic to his
views could be increased and a final vote possibly avoided.

None of these alternatives occurred. The stakes for Edwards's dismissal were too high. Either Northampton would be rid of him or he
would be publicly vindicated and his opponents humiliated. In losing
the controversy, Edwards's wish fulfillment, to become equal or supe-
rior to his grandfather in authority, was frustrated.

Why were options not pursued? Erikson suggests that self-doubt is
reflected in the tendency toward over-manipulation. Self-doubt yields
obsessive thoughts and behavior. Puritan theology and polity may not
have been inherently obsessive; but Puritan methods for resolving disputes took on all the formal aspects of a trial complete with legalistic,
obsessive thinking. It was the Puritan process for pastoral dissolutions
that proved to be a ritual vulnerable to excessively legalistic manipulation. As Donald Capps concludes, Puritan leaders "allowed obsessional
thought processes to overwhelm a judicial ritual with legalistic
excess."[4] Pressed hard by his adversaries, Edwards was determined to
make his case and, if he lost the debate, rise above any attempts to
shame or humiliate him by responding to the council's final decision
with his characteristic dignity and restraint.

Why did Edwards not moderate his views? Edwards wrestled for
years with the thought of opposing Stoddard's practices. His respect
for his maternal grandfather was more than a socially appropriate
deference. Stoddard's authority and prestige were both blessing and
bane. They were a blessing in that Stoddard's choice of Edwards
marked him as the legitimate successor. The familial tie was also a bane
in that any opposition to Stoddard's theology or methods would appear
disrespectful.

These conflicts were both conscious and unconscious. On the
unconscious level, Edwards's relationship with Stoddard included oedipal conflicts. If Edwards were to serve "Mother Church" faithfully, then

4. See chapter 15, p. 224.

he had to overthrow Stoddard's communion practices. Given Edwards's active superego, such an assault on Stoddard could not go without psychic punishment. Edwards's stout resistance to modifying his views in the communion controversy was, on the unconscious level, a way of punishing himself for the sin against Stoddard. In a real sense, Edwards brought the punishment upon himself, unconsciously contributing to the maladaptive ritual process. The self-administered verdict for contradicting Stoddard was the death of his relationship with the church that Stoddard had prepared for him. The punishment for his sin was public humiliation. Edward's sternest judge was his punishing superego. If, as Erikson believes, "doubt is the brother of shame," then Edwards's opponents were determined to deal with their own doubts by shaming him (1980, 70). They were unforgiving because he had aroused their "deadly" sin of anger (Capps 1987, 28–31).

Ritual Elements and Types of Religious Authority

In his analysis of Ann Hibbens, Capps proposes the recognition of the relationship between Erikson's ritual elements and types of religious authority. For each of Erikson's first four types of ritual, Capps supplies a corresponding type of religious authority. Capps's point is that "certain types of religious authority encourage certain types of ritual, and certain types of ritual encourage their corresponding authority structures" (1992, 224). The types of authority are derived from various classifications of authority types (224). The types that parallel each of the ritual elements are illustrative rather than exhaustive combinations. The matching of life stages with the corresponding authority types indicates which excesses are most probable in any stage.

Edwards viewed his ministry as primarily that of an evangelist, pastor, and teacher. These authority types were appropriate until the drama of his dismissal degenerated into a judicial affair. This degeneration was marked by a developmentally regressive shift from proving guilt to invoking shame on a culprit. In the judicial context of his appeals to the special council, Edwards's self-images changed from teacher, pastor, and evangelist to martyr and sage. Edwards's regression into developmentally more primitive authority types conformed to the judicial atmosphere of his dismissal. Edwards felt that Hawley's band attacked him unjustly; but he was willing to be martyred. Moreover, Edwards saw himself as spiritually wiser than his detractors. The more Edwards acted as a martyr, the more ritually appropriate it was for Hawley's compatriots to resort to a judicial process. Instead of being judicious, the council responded maladaptively. They persisted in being judgmental in the dismissal process to bring the open conflict with Edwards to an end. It was the judicial nature of the process that cast it in a maladaptive form certain to inflict shame on Edwards and lasting feelings of guilt among those who deposed him.

Edwards lost the public contest of wills but continued to rage within. The victim of his superego, Edwards's anger turned inward to melancholy. By remaining in Northampton for almost a year after his formal dismissal, he became a daily reminder to the turmoil. His adversaries were very uncomfortable with the Edwards family still living in town. If Edwards was supposed to bear the shame of dismissal, he made certain that he would not suffer alone. Without saying a word, his presence manifested passive-aggressive hostility. His shame became Northampton's shame. Edwards's martyrdom became Northampton's stigma.

Erikson's theory of ritual provides a context for interpreting the individual and collective psychological dynamics of faith communities. When used in conjunction with Capps's models of authority types, Erikson's life cycle theory broadens to encompass the adaptive and maladaptive features of congregational conflicts. The interaction between a "ritual coordinator" and a congregation is extraordinarily complex involving ritual events and authority patterns often overlooked by pastors and parishioners. Attending to Erikson's theories can provide an important interpretive angle of vision on these vital dynamics of religious experience.

17

Jesus and the Age Thirty Transition

JOHN W. MILLER

Recent studies have emphasized the importance, for a deepened understanding of Jesus' mission, of a correct interpretation of certain prior transitional events that occurred soon after he left his parental home: his baptism, temptations, and temporary association with John the Baptist, above all (Jeremias 1971; Meyer 1979; Hollenbach 1982). However, in the investigations to date not much attention has been paid to Luke's suggestion that he might have been "about thirty years old" at the time (Luke 3:23),[1] even though we now realize, thanks to developmental psychology, that abrupt changes of this kind frequently occur in men's lives right at this point, for reasons that are inherent to the process of becoming a mature adult (Erikson 1963; 1964; Levinson et al. 1978; Greenspan and Pollock 1980). Might then an inquiry into this facet of Jesus' life, in this light, sharpen our perceptions of what he was contending with at this time and thereby enrich our picture of him at maturity?[2]

1. On the basis of papyri evidence, where ages are often given in multiples of five, J. Cadbury (1963, 275–76) suggests that Luke's "about thirty" was meant to convey that Jesus was between twenty-five and thirty-five at the time.
2. The importance of utilizing psychological insights in historical Jesus research is astutely analyzed and defended by J. McIntyre (1966, 114–43). For a review of psycho-historical research generally, see W. J. Gilmore (1984). Among the sporadic attempts at

An answer, I suggest, will depend on our response to three additional questions: (1) What is now known about the developmental issues facing men generally at this stage of their lives; (2) Is what is known generally, based as it is on studies of men in modern societies, at all relevant to an understanding of someone living as long ago in another culture as did Jesus; (3) What can be said about the Jesus of history that might be at all germane to such an inquiry?

In the paragraphs that follow I will try to address each of these questions and conclude with a few comments regarding the contemporary relevance of such a psychohistorical probe.

The Age Thirty Transition

What then in general is known about the transitions men often experience at this time of their lives? It was Daniel Levinson's careful study of a cross-section of forty American men that first alerted us to the unique importance of "about thirty" as a specific life stage (Levinson, 1978, 71–135). Building on the life stage research of Sigmund Freud, Carl G. Jung, and especially Erik Erikson, Levinson sought through in-depth "biographical interviews" to gain a fuller picture of what these men had experienced during their adult years from seventeen to forty-five. Since he began his study predisposed to the traditional notion that a crucial transition in adult life occurs around forty, the discovery that already earlier equally significant transitions often take place was somewhat surprising. More specifically, he observed that already during their twenties and early thirties these men typically approached adulthood in two clearly distinguishable phases: an initial casual, exploratory mode, during their early and middle twenties, when a first provisional life structure was fashioned, and then a more serious, urgent mode, during their later twenties and early thirties—followed by the making of stronger commitments and the forming of deeper roots and a new life structure (84). Between the structures of the first provisional phase and those of the "settling down" period in the early thirties there occurred, Levinson noted, an often turbulent "age thirty transition." What brought it about, in part at least, it seemed, was a dawning sense of mortality: the now persistent awareness that life is short and that a start will have to be made soon, if what one hopes to accomplish in life is going to get done before it is too late. As a consequence, the structures and achievements of the initial phase were tested and often found wanting and in need of radical change (85).

---

understanding Jesus in this light the following should be mentioned: G. Berguer (1923); Anton Boisen (1936); R. S. Lee (1948); Erik Erikson (1981); and P. C. Vitz and J. Gartner (1984). To this end no one to date, so far as I know, has made use of Levinson's research.

In his discussion of the tasks or objectives that typically engaged these men during this time of their lives Levinson observed, as had Erikson, the central importance of establishing a truly meaningful vocational identity, as well as "forming love relationships, marriage and family" (101–10). The wider significance of the latter had been especially stressed by Erikson, for it was through this, he had written, that "generativity" emerges—that quality of "caring for" or "taking care of" (that which has been generated) which is so essential to the life and well-being of the succeeding generation (Erikson 1963, 266–68).

But two additional issues surfaced in Levinson's research as of equal importance. In one way or another, he noted, all the men he had interviewed were preoccupied during their age thirty transitions with what he termed "forming a Dream and giving it a place in the life structure," as well as with "forming mentor relationships" that would assist them in this. This Dream, Levinson wrote, had "the quality of a vision, an imagined possibility that generates excitement and vitality" (1978, 91). At the beginning of the age thirty transition it was often still poorly articulated or encased in grandiose aspirations only tenuously connected to reality as in the myth of the hero. But whatever the form, he observed, the age thirty transition was experienced as a time when it was urgent to define this Dream and live it out quite concretely. Therefore, the extent to which the initial life structure was "consonant with and infused by the Dream, or opposed to it" was a matter of great consequence, for if the Dream had remained unconnected to their lives, Levinson wrote, it might simply die, and with it their sense of "aliveness and purpose" (92).

While mentoring relationships have long been recognized as important to emotional development earlier in life, during adolescence, for example, Levinson's research indicated they were crucial as well during this age thirty transition. Ideally the mentor at this stage in life is neither parent nor crypto-parent, he noted, but a slightly older peer who fosters the young adult's development "by believing in him, sharing the youthful Dream and giving it his blessing, helping to define the newly emerging self in its newly discovered world, and creating a space in which the young man can work on a reasonably satisfactory life structure that contains the Dream" (99).

For a few men the age thirty transition went smoothly, according to Levinson, although all of the men he interviewed experienced significant changes. For the great majority this period was extremely stressful; the interviewees felt like a man alone in the water between two islands, unable to move one way or the other and on the verge of drowning (86). A man's difficulties may be accentuated "by specific aspects of his situation—economic recession, discrimination, the rivalries of a highly competitive world—and by his own emotional problems of committing himself to an occupation, relating to women and separating from parents" (82).

Relevance

To what extent are these observations, based as they are on the study of men in twentieth-century North America, valid for a deepened understanding of a historic figure like Jesus, living as he did in first-century Palestine? As noted, a heightened sense of mortality and urgency to do something authentic while there is yet time appears to be a critical factor in the changes that occur in this period. This could be related to the fact that bodily maturation, along with reproductive capacities, reach their peak in humans in their mid-twenties, after which a slow physical decline sets in. If so, this in itself would suggest that a species-wide genetic clock, and not culture alone, may be a triggering factor in the age thirty transition (Levinson, 1978, 326–30). However, that men in all cultures do in fact experience this time of their lives in analogous ways is as yet hard to verify, Levinson admits. Still, he points out, there are a number of texts from a variety of cultures that seem at least to allude to this. In the Talmudic "Sayings of the Fathers," for example, the stages of life from five to one hundred are carefully outlined and thirty is mentioned as the time in life when "full strength" is attained (*Avoth* 5.24). In a Confucian text (*Analects,* book 2) Confucius himself traces the stages of his life from fifteen to seventy and says of his thirtieth year that it was then that he had planted his feet "firm upon the ground." Thirty is also mentioned by Solon of Greece, in a similar sketch of the life cycle, as "the season for courting and begetting sons who will preserve and continue his line" (Levinson 1978, 324–26). In Israel thirty was specified as the lower limit for the census of those fit to bear arms who were liable for service in the temple (Num. 4). Among the Jewish sectarians at Qumran a man was eligible for communal office at twenty-five, but it was not until thirty that he was deemed ready to render judgments or function as a tribal commissioner (*Manual of Discipline for the Future Congregation of Israel*). A scattering of anecdotal data adds color to these transcultural hints. To the famous incident of Gautama Buddha's life-changing encounter with suffering and death at twenty-nine may be added as examples from biblical tradition alone, apart from Jesus, the allusions to age thirty type transitions in the lives of Joseph (Gen. 41:46), David (2 Sam. 5:4), Ezekiel (1:1), and possibly Moses, Hosea, and Isaiah, all of whom were married and having their first children at the time they were called to be prophets.

This does not mean, obviously, that there are no differences at all in the process of becoming an adult in modern America and the small first-century Galilean village where Jesus grew up. Life, we imagine, was much simpler then than today and the social structures shaping adult transitions firmer and more stable. Were we to imagine, however, that our world and his were too different in this respect, a single story, Jesus' parable of the prodigal son (Luke 15:11–32), should remind us that then, too, becoming an adult was not easy. In any case, neither the rebellious prodigal of this story, who left home, nor his obedient brother, who stayed behind, reached adulthood, it seems, in a single bound. The prodigal had first to experiment with being an adult in the wider world before returning to his father's farm, ostensibly to settle down there; his elder brother, while remaining home, was also obviously not altogether content with his initial choice, as his bitter complaint to his father at the time of his younger brother's return reveals. The relevance of contemporary life-stage research to the experience of a first-century Palestinian Jew is hardly thereby proven. It does suggest, however, that its heuristic value ought not to be summarily dismissed either.

Jesus' Age Thirty Transition

Granted the possible relevance of this data, how much do our sources for the life of Jesus actually tell us that might be germane to this theme? Factual information regarding Jesus' life during his childhood, adolescence, and young adulthood is, of course, notoriously scarce. Indeed, even the few accounts we do have of his birth and adolescence are regarded suspiciously by most historians. However, there is no reason to doubt Luke's reference to his role as his parents' firstborn (Luke 2:7), nor that his family eventually included four younger brothers and several sisters (Mark 3:31–35; 6:3; Wilson 1984, 71; Brown et al. 1978, 65–72). Nor need we question that his father was a carpenter (Matt. 13:55), or that Jesus too worked at that trade (Mark 6:3). This does not mean, however, that he was a simple village carpenter necessarily, or poor, as often imagined. Buchanan has sought to demonstrate that "carpenter" might also mean "contractor" and that Paul's allusion to his having once been rich (2 Cor. 8:9) could be historical (Buchanan 1984; 1985). If so, this would be congruent with the preponderance of middle-class figures who people his parables: owners of vineyards with managerial worries (Matt. 20:1–16); fathers with wealth to be distributed (Luke 15:11–32); traveling merchants (Luke 10:29–37; Matt. 13:45–46); farmers with servants (Matt. 13:24–30; 24:45–51); rich entrepreneurs (Matt. 25:14–30; Miller 1980).

But why then by thirty had Jesus not married and founded a family? Some have argued that he had, on the basis that it is inconceivable in an age where marriage by twenty was virtually mandatory that he would not have (Phipps 1971; 1973). Yet, the silence of our sources regarding wife and children is deafening and can hardly be construed otherwise than that there were none. The possible reasons for this ought, however, to be analyzed more carefully than they generally are. Virtually all discussions of this topic focus on the motives Jesus might have had at thirty for remaining single (Sloyan 1983, 129–32; Wilson 1984, 96–97; Buchanan 1984, 184–90). But the Talmud states that it was the father's responsibility to see that his son got married and to do so while the son was young and amenable to the father's advice.[3] Were traditions of this kind at all in vogue among the Jews of Jesus' day, and there is no reason to think otherwise, the question would then be not so much why Jesus at thirty had not yet married, but why his father, much earlier, had failed to make arrangements to this end.

A likely answer is that Joseph had died before the time had come when it would have been appropriate to have done so. That he died prior to Jesus' mission at thirty is almost certain, for he is missing from all the accounts of this period, even those where members of Jesus' family are explicitly identified (Mark 3:31–35; 6:1–6). David Flusser comments that it is his impression that this death took place quite early in Jesus' life, when he was still "quite a child" (Flusser 1969, 17). But that would not have been possible were it true that there were six younger siblings, as Mark 6:3 implies. That Jesus was still unmarried at thirty suggests that his father's death occurred during his early teens, before the time had arrived when a marriage would have certainly been arranged for him, were his father still alive.

According to the traditions of his times, Jesus would have then become, as eldest son, the head of his deceased father's family (Connick 1974, 131; Wilson 1984, 71). With this possibility we arrive at what might well have been the most important factor of all in Jesus' personal development during his growing-up years. The loss of a father by anyone at any time in life is a difficult experience. In a relatively large first-century Jewish family, the loss of a father by an eldest son during his early teens must have been traumatic. Can we imagine what some of the more obvious consequences of such a death might have been for such a son under such circumstances? Although it is admittedly conjectural, the attempt to do so may shed light on several otherwise puzzling features of the life of the "about-thirty"-year-old Jesus.

To begin with, if it is true that prior to his father's death Jesus was indeed working with him in carpentry or contracting, as the Gospels intimate, it will now fall to Jesus' lot to shoulder this trade by himself, for he will have become his family's chief means of support. Not just

---

3. In *Kiddushin* (29a) it is stated that "the father is bound in respect of his son, to circumcise, redeem, teach him Torah, take a wife for him, and teach him a craft. Some say, to teach him to swim too." In *Kiddushin* (30a) it is reported that "Raba said to R. Nathan b. ammi: Whilst your hand is yet upon your son's neck, [marry him], viz., between sixteen and twenty-two. Others state, between eighteen and twenty-four."

financially, however, but in other ways too the leadership once vested in his father would now gravitate toward him. This could be a stimulus to the development of latent talents. He would have to learn quickly how to care for and manage in an efficient, competent manner.[4]

On the other hand, such a demanding role may pose certain risks or "temptations" as well. To become suddenly "father" in a world in which it would still be normal to be "son" sets the stage for a reawakening of oedipal ambivalence. A son might respond with a sense of over-responsibility or grandiosity. In any case, an inner debate is sure to rage over which is to have priority and for how long: remaining as head of his father's family or founding one of his own, concern for his father's wife or finding a wife of his own, care of his father's children or having children of his own? As a result, personal plans for marriage are almost sure to be postponed beyond the time ordinarily set for them, as I have personally observed in the case of several Middle Eastern and North American men in similar circumstances.[5] As time goes on such a son's relation to his mother may prove to be especially problematical, as she, on her part, tries to cope with her own needs and frustrations by leaning more and more on this highly resourceful firstborn. This will not only intensify his ambivalence but also exacerbate sibling rivalries. A welter of other emotions may accompany these developments: anger at the premature loss of his father, guilt at taking his place, fear of going too far or not far enough in this complex new role, idealization of the lost father, anxiety over unknown catastrophes yet to come (Lammers 1975, 75–76).

To summarize, the available evidence, while meager, strongly suggests that during his adolescence Jesus, as eldest son, became the head of his father's family. An especially significant consequence of this would be that, while vocationally successful, he would not be free at

---

4. Parental loss as a factor in high achievement has been carefully researched by J. M. Eisenstadt (1978). In a study of 573 "eminent individuals" he discovered that parental loss among this group was at a significantly earlier age than among the general population. Surprisingly, the statistics for this group were similar to the age of parental loss among psychotic, severely depressed, or suicidal patients. The reason, he concluded, is that a child faced by the loss of one or both parents is suddenly compelled to master a new environment. For some this challenge may prove to be overwhelming, leading to mental and emotional breakdown. But others are able to respond by going through what Eisenstadt calls a process of "creative mourning" and "overcompensation." The potential genius, he writes, translates this struggle for mastery, following the death of a parent, into a personal development that leads to a high degree of competency in an occupational field.

5. In one instance a son whose father was killed in a farming accident when he was an adolescent told me that the dilemma he felt over how long to remain at home was resolved only when his mother remarried. He was twenty-five at the time, but "it was as though a burden had been lifted from my shoulders," he said, and it was this that gave him the emotional freedom soon thereafter to marry and establish a home of his own.

the appointed time to marry and found a family of his own. As can be readily gathered from the fact that at "about thirty" he left his parental family, quite abruptly it seems, to join the masses who were going to the Jordan to be baptized there, he would have been, during these years, increasingly uneasy and dissatisfied with the course his life was taking. Clearly, he would not yet have fulfilled *his* dream.

Jesus at Thirty

A hypothesis is only as good as its power to illumine perplexing data. Does the developmental scenario just outlined do this? I will try to indicate a few of the ways I think it does and add several comments regarding how looking at Jesus in this light may serve to highlight certain otherwise neglected features of his life and mission.

An especially puzzling aspect of the Gospel portraits of Jesus at thirty are references to tensions that seem to have existed at this stage of his life between himself and his mother, brothers, and sisters. His brothers did not believe in him, the fourth Gospel reports (John 7:5), and Mark 3:19–21 states that at one point during the height of his public mission his family thought him "beside himself" and were determined to seize him and bring him back home.[6] We are then also told, as a sequel, that on their visit to his headquarters at Capernaum, ostensibly to carry out their plan, Jesus would not even see them, but sharply distanced himself from them when he said: "Who are my mother and my brothers? . . . Here are my mother and my brothers! Whoever does the will of God is my brother, and sister, and mother" (Mark 3:33–35).[7] Additional hints of this estrangement may be found in the report of his abortive visit to Nazareth (Mark 6:1–6), as well as those sayings that stress the absolute priority of doing God's will over family ties (Matt. 10:35; Luke 9:60/Matt. 8:22; Luke 11:28; 12:51–52; 14:26; 18:29–30). The pathos of this unexpected development is summed up in John's Gospel: "He came to his own home, and his own people received him not" (John 1:11).

All this is consistent, I suggest, with the developmental scenario just outlined. Few situations in life are as demanding and emotionally complex as that of a son caught up in the necessity of assuming his father's

6. For a review of the problems involved in translating Mark 3:19b–21 see R. E. Brown et al. (1978, 51–58). Geza Vermes (1973, 33) comments that "the scandalous incongruity of this statement is the best guarantee of its historicity." For a further understanding of the historical Jesus, see M. Hengel (1981, 64).

7. According to J. Klausner and H. Danby (1925, 280), "respect for his mother, a prominent trait among the Jews, ranked in the Ten Commandments on the same level as respect for the father, required that he should go to her at once" instead of responding in this manner.

role with his mother and her family. If his mother, brothers, and sisters were mystified at this time by his radical shift in loyalty from their family to God's family and thought him "beside himself," then this only means that they, and the mother especially, like others in their predicament, perhaps were more attuned to their own needs and necessities than to his.

John the Baptist's role in Jesus' life may also come into sharper focus in this light. Of no one else, it would appear, did Jesus speak so exuberantly. John is a prophet, Jesus is quoted as saying, yes, more than a prophet, indeed, the greatest man who ever lived (Matt. 11:9, 11/Luke 7:26, 28). Yet after briefly working with John in Judea, even, perhaps, baptizing as John did (John 3:22), he returned to Galilee (John 4:3) and there continued his mission in a manner increasingly unique to himself. While traditionally regarded as Jesus' forerunner, John's part in Jesus' age thirty transition also corresponds precisely to that of the mentor who helps to awaken and realize the still latent Dream.[8] John's person and preaching were, our sources suggest, the catalyst Jesus needed to break free of an increasingly sterile role in his deceased father's family so that he could at last fulfill his own unique destiny and mission.

What Jesus is said to have experienced as a consequence of his association with John, his baptism and temptations especially, may also take on added meaning when looked at more closely in the context of the age thirty transition. Immediately following Jesus' baptism, we are told, God became experientially real to him as gracious father through divine words of acceptance and approval that broke into his consciousness while he prayed (Luke 3:21–22).[9] During the temptations that followed he wrestled with Satan over whether to turn stones into bread, throw himself from the pinnacle of the temple, or rule the world (Matt. 4:1–11/Luke 4:1–13).[10] These were, we may conjecture, thaumaturgical fantasies of a type widely current in his time, for to produce mighty

8. The mentor at thirty is invariably "a transitional figure," writes Levinson (1978, 99), due to the innate drive of the age thirty male to find himself and realize his destiny. This would suggest that there was no one "root cause" of Jesus' eventual independence and differentiation from John, such as the "disconfirmation" of John's eschatological expectations (Riches 1980, 165, 180), or his exorcisms (Hollenbach 1982, 209–16), or the audition and vision at the time of his baptism (Jeremias 1971, 55). These may well have been factors, but at thirty the mentoring relationship is almost always a very temporary one.

9. The way Matthew's Gospel has changed what was undoubtedly a private audition ("*Thou* art my beloved Son." Mark 1:11/Luke 3:22, ital. added) into a public event ("*This* is my beloved Son." Matt. 3:17, ital. added) has often been observed. For a defense of the historicity and life-changing importance of this experience see especially J. Jeremias (1971, 51–56); J. D. G. Dunn (1975, 62–65); I. Wilson (1984, 87).

10. While it is difficult to imagine who in the early church might have invented stories of Jesus being tempted by Satan in this manner, an analysis of Jesus' mission

signs and rule the world were the then prevailing expectations of what the Messiah would do when he appeared.[11] Grandiose thoughts such as these on the part of Jesus would accord with the fantasies of greatness which, as we have seen, are endemic to the struggle for self-definition of the age-thirty male; in Jesus' case these might have been exacerbated by his assumption of his father's role at the time of his death.[12] Nor is it to be doubted that with the help of his baptism and the disclosure experience he had at that time ("Thou art my beloved son . . .") he was finally able to fight free of these fantasies, reconnect with the "Father," and experience what it meant to be a trusting "son" once again. Viewed in this way, something like the battle with Satan described here would help explain Jesus' unprecedented certainty, during the time of his mission, that Satan was retreating and God's fatherly care was being revealed to the world through him.[13]

---

points to a victorious battle over "Satan" as one of its presuppositions (see n. 13). For further arguments for historicity, see Thomas W. Manson (1953, 55); V. McCasland (1964, 31); I. Howard Marshall (1979).

11. Josephus writes in *The Jewish War* (6.312) that the chief inducement for the Jewish rebellion against Rome in the years prior to the fall of Jerusalem in A.D. 70 was an "oracle also found in their sacred scriptures, announcing that at that time a man from their country would become ruler of the world." While Josephus is vague regarding the relevance of this oracle for the various prophetic-messianic type revolutionaries he describes elsewhere as active during the fourth and fifth decades of this first century (see 2.118, 258–65), it is apparent that there must have been some connection. In 2.259, for example, these latter are described as "deceivers and imposters, claiming divine inspiration" and as men who "fostered revolutionary changes by inciting the mob to frenzied enthusiasm and by leading them into the wilderness under the belief that God would show them omens of freedom there." This is as plausible a background for understanding Jesus' wilderness temptations as could be hoped for. Seen in this light Jesus' temptations would appear to be not "temptations of the Messiah," as traditionally thought, but "temptations to messianism." In other words, a spiritual ordeal is alluded to in which Jesus, after his encounter with God as gracious Father at his baptism, came to recognize messianic delusions of grandeur as satanic and thrust them from him.

12. It is worth noting that Satan in these narratives represents patricidal ambition. He tempts Jesus to usurp the role of his true Father (God) and rule the world in his stead. This is precisely the dilemma a son would face in taking charge of a deceased father's family, as we conjecture Jesus did. Suddenly powerful in a realm where only a short time before he had been a subordinate, his identity as "son" will inevitably be threatened by the heady "impossible possibility" of "ruling" in his rightful father's place. Understandably a son in such circumstances will find himself contending with fantasies of greatness which he knows in his more sober moments to be illusory. If he should happen to live in a time when hopes for the coming of a miracle-working Messiah are high, these may well determine the more precise form that such fantasies might take.

13. That a satanic figure was extremely real to the historical Jesus, and had in fact, in his view, already in some sense been defeated, is evident from the following passages: Mark 3:27/Luke 11:21; Luke 10:18; Mark 8:33; Luke 22:31–32. Regarding God's fatherly power see Matt. 6:10/Luke 11:2 ("Father . . . thy kingdom come!"); Matt. 12:28/Luke 11:20; Luke 17:20–21. For a penetrating discussion of Jesus' "Abba-experience" as "source and secret of his being, message, and manner of life," see Eduard Schillebeeckx (256–71).

Regarding the mission itself, what Erikson has written of Gandhi's achievement at a similar stage in his life may apply to Jesus as well. "The true saints," he writes, in his book about Gandhi, "are those who transfer the state of householdership to the house of God, becoming father and mother, brother and sister, son and daughter, to all creation, rather than of their own issue" (Erikson 1969, 399). Erikson was referring to the way Gandhi extended his emerging sense of generative care from his wife and children to the needs of India during a time of crisis. If our conjecture is correct, Jesus too had been a "householder" of sorts; not, however, in a family of his own, but in his deceased father's family. As a result, both ripe experience and a pent-up generativity were still waiting to be released. John was the catalyst, his years as head of his deceased father's family were the apprenticeship, his baptism and temptations were the turning point. Through finally taking matters into his own hands, going out to John and thereby being set free of his past, he was poised and ready now to create a family of his own; one born, however, not of flesh, nor of blood, nor of the will of man, but of God (John 1:12–13).

The focus of his mission, initially at least, was "the lost sheep of the house of Israel" (Matt. 10:6); the sick, the sinners, or the poor, as he preferred to call them.[14] Their numbers were large, for the times were out of joint. Gentiles occupied the Israelite homeland and to many God seemed distant. Only a dedicated few could live up to the high standards of God's Torah and find meaning. The rest lived in a religious twilight zone. The result was that they frequently suffered from guilt, sickness, confusion, or worse (Borg 1984, 51–72). Obviously Jesus' own life experience had prepared him to understand their condition well. All that we know about him during this phase of his life testifies to his swift, uncanny insight into the inner world of these disaffiliated ones. Often, it appeared, only a word was all that was needed for amazing things to happen (Mark 2:5–12). In fact his charismatic effectiveness with this sector of the population quickly thrust him into the center of the Jewish struggle for self-definition where his subjective inward approach to Torah soon rendered him suspect among the Jewish elite.[15] When this happened, he did not retreat, but defended his

---

14. Regarding this alienated sector and the reasons for their alienation see Jeremias (1971, 108–13); A. Oppenheimer (1977); and now also E. P. Sanders (1985, 186–211), who call attention to the failure of earlier discussions of this topic to differentiate between "sinners" and "common people" ('am ha-aretz).

15. Again M. J. Borg's judgment is similar (238). Whereas, he writes, the other renewal movements of the time "intensified the Torah in the direction of holiness, emphasizing various forms of separation: from society as a whole, from the Gentiles, from impurity within society; Jesus intensified the Torah primarily by applying it to internal dimensions of the human psyche: to dispositions, emotions, thoughts and desires." For a comparable analysis, see Vermes (1984, 47).

approach with irenic skill (Farmer 1982, 32–48). There are hints that satanic delusions of grandeur continued to haunt him, but he would not succumb (Mark 8:33).[16] He disliked honorific titles (Matt. 23:6–12),[17] rebuked those who called him "good" (Mark 10:18), and warned against emulating "great men" who lord it over others (Mark 10:42–45). His exuberant thanksgiving, at one point in his mission, for the way God's fatherly love was being revealed to the world through him (Matt. 11:25–27/Luke 10:21–22) would suggest that he was, in that moment at least, a man at last at peace with himself and his God, doing now what he knew he does best, God's gracious will for his life (Matt. 6:33/Luke 12:31).[18]

Concluding Comments

Already the author of Hebrews saw nobility in Jesus being tempted as we are (Heb. 4:15) and maturing through the things that he suffered (Heb. 5:8). But prior to the advent of developmental psychology our knowledge of *how* we are tested and tempted and grow through various life stages, from early childhood onward, was limited. As a result biographies tended to be long at the end in their accounts of the culminating achievements of a man's life, but short at the beginning on analysis of the events leading up to those accomplishments.

This is certainly true of the Gospels. They too focus almost exclusively on Jesus' final public mission and the events leading up to his death. And yet even they are insistent that there were developments leading up to these climactic events without which they cannot properly be understood or appreciated. Although Jesus had lived the greater part of his life in Nazareth, they inform us, his mission did not begin there. Prior to his mission at thirty he had left Nazareth and gone out to the Jordan where he was baptized and tempted and asso-

16. The emotional dimensions of Jesus' reaction to Peter's insistence on projecting a messianic identity upon him are too seldom noted. It can be argued, I suggest, that Jesus not only did not think of himself as Messiah (Vermes 1973, 149), but that he was inwardly tormented over this issue, and feared succumbing to such an identity. It was, so to speak, the dark side of his inner world, one which he thrust from him on this occasion (Mark 8:33) with an outburst of emotion that apparently startled his disciples ("Get behind me, Satan! for you are not on the side of God, but of men").

17. According to Jeremias (1971, 258), "the only title used by Jesus of himself whose authenticity is to be taken seriously" is "Son of Man," but Vermes (1973, 160–91; 1984, 89–99), has shown that even this (Aramaic: *bar enash*) was not a title in the world of Jesus, but an idiom meaning "man," "someone," or used occasionally as a self-effacing circumlocution for "I."

18. Jeremias (1978, 45), documents the "turning of the tide" in favor of the historicity of these important texts. See also Jeremias (1971, 57–59); Dunn (1975, 27–34); B. F. Meyer (1979, 152).

ciated for a time with one of the great men of his world. And it was then, the Gospels intimate, that something happened without which there might possibly have been no mission. Jesus had to face and surmount certain inner problems: fantasies of power and miracle-working greatness above all. Only after that, and the arrest of his mentor John, did he return to Galilee "in the power of the Spirit" and begin that mission for which he became famous (Luke 4:14–15/Mark 1:14/Matt. 4:12).

A sharper focus on Jesus' age-thirty transition could have contemporary relevance, for problems of this nature—pseudoattachments, misshapen identities, and fantasies of power in men of this age group—remain with us as one of our intransigent problems. The world-famous martyr-theologian, Dietrich Bonhoeffer, a recent psychobiography informs us (Green 1977, 169), was also conflicted in this way at this time of his life. Theology itself was initially embraced by him, we are told, partly as a tactic for surpassing his prestigious father and brothers. In a memoir written when he was twenty-six he refers to the "contemptible vanity" that had plagued him in doing so. "How often," he lamented, "he had sought to master it [this vanity]. But it always crept back again and . . . forced an entry into the house of his soul and made him afraid" (Green 1977, 169). Only through a deep-seated conversion to the God of the Bible and to Jesus was he released from this agonizing state of mind and set free at last to pursue his life's work. Pope John XXIII also tells, in his posthumously published *Journal of a Soul*, of the "fantastic dreams" of "positions and honors" that assailed him all his life. His "enemy within," he called them. "In the end," he says, "I was able to get the better of it. But I was mortified to feel it constantly returning." Hitler may be cited as an example of someone who, beset by similar problems and grandiose dreams, not only yielded, but in yielding brought the world with him to the brink of destruction. It would appear that the great men who fail in this crucial encounter with hubris, especially at this time of their lives, may descend to the depths and become the tragic antichrists of history, while those who instead come "to their senses" (Luke 15:17 NIV) are the pillars upon whom whatever sanity the world has is continually being built and rebuilt.

Through the centuries the portraits of Jesus have varied from age to age and place to place: "good shepherd" during the early church persecutions; "cosmic ruler" during the triumph of Christianity in the Roman Empire; "the crucified" in the late Middle Ages (Bainton 1974). A psychohistorical probe of the kind undertaken here may help us appropriate still another dimension of Jesus' achievement, one of special importance, perhaps, in an age grasping for ways to check the indulgent and sometimes dangerous ambitions of too many of its age-thirty-and-over males: Jesus, "the tempted one," who at the right time finds a wise mentor, humbles himself in baptism, says no to grandiosity, and with God's help goes on to become what he was meant to be: the prototypical, caring, "generative man."[19]

19. For an incisive discussion of this prototype and its contemporary relevance, see D. S. Browning (1973).

Conclusion

DAVID G. BENNER
AND J. HAROLD ELLENS

This book is about growth. It presents a clear description of human life and experience, in God's grace and providence, as an intriguing process of predictable patterns in personality development. The focus of this volume is upon the role that Christian faith and life play in human spiritual and psychological growth.

The authors of our book have demonstrated how fertile a field of interest and work the science of developmental theory can be for Christians who are seriously interested in deeply understanding faith, maturity, and ministry. As Professor Aden suggested in the introduction, developmental psychology brings to our attention the fact that we are historical creatures and that we can only begin to understand the human condition when we view it through a developmental perspective.

Static views of our nature and life as persons fail to reflect the fact that our experience is one of change during growth. The developmental models we have considered here are, in that sense, dynamic theories in as much as they present humans as persons in process. The image we receive from such developmental theories is more like a moving picture of ourselves than like a snapshot. Snapshots fail to capture the dynamism of the subject matter. So also do many attempts to describe the unfolding of human personality. Developmental theories, such as those which the structuralists have proposed, illumine our understanding with the insight that personality growth always involves a process that moves in one direction or another.

It is just at this juncture and for that reason that faith is of such central importance in our growth, and in understanding the nature and dynamics of human growth. Faith reflects and provides the orientation that a person has and thus the direction a person's growth takes. Faith has the unique ability, according to R. C. Fuller in chapter 9, to give the crucial impetus and direction the maturing personality needs. The object upon which our faith is fixed, and the commitment we hold toward faith objects, determines the direction of our lives. Depending upon the object of our faith, our commitments can bring integration to our personalities and healing to our persons that cannot be obtained from any other source.

Models and theories of development are not the development itself. In like fashion, a map is not the same as the territory that the map describes. But models and theories, just as maps, are an enormous help in understanding where we are going and what we are doing, and afford us a real understanding of what the territory actually looks like. They help us see the big picture, so to speak.

Models and theories of human development help us understand and focus upon the important directionality of human personality, as it moves through the God-given patterns and dynamics that constitute our growth. They help us appreciate how important our faith objects are, the direction these faith commitments give to our lives, and the integrating and unifying effects that these centering objects of our heart's desire provide us with.

To be human is to be a creature of faith. We do not and cannot choose whether to be creatures of faith. While we have some freedom of will and choice, we are free in our wills to choose only those things to which our hearts are committed. That commitment sets the boundaries around what is possible for us to will and to choose.

So models and theories of human development are of great importance to Christians who seek to understand themselves more completely and allow their lives of Christian dedication to be informed and illumined by such understanding. Christian perspectives are equally crucial for models and theories of human development. They ensure that such theories include the full range of human dynamics, including religious and spiritual dynamics.

This book makes a strenuous effort to articulate Christian perspectives on human development. It is an early step in this crucial enterprise. Christian developmental perspectives and models must be applied to many more aspects of human experience than we have been able to address here. Sexuality, identity, sin, self-esteem, empathy, creativity, spirituality itself, and relational styles in human feeling and behavior, all need to be examined carefully and understood thoroughly in Christian developmental perspectives. The structuralists have given us a set of remarkably useful tools for that work.

That work will be the task of future volumes. If this book has set the course and generated the motivation for a comparable undertaking in those remaining areas of scholarship, it will have succeeded in one of its two most important objectives.

Thus we offer this volume, first, in the hope that it informs and inspires Christians to profound understanding and appreciation of what God has wrought in his majestic and mysterious creation of humans in his image. We trust, secondly, that it will motivate much creative Christian scholarship in those areas of human growth which require further careful investigation.

Bibliography

Aden, L. 1969. Rogerian therapy and optimal pastoral counseling. In *The new shape of pastoral theology: Essays in honor of Seward Hiltner,* ed. W. B. Oglesby, Jr. New York: Abingdon.

Adler, A. 1927. *Practice and theory of individual psychology.* New York: Harcourt, Brace.

Ainsworth, M. D. S., and S. M. Bell. 1970. Attachment exploration and separation: Illustrated by the behavior of one-year-olds in a strange situation. *Child Development* 41: 49–67.

Allport, G. W. 1937. *Personality: A psychological interpretation.* New York: Henry Holt.

———. 1950. *The individual and his religion: A psychological interpretation.* New York: Macmillan.

———. 1960. *Personality and social encounter: Selected essays.* Boston: Beacon.

———. 1961. *Pattern and growth in personality.* New York: Holt, Rinehart, and Winston.

Anderson, J. F. 1972. *Paul Tillich: Basics in his thought.* Albany, N. Y.: Magi.

Armstrong, R. C., G. L. Larsen, and S. A. Mourer. 1962. Religious attitudes and emotional adjustment. *Journal of Psychological Studies* 13: 35–47.

Bainton, R. H. 1950. *Here I stand: A life of Martin Luther.* New York: Abingdon-Cokesbury.

Bainton, R. H., and S. Devasahayam. 1974. *Behold the Christ: A portrayal in words and pictures.* New York: Harper and Row.

Bakan, D. 1966. *The duality of human existence.* Chicago: Univ. of Chicago Press.

Barshinger, C. 1977. Intimacy and spiritual growth. *CAPS Bulletin* 2: 19–21.

Baruch, G. K. 1976. Girls who perceive themselves as competent: Some antecedents and correlates. *Psychology of Women Quarterly* 1: 38–49.

Beck, J. R. 1978. Mutuality in marriage. *Journal of Psychology and Theology* 6, 2: 141–48.

Bellah, R. N., R. Madsen, W. M. Sullivan, A. Swidler, and S. M. Tipton. 1985. *Habits of the heart: Individualism and commitment in American life.* New York: Harper and Row.

Benner, D. G. 1983. The incarnation as a metaphor for psychotherapy. *Journal of Psychology and Theology* 11: 287–94.

———. 1988. *Psychotherapy and the spiritual quest.* Grand Rapids: Baker.

255

Berger, P. L. 1975. *A rumor of angels: Modern society and the rediscovery of the supernatural.* Garden City, N. Y.: Doubleday, Anchor Books.

———. 1979. *The heretical imperative: Contemporary possibilities of religious affirmation.* Garden City, N. Y.: Doubleday, Anchor Books.

Berguer, G. 1923. *Some aspects of the life of Jesus from the psychological and psychoanalytic point of view.* New York: Harcourt, Brace.

Berkouwer, G. C. 1962. *Man: The image of God.* Grand Rapids: Eerdmans.

Board of Publications of the Christian Reformed Church. 1980. *Acts of Synod 1980.* Grand Rapids: Board of Publications of the Christian Reformed Church.

Boisen, A. 1936. *The exploration of the inner world: A study of mental disorder and religious experience.* New York: Harper.

Bonhoeffer, D. 1954. *Life together.* New York: Harper and Brothers.

Borg, M. J. 1984. *Conflict, holiness and politics in the teaching of Jesus.* New York: Edwin Mellen.

Bowlby, J. 1969. *Attachment and loss.* New York: Basic.

Brainerd, C. J. 1978. *Piaget's theory of intelligence.* Englewood Cliffs, N. J.: Prentice-Hall.

Bregman, L. 1982. *The rediscovery of inner experience.* Chicago: Nelson-Hall.

Broverman, I. K. 1972. Sex-role stereotypes: A current appraisal. *Journal of Social Issues* 28: 59–78.

Brown, R. E., et al., eds. 1978. *Mary in the New Testament: A collaborative assessment by Protestant and Roman Catholic scholars.* Philadelphia: Fortress.

Browning, D. S. 1973. *Generative man: Psychoanalytic perspectives.* Philadelphia: Westminster.

Buber, M. 1961. *Two types of faith.* Trans. N. P. Goldhawk. New York: Harper and Row.

Buchanan, G. W. 1984. *Jesus, the king and his kingdom.* Macon, Ga.: Mercer Univ. Press.

———. 1985. Jesus and the upper classes. In *Novum Testamentum* 7: 195–209.

Bucke, R. M. 1901. *Cosmic consciousness: A study in the evolution of the human mind.* New York: E. P. Dutton.

Bugental, J. F. T., ed. 1967. *Challenges of humanistic psychology.* New York: McGraw-Hill.

Buzin, W. E. 1958. Luther on music. *Lutheran Society of Worship, Music and the Arts,* 3. St. Paul: North Central.

Cadbury, H. J. 1963. Some Lukan expressions of time (lexical notes on Luke-Acts 7). *Journal of Biblical Literature* 82: 272–78.

Calvin, J. 1960. *Institutes of the Christian religion.* Ed. J. T. McNeill. Trans. F. L. Battles. Philadelphia: Westminster.

Capps, D. 1974. Contemporary psychology of religion: The task of theoretical reconstruction. *Social Research* 41: 362–83.

———. 1979. *Pastoral care: A thematic approach.* Philadelphia: Westminster.

———. 1983. *Life cycle theory and pastoral care.* Philadelphia: Fortress.

———. 1984. Erikson's life-cycle theory: Religious dimensions. *Religious Studies Review* 10, 2: 120–27.

———. 1987. *Deadly sins and saving virtues.* Philadelphia: Fortress.

———. 1991. Religious ritual and the excommunication of Ann Hibbens. See chapter 15 of present volume.

Capps, D., P. Ransohoff, and L. Rambo. 1976. Publication trends in the psychology of religion. *Journal for the Scientific Study of Religion* 15, 1: 15–28.

Carter, J. D. 1974. Maturity: psychological and biblical. *Journal of Psychology and Theology* 2, 2: 89–96.

———. 1980. Towards a biblical model of counselling. *Journal of Psychology and Theology* 8, 1: 45–52.

Chapko, J. J. 1985. *Faith in search of a focus, an internal critique of the faith development theory of James Fowler.* Toronto: Institute for Christian Studies.

Clines, D. J. A. 1977. Sin and maturity. *Journal of Psychology and Theology* 5, 3: 183–96.

Cobble, J. F. 1985. *Faith and crisis in the stages of life.* Peabody, Mass.: Hendrickson.

Connick, C. M. 1974. *Jesus: The man, the mission, and the message.* 2d ed. Englewood Cliffs, N. J.: Prentice-Hall.

Cornfled, G., ed. 1982. *Josephus: The Jewish wars, newly translated with extensive commentary and archaeological background illustrations.* Grand Rapids: Zondervan.

Corsini, R. J., ed. 1977. *Current personality theories.* Itasca, Ill.: F. E. Peacock.

de Castillejo, I. C. 1973. *Knowing women.* New York: Harper and Row.

Demos, J. 1970. *A little commonwealth: Early family life in Plymouth Colony.* New York: Oxford Univ. Press.

Droege, T. A. 1966. A developmental view of faith. Ph.D. diss., Divinity School, Univ. of Chicago.

———. 1974. A developmental view of faith. *Journal of Religion and Health* 3: 313–29.

———. 1987. *Guided grief imagery: A resource for grief ministry and death education.* New York: Paulist.

Dunn, J. D. G. 1975. *Jesus and the spirit: A study of the religious and charismatic experience of Jesus and the first Christians as reflected in the New Testament.* London: SCM.

Dykstra, C. R. 1981. *Vision and character, a Christian educator's alternative to Kohlberg.* New York: Paulist.

———. 1982. Theological tabletalk: Transformation in faith and morals. *Theology Today* 39, 1: 56–64.

Dykstra, C. R., and S. Parks, eds. 1986. *Faith development and Fowler.* Birmingham, Ala.: Religious Education Press.

Ehrenwald, J. 1966. *Psychotherapy: Myth and method, an integrative approach.* New York: Grune and Stratton.

Eisenstadt, J. M. 1978. Parental loss and genius. *American Psychologist* 33, 3: 211–23.

Eliade, M. 1960. *Myths, dreams, and mysteries: The encounter between contemporary faiths and archaic realities.* New York: Harper and Brothers.

———. 1967. *From primitives to Zen: A thematic sourcebook of the history of religions.* New York: Harper.

Elkind, D. 1974. *Children and adolescents: Interpretive essays on Jean Piaget.* 2d ed. New York: Oxford Univ. Press.

———. 1984. *All grown up and no place to go: Teenagers in crisis.* Reading, Mass.: Addison-Wesley.

Ellenberger, H. F. 1970. *The discovery of the unconscious: The history and evolution of dynamic psychiatry.* New York: Basic.

Ellens, J. H. 1982. *God's grace and human health.* Nashville: Abingdon.

———. 1987a. Andrew's anxiety. In *Christian counseling and psychotherapy,* ed. D. G. Benner. Grand Rapids: Baker.

———. 1987b. Biblical themes in psychological theory and practice. In *Christian counseling and psychotherapy,* ed. D. G. Benner. Grand Rapids: Baker.

———. 1987c. Ritual. In *Psychology and religion,* ed. D. G. Benner. Grand Rapids: Baker.

———. 1987d. *Psychotheology: Key issues.* Pretoria: UNISA.

———. 1987e. Theology and psychotherapy. In *Psychotherapy in Christian perspective,* ed. D. G. Benner. Grand Rapids: Baker.

———. 1987f. Worship. In *Psychology and religion*, ed. D. G. Benner. Grand Rapids: Baker.

———. 1988. The psychodynamics of Christian conversion. In *The church and pastoral care*, ed. L. Aden and J. H. Ellens. Grand Rapids: Baker.

———. 1989a. The Christian way, faith or heresy? In *God se genade is genoeg*, ed. H. J. C. Pieterse et al. Johannesburg: NGKB.

———. 1989b. A psychospiritual view of sin. In *Counseling and the human predicament*, ed. L. Aden and D. G. Benner. Grand Rapids: Baker.

———. 1989c. Sin and sickness: The nature of human failure. In *Counseling and the human predicament*, ed. L. Aden and D. G. Benner. Grand Rapids: Baker.

Ellens, J. H., and L. Aden. 1988. The church and pastoral care. Grand Rapids: Baker.

———. 1990. *Turning points in pastoral care: The legacy of Anton Boisen and Seward Hiltner.* Grand Rapids: Baker.

English, H. B., and A. C. English. 1958. *A comprehensive dictionary of psychological and psychoanalytical terms: A guide to usage.* New York: Longmans, Green.

Erikson, K. T. 1966. *Wayward Puritans: A study in the sociology of deviance.* New York: Wiley.

Erikson, E. H. [1958] 1962. *Young man Luther: A study in psychoanalysis and history.* New York: Norton.

———. [1959] 1980. *Identity and the life cycle.* New York: Norton.

———. 1963. *Childhood and society.* 2d. ed. New York: Norton.

———. 1964. *Insight and responsibility: Lectures on the ethical implication of psychoanalytic insight.* New York: Norton.

———. 1966. Ontogeny of ritualization. In *Psychoanalysis—a general psychology: Essays in honor of Heinz Hartmann*, ed. R. Loewenstein et al. New York: International Universities Press.

———. 1968. *Identity: Youth and crisis.* New York: Norton.

———. 1969. *Gandhi's truth: On the origins of militant nonviolence.* New York: Norton.

———. 1975. *Life history and the historical movement.* New York: Norton.

———. 1977a. *Childhood and society.* 2d ed. London: Triad/Paladin.

———. 1977b. *Toys and reasons: Stages in the ritualization of experience.* New York: Norton.

———. 1981. The Galilean sayings and the sense of "I." *The Yale Review* 70: 321–62.

———. 1982. *The life cycle completed: A review.* New York: Norton.

———. 1987. *A way of looking at things, Selected papers from 1930 to 1980.* Ed. S. Schlein. New York: Norton.

Evans, R. I. 1969. *Dialogue with Erik Erikson.* New York: Dutton.

Farmer, W. R. 1982. *Jesus and the gospel: Tradition, Scripture, and canon.* Philadelphia: Fortress.

Faust, C. H., and H. Johnson, eds. 1962. *Jonathon Edwards: Representative selections, with introduction, bibliography and notes.* New York: Hill and Wang.

Flusser, D. 1969. *Jesus.* New York: Herder and Herder.

Foder, J. 1980. Methodological solipsism. *The Behavioral and Brain Sciences* 3: 63–109.

Fowler, J. W. 1976. Faith development theory and the aims of religious socialization. In *Emerging issues in religious education*, ed. G. Durka and J. Smith. New York: Paulist.

———. 1980. Moral stages and the development of faith. In *Moral development, moral education, and Kohlberg: Basic issues in philosophy, psychology, religion, and education*, ed. B. Munsey. Birmingham, Ala.: Religious Education Press.

———. 1981. *Stages of faith: The psychology of human development and the quest for meaning.* San Francisco: Harper and Row.

———. 1982. Theology and psychology in the study of faith development. In *Concilium: The challenge of psychology to faith*, ed. S. Kepnes, D. Tracy, and M. Lefebure. New York: Seabury.

———. 1984. *Becoming adult, becoming Christian: Adult development and Christian faith*. San Francisco: Harper and Row.

Fowler, J. W., S. Keen, and J. Berryman. 1978. *Life-maps: Conversations on the journey of faith*. Waco: Word.

Fowler, J. W., and J. W. Loder. 1982. Conversations on Fowler's *Stages of faith* and Loder's *The transforming moment*. *Religious Education* 77 (2).

Frankl, V. E. 1962. *Man's search for meaning: An introduction to logotherapy*. Boston: Beacon.

———. 1975. *The unconscious God: Psychotherapy and theology*. New York: Simon and Schuster.

Frankl, V. E., and J. C. Crumbaugh. 1967. *Psychotherapy and existentialism: Selected papers on logotherapy*. New York: Washington Square Press.

Freud, S. 1964. *The future of an illusion*. New York: Doubleday.

Fuller, R. C. 1988. *Religion and the life cycle*. Philadelphia: Fortress.

Gay, V. P. 1975. Psychopathology and ritual: Freud's essay "obsessive actions and religious practises." *The Psychoanalytic Review* 62: 493–507.

———. 1978. Public rituals versus private treatment: Psychodynamics of prayer. *Journal of Religion and Health* 17: 244–60.

Gerkin, C. V. 1979. *Crisis experience in modern life: Theory and theology in pastoral care*. Nashville: Abingdon.

———. 1984. *The living human document: Re-visioning pastoral counseling in a hermeneutic mold*. Nashville: Abingdon.

———. 1986. *Widening the horizons: Pastoral responses to a fragmented society*. Philadelphia: Westminster.

Getz, G. A. 1976. *Building up one another*. Wheaton: Victor.

Gilbert, A. R. 1951. Recent German theories of stratification of personality. *The Journal of Psychology* 31: 3–19.

———. 1967. Neuere deutsche schichtentheorien der personlichkeit. In *Zur psychologie der personlichkeit*, ed. M. Pertilovitsch. Darmstadt: Wissenschaftliche Buchgesellschaft.

Gilligan, C. 1982. *In a different voice: Psychological theory and women's development*. Cambridge: Harvard Univ. Press.

Gilmore, W. J. 1984. *Psychohistorical inquiry: A comprehensive research bibliography*. New York and London: Garland.

Goldbrunner, J. 1964. *Individuation: A study of the depth psychology of Carl Gustav Jung*. Notre Dame, Ind.: University of Notre Dame Press.

Goldman, R. 1964. *Religious thinking from childhood to adolescence*. New York: Seabury.

———. 1965. *Readiness for religion: A basis for developmental religious education*. New York: Seabury.

Gould, R. L. 1975. Adult life stages: Growth toward self-tolerance. *Psychology Today* 8: 74–78.

———. 1978. *Transformations, growth and change in adult life*. New York: Simon and Schuster.

Green, C. 1977. Bonhoeffer in the context of Erikson's Luther study. In *Psychohistory and religion: The case of young man Luther*, ed. R. H. Bainton. Philadelphia: Fortress.

Greenblatt, M. 1978. The grieving spouse. *American Journal of Psychiatry* 8: 43–47.

Greenspan, S. I., and G. H. Pollock, eds. 1980. *The course of life: Psychoanalytic contributions toward understanding personality development, III: Adulthood and the aging process*. Adelphi, Md.: NIMH.

Groeschel, B. J. 1984. *Spiritual passages: The psychology of spiritual development "for those who seek."* New York: Crossroad.

Guidelines for therapy with women. *American Psychologist* 33: 1122–23.

Guntrip, H. 1969. Religion in relation to personal integration. *The British Journal of Medical Psychology* 42: 323–33.

———. 1971. *Psychoanalytic theory, therapy, and the self.* New York: Basic.

Gustafson, J. M. 1977. Interdependence, finitude, and sin: Reflections on scarcity. *Journal of Religion* 57, 2: 156–58.

Hagner, D. A. 1984. The battle for inerrancy. *The Reformed Journal* 34, 4: 19–22.

Hall, C. S., and G. Lindzey. 1970. *Theories of personality.* New York: Wiley.

Harding, M. E. 1970. *The way of all women: A psychological interpretation.* New York: Harper and Row.

Hartmann, H. 1950. *Ego psychology and the problem of adaptation.* New York: International Universities Press.

Havighurst, R. J. 1972. *Developmental tasks and education.* New York: McKay.

Hengel, M. 1981. *The charismatic leader and his followers.* New York: Crossroad.

Herink, R., ed. 1980. *The psychotherapy handbook.* New York: New American Library.

Hillman, J. 1967. *Insearch: Psychology and religion.* New York: Scribner's.

Hodge, M. B. 1967. *Your fear of love.* New York: Doubleday.

Hollenbach, P. 1982. The conversion of Jesus: From Jesus the baptizer to Jesus the healer. In *Aufstieg und Niedergang der Romischen Welt,* 2, 55: 196–219.

Holmes, U. T. 1982. *Spirituality for ministry.* San Francisco: Harper and Row.

Homans, P. 1976. Protestant theology and dynamic psychology: New thoughts on an old problem. *Anglican Theological Review: Supplementary Series* 7: 125–38.

———. 1989. *The ability to mourn; disillusionment and the social origins of psychoanalysis.* Chicago: Univ. of Chicago Press.

Homans, P., ed. 1978. *Childhood and selfhood: Essays on tradition, religion and modernity in the psychology of Erik H. Erikson.* Lewisburg, Penn.: Bucknell Univ. Press.

Horowitz, F. D. 1987. *Exploring developmental theories: Toward a structural/behavioral model of development.* Hillsdale, N. J.: Lawrence Erlbaum.

Jaekle, C. R., and W. A. Clebsch. 1975. Reprint. *Pastoral care in historical perspective.* New York: Aronson.

Jahoda, M. 1950. Towards a social psychology of mental health. In *Symposium on the healthy personality,* ed. M. J. E. Benn. New York: Josiah Macy, Jr., Foundation.

James, W. 1956. *The will to believe.* New York: Dove.

———. 1958. *The varieties of religious experience.* New York: Mentor.

———. 1961. *The varieties of religious experience.* New York: Collier.

Janeway, E. 1974. *Between myth and morning: Women awakening.* New York: Morrow.

Jeremias, J. 1971. *New Testament theology, part one: The proclamation of Jesus.* London: SCM.

———. 1978. *The prayers of Jesus.* Philadelphia: Fortress.

Johannes XXII, Pope. 1965. *Journal of a soul.* Montreal: Paul Publishers.

Johnson, S. 1989. *Christian spiritual formation in the church and classroom.* Nashville: Abingdon.

Joy, D. M., et al. 1983. *Moral development foundations, Judeo-Christian alternatives to Piaget/Kohlberg.* Nashville: Abingdon.

Jung, C. G. 1933. *Modern man in search of a soul.* New York: Harcourt, Brace.

———. [1938] 1958. *Psychology and religion: West and east.* London: Routledge.

————. 1940. *The integration of the personality.* London: Kegan Paul.

————. 1964. *Man and his symbols.* New York: Doubleday.

Kao, C. C. L. 1975. *Search for maturity.* Philadelphia: Westminster.

————. 1981. *Psychological and religious development: Maturity and maturation.* Washington, D. C.: Univ. Press.

Keaynes, R. 1972. Proceedings of excommunication against Mistress Ann Hibbens of Boston (1640). In *Remarkable providences,* ed. J. Demos. New York: Braziller.

Kerr, H. T., and J. M. Mulder. 1983. *Conversions: The Christian experience.* Grand Rapids: Eerdmans.

Kierkegaard, S. 1941. *Fear and trembling and the sickness unto death.* Princeton, N. J.: Princeton Univ. Press.

Klausner, J., and H. Danby. 1925. *Jesus of Nazareth: His life, times, and teaching.* London: Allen and Unwin.

Knapp, R. R. 1964. Relationship of a measure of self-actualization to neuroticism and extraversion. *Journal of Consulting Psychology* 29: 168–72.

Kobes, W. A. 1983. Faith development: A view of James W. Fowler's theory. *Pro Rege* 12, 1: 24–34.

Kohlberg, L. 1963. Development of children's orientation toward a moral order. *Vita Humana* 6: 11–36.

————. 1973. Continuities in childhood and adult moral development revisited. In *Life-span developmental psychology: Personality and socialization,* ed. P. Baltes and K. Schaie, 202ff. New York: Academic.

————. 1974. Education, moral development and faith. *Journal of Moral Education,* 4, 1: 5–16.

————. 1976. Moral stages and moralization. In *Moral development and behavior: Theory, research and social issues,* ed. T. Likona. New York: Holt, Rinehart, and Winston.

Kübler-Ross, E. 1969. *On death and dying.* New York: Macmillan.

Kuhn, D. 1984. Cognitive development. In *Developmental psychology: An advanced textbook,* ed. M. H. Bornstein and M. E. Lamb. Hillsdale, N. J.: Lawrence Erlbaum.

Lain Entralgo, P. 1970. *The therapy of the word in classical antiquity.* Trans. L. J. Rather and J. M. Sharp. New Haven, Conn.: Yale Univ. Press.

Lammers, W., Jr. 1977. The absent father. In *Fathering, fact or fable?,* ed. E. V. Stein. Nashville: Abingdon.

Langer, W. C. 1972. *The mind of Adolf Hitler.* New York: New American Library.

Leader, A. L. 1976. Denied dependence in family therapy. *Social Casework* 57, 10: 637–43.

Lee, R. S. 1948. *Freud and Christianity.* Hammondsworth, Middlesex, England: Penguin.

Lerner, H. E. 1978. Adaptive and pathogenic aspects of sex-role stereotypes: Implications for parenting and psychotherapy. *American Journal of Psychiatry* 135: 29–33.

Lerner, R. M. 1986. *Concepts and theories of human development.* 2d ed. New York: Random House.

Levinson, D. J. 1978. Eras: The anatomy of the life cycle. *Psychiatric Opinion* 15: 39–48.

Levinson, D. J., et al. 1978. *The seasons of man's life.* New York: Knopf.

Lewis, C. S. 1960. *The four loves.* New York: Harcourt, Brace.

Luther, M. 1945. Letters of spiritual counsel. In *Library of Christian classics,* vol. 18. Philadelphia: Westminster.

————. 1957. Explanations of the ninety-five theses. In *Luther's Works,* vol. 31. Philadelphia: Fortress.

————. 1959. The small catechism. In *The book of concord,* ed. and trans. T. Tappert. Philadelphia: Fortress.

——. 1967. *Table talk.* In *Luther's works,* vol. 54. Philadelphia: Fortress.

Lyon, K. B. 1985. *Toward a practical theology of aging.* Philadelphia: Fortress.

McCasland, V. 1964. *The pioneer of our faith: A new life of Jesus.* New York: McGraw-Hill.

McCool, G. A., 1975. *A Rahner reader.* London: Darton, Longman and Todd.

McDargh, J. 1983. *Psychoanalytic object relations theory and the study of religion on faith and the imaging of God.* Lanham, Md.: Univ. Press of America.

McIntyre, J. 1966. *The shape of Christology.* London: SCM.

Manson, T. W. 1953. *The servant-Messiah: A study of the public ministry of Jesus.* Cambridge: Cambridge Univ. Press.

Marshall, I. H. 1978. *The gospel of Luke: A commentary on the Greek text.* Grand Rapids: Eerdmans; Exeter: Paternoster.

Maslow, A. H. 1954. *Motivation and personality.* New York: Harper.

——. 1968. *Toward a psychology of being.* 2d ed. New York: Van Nostrand.

——. 1970. *Religions, values, and peak experiences.* New York: Viking.

May, G. 1982. *Will and spirit: A contemplative psychology.* San Francisco: Harper and Row.

May, R. 1969. *Love and will.* New York: Norton.

——. 1972. *Power and innocence: A search for the sources of violence.* New York: Norton.

May, R., ed. 1966. *Existential psychology.* New York: Random House.

Merton, T. 1955. *No man is an island.* New York: Harcourt, Brace.

Meyer, B. F. 1979. *The aims of Jesus.* London: SCM.

Miller, J. W. 1980. Jesus' personality as reflected in his parables. In *The new way of Jesus: Essays presented to Charles Howard,* ed. W. Klassen. Newton, Kans.: Faith and Life Press.

Millon, T. 1969. *Modern psychopathology: A bisocial approach to maladaptive learning and functioning.* Philadelphia: W. B. Saunders.

Minirth, F. B. 1970. *Christian psychiatry.* Old Tappan, N. J.: Revell.

Moody, R. A. 1976. *Life after life: The investigation of a phenomenon—survival of bodily death.* New York: Bantam.

Moran, G. 1983. *Religious education development: Images for the future.* Minneapolis: Winston.

Nadelson, C. C., et al. 1978. Marital stress and symptom formation in mid-life. *Psychiatric Opinion* 15: 29–33.

Neaman, J. 1975. *Suggestions of the devil: The origins of madness.* New York: Doubleday, Anchor Books.

Nelson, C. E. 1989. *How faith matures.* Louisville: Westminster/John Knox.

Neugarten, B. L. 1968. *Middle age and aging: A reader in social psychology.* Chicago: Univ. of Chicago Press.

——. 1975. Adult personality: Toward a psychology of the life cycle. In *Human life cycle,* ed. W. C. Sze. New York: Aronson.

Noll, M. A. 1984. Evangelicals and the study of the Bible. *The Reformed Journal* 34, 4.

Notman, M. T. 1978. Women and mid-life: A different perspective. *Psychiatric Opinion* 15: 15–25.

Nouwen, H. J. M. 1975. *Reaching out: The three movements of spiritual life.* Garden City, N. Y.: Doubleday.

Nouwen, H. J. M., and W. Gaffney. 1976. *Aging: The fulfillment of life.* Garden City, N. Y.: Image.

Oden, T. C. 1964. *Radical obedience: The ethics of Rudolf Bultmann.* Philadelphia: Westminster.

Oldham, J. H. 1959. *Life is commitment.* New York: Association.

Oppenheimer, A. 1977. *The 'Am Ha-aretz: A study in the social history of the Jewish people in the Hellenistic Roman period.* Leiden: Brill.

Otto, R. [1936] 1966. *The idea of the holy.* New York: Oxford Univ. Press.

Oxford English Dictionary. 1933. Ed. J. A. Murray et al. Oxford: Oxford Univ. Press.

Parens, H., and L. Saul. 1971. *Dependence in man.* New York: International Univ. Press.

Parlee, M. B. 1978. Psychological aspects of the climacteric in women. *Psychiatric Opinion* 15: 36–40.

Phipps, W. E. 1970. *Was Jesus married? The distortion of sexuality in the Christian tradition.* New York: Harper.

———. 1973. *The sexuality of Jesus: Theological and literary perspectives.* New York: Harper.

Piaget, J. 1967. *Six psychological studies.* New York: Random House.

———. 1969. *The psychology of the child.* New York: Random House.

———. 1970. *Genetic epistemology.* Trans. E. Duckworth. New York: Columbia Univ. Press.

———. 1977. *The development of thought: Equilibration of cognitive structures.* Trans. A. Rosin. New York: Viking.

Price, E. J. 1959. The limitations of the psychology of religion. In *Readings in the psychology of religion,* ed. O. Strunk, Jr. New York: Adingdon.

Pruyser, P. W. 1974. *Between belief and unbelief.* New York: Harper and Row.

Pulaski, M. A. S. 1980. *Understanding Piaget: An introduction to children's cognitive development.* Rev. ed. New York: Harper and Row.

Rahner, K. 1974. Anonymous Christians. In *Theological investigations,* vol. 6. London: Darton, Longman and Todd.

———. 1977. *Meditations on freedom and the Spirit.* London: Burns and Oates.

———. 1979. Anonymous and explicit faith. In *Theological investigations,* vol. 16. London: Darton, Longman and Todd.

Reifsnyder, W. E., and E. I. Campbell. 1960. Religious attitudes of male neuropsychiatric patients. *Journal of Pastoral Care* 14: 150–59.

Religious Education Association. 1987. *Faith development in the adult life cycle.* Minneapolis: Religious Education Association.

Reynolds, L. 1983. Lawrence Kohlberg: Pursuing John Dewey's vision. *Pro Rege* 12, 1: 2–13.

Riches, J. 1980. *Jesus and the transformation of Judaism.* London: Darton, Longman and Todd.

Rickel, W. 1954. Editorial. *Journal of Psychotherapy as a Religious Process* 1: 97.

Rizzuto, M. 1979. *The birth of the living God: A psychoanalytic study.* Chicago: Univ. of Chicago Press.

Robinson, J. A. T. 1963. *Honest to God.* Philadelphia: Westminster.

———. 1965. *The new Reformation?* Philadelphia: Westminster.

Rogers, C. R. 1961. *On becoming a person: A therapist's view of psychotherapy.* Boston: Houghton Mifflin.

Rosen, I. M. 1973. Ego psychology of dependence. *Journal of Religion and Health* 11: 349–56.

Rosenthal, D. 1955. Changes in some moral values following psychotherapy. *Journal of Consulting and Clinical Psychology* 19: 431–36.

Rossi, A. 1973. Transition to parenthood. *Journal of Marriage and the Family* 38: 92–99.

Rottschafer, R. H. 1980. Giving and getting: A clinical and spiritual evaluation. *The Bulletin* 6, 2: 23–29.

———. 1984. The passive Christian. *Journal of Psychology and Christianity* 3, 1.

Royce, J. R. 1964. *The encapsulated man: An interdisciplinary essay on the search of meaning.* New York: Van Nostrand.

Salinger, R. J. 1979. Toward a biblical framework for family therapy. *Journal of Psychology and Theology* 7, 4: 241–50.

Sanders, E. P. 1985. *Jesus and Judaism.* Philadelphia: Fortress.

Schachtel, E. G. 1954. *Metamorphosis: On the development of affect, perception, attention and memory.* New York: Basic.

Schillebeeckx, E. 1979. *Jesus: An experiment in Christology.* New York: Seabury.

Schoeps, H. J. 1968. *The religions of mankind.* Trans. R. and C. Winston. Garden City, N.Y.: Doubleday.

Schuller, R. 1977. *Peace of mind through possibility thinking.* Garden City, N.Y.: Doubleday.

Shackleford, J. F. 1978. *A comparison of psychological and theological concepts of dependency.* Unpublished Ph.D. diss. Rosemead Graduate School of Professional Psychology.

Shakespeare, W. 1917. *The complete works of William Shakespeare.* New York: Walter J. Black.

Sheehy, G. 1976. *Passages: Predictable crises of adult life.* New York: E. P. Dutton.

Shostrom, E. L. 1966. *Personal orientation inventory.* San Diego: Educational and Industrial Testing Services.

Shostrom, E. L., and R. R. Knapp. 1966. The relationship of a measure of self-actualization (POI) to a measure of pathology (MMPI) and the therapeutic growth. *American Journal of Psychotherapy* 20, 1: 193–202.

Singer, J. 1976. *Androgyny: Toward a new theory of sexuality.* New York: Anchor.

Sloyan, G. S. 1983. *Jesus in focus: A life in its setting.* Mystic, Conn.: Twenty-Third Publications.

Smart, N. 1983. *World views, crosscultural explorations of human beliefs.* New York: Scribner's.

Smith, M. J. 1975. *When I say no, I feel guilty: How to cope—using the skills of systematic assertive therapy.* New York: Dial Press.

Smith, W. C. 1963. *The meaning and end of religion, a new approach to the religious traditions of mankind.* New York: Macmillan.

Stott, J. R. W. 1978. Must I really love myself? *Christianity Today* 22, 15.

———. 1984. Am I supposed to love myself or hate myself? *Christianity Today* 28, 7.

Streng, R. F. J. 1985. 3d. ed. *Understanding religious life.* Belmont, Calif.: Wadsworth.

Strommen, M. P. 1971. *Research on religious development: A comprehensive handbook.* New York: Hawthorn.

Stronks, G. G. 1983. Stages of intellectual development: A scheme. *Pro Rege* 12, 1: 14–23.

Strunk, O., Jr. 1965. *Mature religion: A psychological study.* New York: Abingdon.

———. 1968. *The choice called atheism.* New York: Abingdon.

———. 1969. *In faith and love.* Nashville: Graded.

Szasz, T. 1978. *The myth of psychotherapy.* Garden City, N. Y.: Anchor.

Tart, C. 1975. *Transpersonal psychologies.* New York: Harper and Row.

Tillich, P. [1952] 1977. *The courage to be.* New Haven, Conn.: Yale Univ. Press.

———. 1957. *Dynamics of faith.* New York: Harper and Brothers.

———. 1964. *Systematic theology.* 3d. ed. Welwyn, England: James Nisbet.

———. 1965. *Ultimate concern: Tillich in dialogue*. Ed. D. Mackenzie Brown. London: SCM.

———. 1968. *A history of Christian thought*. Ed. C. E. Braaten. New York: Harper and Row.

Tozer, A. W. 1948. *The pursuit of God*. Wheaton: Tyndale.

Tracy, D. 1975. *Blessed rage for order: The new pluralism in theology*. New York: Seabury.

Tracy, P. J. 1980. *Jonathan Edwards, pastor: Religion and society in eighteenth-century Northampton*. New York: Hill and Wang.

Vande Kemp, H. 1983. Spirit and soul in no-man's land: Reflections on Haule's "Care of Souls." *Journal of Psychology and Theology* 11: 117–22.

van Kaam, A. L. 1972. *On being yourself: Reflections on spirituality and originality*. Denvill, N. J.: Dimension.

Vermes, G. 1973. *Jesus the Jew: A historian's reading of the Gospels*. New York: Macmillan.

———. 1984. *Jesus and the world of Judaism*. Philadelphia: Fortress.

Vitz, P. C., and J. Gartner. 1984. Jesus as the anti-oedipus. *Journal of Psychology and Theology* 12: 4–14.

Vrieze, M. 1984. Kinds and contexts of knowing. In *Christian approaches to learning theory: A symposium*, ed. N. De Jong. New York: Univ. Press of America.

Wach, J. 1944. *Sociology of religion*. Chicago: Univ. of Chicago Press.

Walters, O. S. 1968. Theology and changing concepts of the unconscious. *Religion in Life* 37, 1.

Weber, M. 1963. *The sociology of religion*. Trans. E. Fischoff. Boston: Beacon.

Weger, K.-H. 1980. *Karl Rahner: An introduction to his theology*. London: Burns and Oates.

Welch, R. 1973. *We really do need each other*. Nashville: Impact.

Welkowitz, J., J. Cohen, and D. Ortmeyer. 1967. Value system similarity: Investigation of patient-therapist dyads. *Journal of Consulting Psychology* 31, 1: 48–55.

Westerhof, J. H. 1976. *Will our children have faith?* New York: Seabury.

Westley, D. 1981. *Redemptive intimacy, a new perspective for the journey to adult faith*. Mystic, Conn.: Twenty-Third Publications.

White, E., B. Elsom, and R. Prawat. 1978. Children's conceptions of death. *Child Development* 49: 307–10.

Whitehead, E. E., and J. D. Whitehead. 1984. *Seasons of strength; new visions of adult Christian maturing*. Garden City, N. Y.: Doubleday, Image.

Williams, D. D. 1949. *God's grace and man's hope*. New York: Harper and Brothers.

Wilson, I. 1984. *Jesus: The evidence*. London: Weidenfeld and Nicolson.

Winicott, D. W. 1958. Transitional objects and transitional phenomena. In *Collected papers*. London: Tavistock.

Winslow, O. E. 1940. *Jonathon Edwards, 1703–1758: A biography*. New York: Macmillan.

Winslow, O. E., ed. 1966. *Jonathan Edwards: Basic writings*. New York: New American Library.

Wuthnow, R. 1982. A sociological perspective on faith development. In *Faith development in the adult life cycle*, ed. K. Stokes. New York: Sadlier.

Zabriskie, F. C. 1976. A psychological analysis of biblical interpretations pertaining to women. *Journal of Psychology and Theology* 4: 304–12.

Index of Authors
and Subjects

Index of Scripture

Index of Scripture

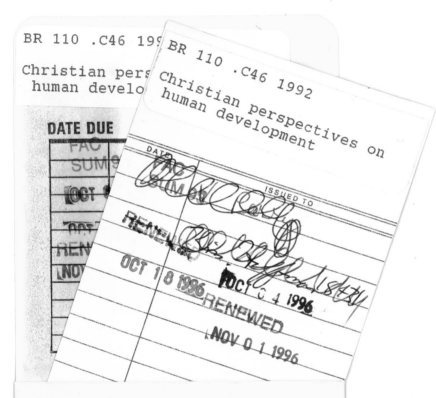
Gardner-Webb Library
P.O. Box 836
Boiling Springs, NC 28017

DEMCO